I0819801

Between Revolution and State

The Institute of Ismaili Studies
Ismaili Heritage Series, 11
General Editor: Farhad Daftary

Previously published titles:

1. Paul E. Walker, *Abū Yaʿqūb al-Sijistānī: Intellectual Missionary* (1996)
2. Heinz Halm, *The Fatimids and their Traditions of Learning* (1997)
3. Paul E. Walker, *Ḥamīd al-Dīn al-Kirmānī: Ismaili Thought in the Age of al-Ḥākim* (1999)
4. Alice C. Hunsberger, *Nasir Khusraw, The Ruby of Badakhshan: A Portrait of the Persian Poet, Traveller and Philosopher* (2000)
5. Farouk Mitha, *Al-Ghazālī and the Ismailis: A Debate on Reason and Authority in Medieval Islam* (2001)
6. Ali S. Asani, *Ecstasy and Enlightenment: The Ismaili Devotional Literature of South Asia* (2002)
7. Paul E. Walker, *Exploring an Islamic Empire: Fatimid History and its Sources* (2002)
8. Nadia Eboo Jamal, *Surviving the Mongols: Nizārī Quhistānī and the Continuity of Ismaili Tradition in Persia* (2002)
9. Verena Klemm, *Memoirs of a Mission. The Ismaili Scholar, Statesman and Poet al-Mu'ayyad fi'l-Dīn al-Shīrāzī* (2003)
10. Peter Willey, *Eagle's Nest: Ismaili Castles in Iran and Syria* (2005)
11. Sumaiya A. Hamdani, *Between Revolution and State: The Path to Fatimid Statehood* (2006)
12. Farhad Daftary, *Ismailis in Medieval Muslim Societies* (2005)

Between Revolution and State

The Path to Fatimid Statehood

Qadi al-Nuʿman and the Construction of Fatimid Legitimacy

Sumaiya A. Hamdani

I.B.Tauris *Publishers*
LONDON • NEW YORK
in association with
The Institute of Ismaili Studies
London

Published in 2006 by I.B.Tauris & Co. Ltd
6 Salem Road, London W2 4BU
175 Fifth Avenue, New York, NY 10010
www.ibtauris.com

in association with The Institute of Ismaili Studies
42–44 Grosvenor Gardens, London SW1W 0EB
www.iis.ac.uk

ISBN: 978 1 85043 882 3

A full CIP record for this book is available from the British Library
A full CIP record for this book is available from the Library of Congress

Library of Congress catalog card: available

Typeset in Minion Tra for The Institute of Ismaili Studies

The Institute of Ismaili Studies

The Institute of Ismaili Studies was established in 1977 with the object of promoting scholarship and learning on Islam, in the historical as well as contemporary contexts, and a better understanding of its relationship with other societies and faiths.

The Institute's programmes encourage a perspective which is not confined to the theological and religious heritage of Islam, but seeks to explore the relationship of religious ideas to broader dimensions of society and culture. The programmes thus encourage an interdisciplinary approach to the materials of Islamic history and thought. Particular attention is also given to issues of modernity that arise as Muslims seek to relate their heritage to the contemporary situation.

Within the Islamic tradition, the Institute's programmes seek to promote research on those areas which have, to date, received relatively little attention from scholars. These include the intellectual and literary expressions of Shiʿism in general, and Ismailism in particular.

In the context of Islamic societies, the Institute's programmes are informed by the full range and diversity of cultures in which Islam is practised today, from the Middle East, South and Central Asia, and Africa to the industrialized societies of the West, thus taking into consideration the variety of contexts which shape the ideals, beliefs and practices of the faith.

These objectives are realized through concrete programmes and activities organized and implemented by various departments of the Institute. The Institute also collaborates periodically, on a programme-specific basis, with other institutions of learning in the United Kingdom and abroad.

The Institute's academic publications fall into several distinct and interrelated categories:

1. Occasional papers or essays addressing broad themes of the relationship between religion and society in the historical as well as modern contexts, with special reference to Islam.
2. Monographs exploring specific aspects of Islamic faith and culture, or the contributions of individual Muslim figures or writers.
3. Editions or translations of significant primary or secondary texts.
4. Translations of poetic or literary texts which illustrate the rich heritage of spiritual, devotional and symbolic expressions in Muslim history.
5. Works on Ismaili history and thought, and the relationship of the Ismailis to other traditions, communities and schools of thought in Islam.
6. Proceedings of conferences and seminars sponsored by the Institute.
7. Bibliographical works and catalogues which document manuscripts, printed texts and other source materials.

This book falls into category five listed above.

In facilitating these and other publications, the Institute's sole aim is to encourage original research and analysis of relevant issues. While every effort is made to ensure that the publications are of a high academic standard, there is naturally bound to be a diversity of views, ideas and interpretations. As such, the opinions expressed in these publications must be understood as belonging to their authors alone.

Ismaili Heritage Series

A major Shiʿi Muslim community, the Ismailis have had a long and eventful history. Scattered in many regions of the world, in Asia, Africa, and now also in Europe and North America, the Ismailis have elaborated diverse intellectual and literary traditions in different languages. On two occasions they had states of their own, the Fatimid caliphate and the Nizari state of Iran and Syria during the Alamut period. While pursuing particular religio-political aims, the leaders of these Ismaili states also variously encouraged intellectual, scientific, artistic and commercial activities.

Until recently, the Ismailis were studied and judged almost exclusively on the basis of the evidence collected or fabricated by their enemies, including the bulk of the medieval heresiographers and polemicists who were hostile towards the Shiʿis in general and the Ismailis among them in particular. These authors in fact treated the Shiʿi interpretations of Islam as expressions of heterodoxy or even heresy. As a result, a 'black legend' was gradually developed and put into circulation in the Muslim world to discredit the Ismailis and their interpretation of Islam. The Christian Crusaders and their occidental chroniclers, who remained almost completely ignorant of Islam and its internal divisions, disseminated their own myths of the Ismailis, which came to be accepted in Europe as true descriptions of Ismaili teachings and practices. Modern orientalists, too, have studied the Ismailis on the basis of these hostile sources and fanciful accounts of medieval times. Thus, legends and misconceptions have continued to surround the Ismailis through the 20th century.

In more recent decades, however, the field of Ismaili studies has been revolutionized due to the recovery and study of genuine Ismaili sources on a large scale – manuscript materials which in different ways survived the destruction of the Fatimid and Nizari Ismaili libraries. These sources, representing diverse literary traditions produced in Arabic, Persian and Indic languages, had hitherto been secretly preserved in private collections in India, Central Asia, Iran, Afghanistan, Syria and the Yemen.

Modern progress in Ismaili studies has already necessitated a complete re-writing of the history of the Ismailis and their contributions to Islamic civilization. It has now become clear that the Ismailis founded important libraries and institutions of learning such as al-Azhar and the Dar al-ʿIlm in Cairo, while some of their learned *daʿis* or missionaries developed unique intellectual traditions amalgamating their theological doctrine with a diversity of philosophical traditions in complex metaphysical systems. The Ismaili patronage of learning and extension of hospitality to non-Ismaili scholars was maintained even in such difficult times as the Alamut period, when the community was preoccupied with its survival in an extremely hostile milieu.

The Ismaili Heritage Series, published under the auspices of the Department of Academic Research and Publications of the Institute of Ismaili Studies, aims to make available to wide audiences the results of modern scholarship on the Ismailis and their rich intellectual and cultural heritage, as well as certain aspects of their more recent history and achievements.

Contents

Acknowledgements

This book began as a dissertation submitted to the Near East Studies Department of Princeton University ten years ago, and its journey to this point has been made possible thanks to the support of many institutions. The History and Art History Department at George Mason University provided necessary summer research grants and a generous leave in 1998–1999. From the Social Science Research Council I received a postdoctoral grant that enabled me to travel to Tunisia and Egypt in 1999, where I additionally had the support of and institutional affiliation to the American University in Cairo. And most importantly, I owe The Institute of Ismaili Studies (IIS) in London thanks for financial support in 1998 and commitment to the publication of this book in the Ismaili Heritage Series.

In the long journey this book has taken, many and varied debts have been incurred. My teachers along the path have been numerous, but among them have been those who have stood out as *maraji*ʿ *al-taqlid*. First and foremost is my father, Abbas Hamdani, to whom I owe more than the usual debt, and through whose long and thoughtful conversations with me this project has evolved. It has been nurtured in turn, with constant encouragement and support, by Dr Farhad Daftary of the IIS, who has, with infinite patience, endured my countless delays and detours. And the project would not have been undertaken had it not been for the enthusiasm shown for my early efforts by James Morris, with whom I first read the works of al-Qadi al-Nuʿman; Paul Walker, who, as he has to many others, always gave me opportunities to grow as a scholar; and Ismail K. Poonawala, who has kept me up to speed on all things related to al-Qadi al-Nuʿman. Any errors and shortcomings are my own.

Alongside my teachers, I am grateful to many friends who have provided necessary interventions and needed distractions. To single out a few: David Sims and Caroline Hawley for the loan of computers at critical junctures; David and Iman Amer, who provided solace in the form of many meals and much laughter in Cairo; the family of Maneeza Hussein for the use of their luxurious digs in London *fi sabil talab al-ʿilm*; Julia Kolb and Luisa Zenobi for their warm welcome and friendship at the IIS; and my colleagues in the History Department who provided support and advice that helped me through the many revisions this book required; and my editors at the IIS, Isabel Miller and Kutub Kassam, for the realization of this project. Finally, I am indebted above all to my parents who have remained throughout pillars of faith, and to my late sister, who is always an inspiring presence despite her absence.

S.H.

Abbreviations

BIFAO	*Bulletin de l'Institut Français d'Archéologie Orientale*
BSMESB	*British Society for Middle Eastern Studies Bulletin*
BSOAS	*Bulletin of the School of Oriental and African Studies*
EI2	*The Encyclopaedia of Islam, New edition*
IJMES	*International Journal of Middle East Studies*
JA	*Journal Asiatique*
JAOS	*Journal of the American Oriental Society*
JBBRAS	*Journal of the Bombay Branch of the Royal Asiatic Society*
JNES	*Journal of Near Eastern Studies*
JRAS	*Journal of the Royal Asiatic Society*
SI	*Studia Islamica*

Introduction

The Fatimids and the Ismaili Shiʿi Century

The historian al-Tabari noted in his entry for the year 282 AH/895 CE that the Abbasid caliph al-Muʿtadid (d. 289/902) had had a troubling dream.[1] In it, the caliph was riding among cheering crowds of people when he spied an old man at a distance from him who was quietly ignoring him and the crowds by performing his prayers. Al-Muʿtadid stopped his horse by the old man and asked him what he meant by this show of disrespect. The old man identified himself as the Prophet Muhammad's cousin and son-in-law, ʿAli b. Abi Talib, and then rebuked the caliph for not treating his descendants and their supporters, the Shiʿa, well.[2] As a result of this reproach, the account goes, al-Muʿtadid decided to release a Shiʿi who had just been caught smuggling money to groups in the capital that were agitating against his government.[3] In 284/897 he followed up this amnesty with an order banning storytellers and discussion groups gathering at mosques in Baghdad, because of reports that they, as well as waterboys plying their trade in the city, were provoking the Shiʿa by invoking blessings on ʿAli b. Abi Talib's enemy, Muʿawiya b. Abi Sufyan.[4] And to make further amends al-Muʿtadid asked his vizier to compose a proclamation, to be read out in all mosques, reviling Muʿawiya b. Abi Sufyan and defending the Prophet's family.[5]

The proclamation, the full text of which is preserved in al-Tabari's history, was in the end never actually issued for fear that it would backfire altogether, by going so far in defence of the Prophet's ʿAlid descendants as to appear to undermine the legitimacy of the Abbasids themselves.[6] Nevertheless, al-Muʿtadid continued to try to solicit Shiʿi support, possibly because of his dream, but more probably because he was aware that pro-Shiʿi sentiment pervaded his territories. By the end of his reign and the turn of the 4th/10th century, in fact, it had led to the establishment of Shiʿi states in many areas of the Islamic world, and eventually by 334/945 the control of the Abbasid state fell into the hands of the Buyids, an Iranian Shiʿi military family.[7] Shiʿi kingdoms were already established in Daylam, Tabaristan and Gilan, the provinces in northern Iran from where the Buyids originated. Other Shiʿi states or dynasties held sway in various parts of the Islamic world, such as the Idrisids in Morocco,[8] the Hamdanids and their successors, the ʿUqaylids and Mazyadids, in northern Syria and central Iraq, and the Qaramita in central Syria and parts of Iraq, and later eastern Arabia.[9] Yemen was controlled by a Zaydi Shiʿi state from 284/897 to 1382/1962, and the cities of Abbasid Iraq itself became the arenas for significant doctrinal developments in Ithnaʿashari or Twelver Shiʿism.

Surrounded by Shiʿi states and communities, and eventually dominated by a Shiʿi military family, it is no wonder that the Abbasid caliphs like al-Muʿtadid were worried enough to dream of being rebuked by ʿAli. Despite the apparent success of Shiʿism by the 4th/10th century, however, the modern scholarly opinion has been that it represented an inherently divergent phenomenon in Islam. In part, this is due to the fact that investigations of Shiʿism have often been based on Sunni texts. Since these sources constructed Shiʿism as a heresy, its emergence and appeal have variously been attributed, at different times, to ethnic discontent, the radicalism of socio-economically marginalized groups, or the resurgence of non-Islamic beliefs and ritual practices in Islamic guise.[10] In part also, academic discourse and the structure of its disciplines have contributed to Shiʿism's treatment as anomalous because they have been focused on establishing a normative Islam and on emphasizing, therefore, the distinctions between Sunni and Shiʿi forms of Islam.[11] As a result, the political achievements of Shiʿism by the 4th/10th century have been explained as a consequence of the fragmentation of the Islamic empire under Abbasid rule, which accompanied a breakdown in the system of government and a rupture in the Islamic community.

In the academic study of Islam, the association of religion and politics has often been held to be uniquely Islamic; institutions like the caliphate, which combined religious and political leadership, have been contrasted with a separation of church and state in the Christian West. However, recent studies on Late Antiquity have argued that, in fact, a close relationship existed between religion (in this case monotheism, and in particular Christianity) and politics in the Eastern Roman Empire, if only because belief in a universal God tended to complement the project of universal empire.[12] Accordingly, the next form of monotheism to appear on the scene, Islam, inherited this relationship between monotheism and empire, especially in the form of the caliphate, thus continuing rather than disrupting the experience of Late Antiquity.[13] Yet arguments that have connected religion and politics in the consolidation of empire (Islamic and otherwise) view that relationship as leading ultimately to ideological rigidity, fragmentation and, in the case of Islam, to the emergence of Shiʿism.[14]

To view Shiʿism merely as a consequence of political fragmentation and a reflection of ideological rigidity in Islam, however, is to ignore other causes for the disintegration of empire under the Abbasids, and to assume that the process of ideological crystalization in Islam was a straightforward movement completed by the 4th/10th century.[15] It also disregards Shiʿism's origins and original impetus, which predate the Islamic empire if not the formation of an Islamic state.[16] The definition of orthodoxy and heresy and the project of universal empire was not as yet resolved in the 4th/10th century, as indicated by one Shiʿi movement which established a rival caliphate a few years after al-Muʿtadid's reign, contesting Abbasid leadership of the Islamic world, and realizing Shiʿism's aim to revive the idea of the unity of the Muslim community, religiously and politically. The establishment of this caliphate of the Ismaili Shiʿi Fatimids (297–567/909–1171) is the focus of this book, and it offers an opportunity to re-examine both the relationship between monotheism and empire, and the role of Shiʿism within Islam. It suggests that the Fatimid experience reflects the continuing saliency of the idea of universalism in Islam, and as such represents the continuation and indeed culmination, rather than rupture, of a historical process.

As is well known, Shiʿism originated in the succession crisis after the Prophet's death in 10/632, as the party that unsuccessfully supported the succession of ʿAli b. Abi Talib over that of Abu Bakr, and then ʿUmar and ʿUthman. ʿAli b. Abi Talib's supporters maintained that his blood kinship with the Prophet, marriage to the Prophet's daughter, early conversion to Islam and public designation by the Prophet in 10/632 at Ghadir Khumm gave him a better title to leadership than the other Companions of the Prophet.[17] Eventually ʿAli b. Abi Talib did succeed as the fourth and last of the Rashidun or 'rightly guided' caliphs (10–40/632–661), but his rule (36–40/656–661) was marred by rebellion,[18] a civil war that led to the takeover of the Islamic state by the Umayyad dynasty,[19] and culminated in his assassination in 40/661 by a member of the dissident Kharijiyya movement.[20] This tragic ending, and the fate of his politically disenfranchised and often persecuted progeny,[21] became the focus of subsequent Shiʿi revolts, such as that of al-Mukhtar on behalf of Muhammad b. al-Hanafiyya, and the revolt of Zayd b. ʿAli during the Umayyad caliphate.[22] It also became the basis for the growth of Shiʿism, which by the 4th/10th century had evolved into three main sub-branches: Zaydi, Ithnaʿashari and Ismaili.[23]

Shiʿism's origins as a political and religious cause, however, continued to drive the establishment of Shiʿi states and dynasties even after the end of the Umayyad and the beginning of the Abbasid period, as already noted. Abbasid caliphs like al-Muʿtadid, for this reason, went to great lengths to appease the Shiʿi communities in their territories: pardoning conspirators, banning anti-Shiʿi polemicists, issuing declarations in defence of ʿAli and his descendents. That they did so was due to the uneasy relationship between the house of ʿAbbas and the supporters of ʿAlid descendants. At the time of their revolution in 132/750, the Abbasids were simply one of many opponents to the Umayyad regime, and one of the many claimants to leadership of the Islamic world on the strength of their relation to the Prophet Muhammad. Like other branches of the Prophet's family and their Shiʿi supporters, they claimed that leadership rested with the Prophet's family because they were the only guarantors of a truly Islamic and just state. Their revolution was thus waged on the basis of ideas expressed in slogans such as '*al-rida min Al-i Muhammad*' or '*al-rida min ahl al-bayt*' (an agreed-upon member of the Prophet's family).

Such a claim was a reaction to the manner in which the Umayyads came to power, through the civil war instigated by Muʿawiya b. Abi Sufyan against ʿAli b. Abi Talib, as well as to the rapid expansion of the Islamic empire to include diverse peoples, which subsequently led to a sense of alienation from the politics and tribal patronage systems of the Umayyads. The Prophet's family, by contrast, came increasingly to be viewed as transcending the particular culture and interests of the Meccan aristocracy, and as representing, like the Prophet himself, the community as a whole. Thus Shiʿism as the cause of the Prophet's family became a powerful ideological challenge to the legitimacy of the Umayyad dynasty, as well as a response to the challenges of empire.

The Abbasids emphasized their kinship with the Prophet through his uncle Ibn ʿAbbas, and were thereby able to commandeer an underground revolutionary organization. They succeeded in attracting a wider following and raising an army from discontented Arabs and others within Umayyad society, and by these means wrested power from the Umayyad dynasty in 132/750.[24] Their revolution succeeded, however, at the expense of Shiʿi solidarity. Once in power, the Abbasids dominated and persecuted rival branches of the Prophet's family, and preferred policies and doctrines that appealed to their non-Shiʿi constituencies, a process which eventually resulted in the formation of Sunni Islam.[25] This, of course, left them open to the very same criticism they had made of the Umayyads, that they had abandoned the true faith, suppressed the authority of the Prophet's family and in particular of his descendants through ʿAli, and did not constitute a legitimate leadership. This criticism continued to haunt the Abbasid caliphate and provoked not only minor rebellions, breakaway states and, as has been seen, the takeover of their regime by a Shiʿi military family, but also, most dramatically, the emergence of the Fatimid revolutionary movement, and the caliphate it established in 297/909 in North Africa.

The Fatimid caliphate was ruled by Ismaili imams[26] who claimed descent from ʿAli through Ismaʿil, the eldest son and designated successor of Jaʿfar al-Sadiq (d. 148/765). At its height their empire extended from North Africa, through Egypt, to Syria and into the Hijaz and the Yemen. Control over such a vast territory enabled the Fatimids to extend their hegemony further into the Mediterranean, the Red Sea and the Indian Ocean, bringing about the development of a thriving new trade economy that reached far beyond the Middle East. The wealth generated by these territories and sea routes enhanced their capital, Cairo, making it a vibrant cultural and intellectual counterpart to Abbasid Baghdad. And the patronage of the ruling imams enabled Ismaili Shiʿism to experience a golden age both inside and outside Fatimid territories through the activity and scholarly output of their *daʿis* or missionaries. For all these reasons, the Fatimid empire represented the apex of Shiʿi success at that time. Hence Massignon's characterization of the 4th/10th century as the 'Ismaili Shiʿi Century'.[27]

Nevertheless, the Abbasids retained their position in Iraq, albeit under the control of the Seljuk Turks from 447/1055, and the institutions, social groups and structures of Sunni Islam, which they supported, survived to flourish and overwhelm Fatimid achievements, even in their own territories, in subsequent periods. As noted above, this has contributed to the view in modern scholarship of Shiʿism's inherent marginality in Islam, as has its reliance on Sunni heresiography.[28] With regard to Ismaili Shiʿism in particular, its importance has not been explicitly addressed except by a few recent studies. One of the most ambitious of these is Michael Brett's *Rise of the Fatimids.*[29] Earlier studies suggested that Fatimid success prompted a Sunni response in the form of the Seljuk takeover of the Abbasid caliphate.[30] Brett further argues that the importance of the Fatimid rise to power not only provoked the hardening of Sunni–Shiʿi distinctions, but also Christian hostility towards Islam as illustrated by the Crusades.[31] But in exploring such opposition, Brett does not question the issue of the marginalization of Shiʿism, and Ismaʿilism in particular, within Islam itself. Rather, he assumes explicitly sectarian identities and boundaries, which hardened somewhat predictably as a result of political events.

The task of exploring the role of Ismaili Shiʿism within Islam has been largely eschewed in most studies in favour of recovering and further elaborating the history of the Ismailis and the Fatimid dynasty.[32] To a large extent such studies see their efforts as a corrective to those based on Sunni polemical sources,[33] and have been aided by the relatively recent availability of Ismaili sources dating both from before and after the Fatimid period.[34] Those who have benefitted most from these sources are the Ismaili historians who have focused on bringing to light new information on origins and doctrines, as well as constructing a historical narrative that connects the now disparate Ismaili communities to a common past. Examples of such works include Zahid ʿAli's *Hamare Ismaʿili madhhab ki haqiqat* ('The Truth about Our Ismaili Religion', Hyderabad, 1954); Husayn al-Hamdani's *al-Sulayhiyyun wa'l-haraka al-Fatimiyya fi'l-Yaman* ('The Sulayhids and the Fatimid Movement in Yemen', Cairo, 1955); Abbas Hamdani's *The Beginnings of the Ismaʿili Daʿwa in Northern India* (Cairo, 1956) and *The Fatimids* (Karachi, 1962); Mustafa Ghalib's *Ta'rikh al-daʿwa al-Ismaʿiliyya* ('History of the Ismaili Movement', Beirut, 1965); and Azim Nanji's *The Nizari Ismaʿili Tradition in the Indo-Pakistan Subcontinent* (Delmar, NY, 1978), to name but a few. Each of these works represents an attempt at reconstructing the history of the various branches of the Ismaili community based on information available in Ismaili sources.

This information was also made available through the loan of manuscripts from the Ismaili community's private libraries, and the edition and translation of many manuscripts by Ismaili scholars, such as the numerous works edited by the late Syrian Ismaili scholars Mustafa Ghalib and ʿArif Tamir, and by Indian Ismailis such as the late Asaf A.A. Fyzee, who edited the Ismaili legal text, *Daʿa'im al-Islam* ('Pillars of Islam', Cairo, 1951–61), and Ismail K. Poonawala, who has revised and edited Fyzee's translation of the *Daʿa'im* (New Delhi, 2002) and edited numerous important Ismaili texts, in addition to compiling the definitive

Biobibliography of Isma'ili Literature (Malibu, CA, 1977).[35]

The efforts of Ismaili scholars to construct or reconstruct a more accurate understanding of Ismaili Shi'ism and of the Fatimid period in particular was simultaneously complemented by the work of Tunisian and Egyptian scholars, who, especially in the post-colonial period, addressed the Fatimid chapter of their own national histories and likewise produced dynastic histories of the Fatimids and editions of Ismaili texts, or those dating from the Fatimid period, held in their respective national libraries. Among the works of Egyptian scholars there are, for example, Muhammad K. Husayn's *Fi adab Misr al-Fatimiyya* ('On the Literature of Fatimid Egypt', Cairo 1950); Muhammad J. Surur's *Misr fi 'asr al-dawla al-Fatimiyya* ('Egypt in the Time of the Fatimid State', Cairo, 1960), and *al-Nufudh al-Fatimi fi bilad al-Sham wa'l-Iraq* ('Fatimid Authority in Syria and Iraq', Cairo, 1964); Hasan I. Hasan's *Ta'rikh al-dawla al-Fatimiyya* ('The History of the Fatimid State', Cairo, 1964); Abdel-Maguid Magued's *Zuhur khilafat al-Fatimiyyin wa suqutuha fi Misr* ('The Rise and Fall of the Fatimids in Egypt', Cairo, 1968); and Ayman F. Sayyid's numerous surveys of Fatimid history and institutions in Egypt, the most recent of which is *al-Dawla al-Fatimiyya fi Misr* ('The Fatimid State in Egypt', Cairo, 2000). In addition, M.K. Husayn, A.M. Magued and A.F. Sayyid have also edited many important manuscripts of the Fatimid period.[36]

As for Tunisian scholarship, Muhammad Ya'lawi has produced many editions of important Fatimid or Ismaili sources such as the *'Uyun al-akhbar* (loosely meaning, 'The Wells of Historical Knowledge') under the title *al-Khulafa' al-Fatimiyyin bi'l-Maghrib* ('The Fatimid Caliphs of North Africa', Beirut, 1985) and the *Kitab al-majalis wa'l-musayarat* ('The Book of Sessions and Excursions'), originially edited with Farhat Dachraoui and Habib Feqi (Tunis, 1978, repr. Beirut, 1998). F. Dachraoui has edited the important narrative of the founding of the Fatimid state, the *Kitab iftitah al-da'wa wa ibtida' al-dawla* ('The Beginning of the Mission and Establishment of the State', Beirut, 1975), and written *Le califat Fatimide au Maghreb* (Tunis, 1981), in Arabic *al-Khilafa al-Fatimiyya bi'l-Maghrib* ('The Fatimid Caliphate in

North Africa', Beirut, 1994).[37]

As Farhad Daftary has explained in his *Assassin Legends*, modern Western scholarship on Ismailism initially grew out of an interest in the Crusades, and derived from the primitive ethnographies of European aides-de-camp and observers of the medieval period. These early descriptions of the Holy Land included sections on the Ismaili communities of Syria which were largely based on hearsay. From these beginnings, the discovery of Ismaili sources led to new appraisals of the Syrian Ismaili community, especially when Europeans developed an imperial interest in the region in the 19th century,[38] and subsequently in Ismaili and Fatimid history generally. Again the emphasis was on the origins and doctrines of Ismaili Shiʿism. Thus, alongside Ivanow,[39] the research of other early pioneers, such as Louis Massignon,[40] Claude Cahen[41] and Maurice Canard[42] contributed to or coincided with the first monographs reassessing the nature of Ismaili Shiʿism, such as Bernard Lewis's *The Origins of Ismaʿilism* and Marshall G.S. Hodgson's *The Order of Assassins.* Afterwards, there were contributions to the understanding of Ismaili doctrines and philosophy, especially by Henry Corbin,[43] and these have been augmented by A. Hamdani's studies on the epistles of the Ikhwan al-Safa' (Brethren of Purity), Paul E. Walker's studies on Ismaili philosophers such as Abu Yaʿqub al-Sijistani, and more recently by Alice H. Hunsberger's work on Nasir-i Khusraw.[44] As for the Fatimids, Wilferd Madelung and Samuel M. Stern in numerous articles extended knowledge of both the early Fatimid movement and later Fatimid doctrine and developments.[45] More recently, these efforts have born fruit in an intensely descriptive history of the early Fatimid period, Heinz Halm's *The Empire of the Mahdi*, translated from the German by M. Bonner (Leiden, 1996), and Daftary's *The Ismaʿilis*, a master narrative of Ismaili history from its beginnings to the present, as well as his *A Short History of the Ismailis* which has been translated into numerous languages.[46]

Subsequently, and while the effort to properly define, describe and chart the evolution of Ismaili Shiʿism continues, new directions in historical research generally have led to a new emphasis in Fatimid studies. As a result, the Fatimid period has been approached from the perspective of social history, as in Schlomo D. Goitein's five-volume *Mediterranean Society* (Berkeley, 1967–93), which deals in particular with the life of the medieval Jewish community in Cairo;[47] cultural history as illustrated in the work of Paula Sanders, *Ritual, Politics and the City in Fatimid Cairo* (New York, 1994);[48] institutional history as explored in Halm's *The Fatimids and their Institutions of Learning* (London, 1997),[49] and even military history as in Yaacov Lev's *State and Society in Fatimid Egypt* (Leiden, 1991).

All in all, much of the research noted above has been driven by the 'discovery' of new sources.[50] While such discoveries have resulted in better-documented facts, filled in gaps and produced a more diversified coverage of the Ismailis and the Fatimid period in recent scholarship, the framework remains largely the same. So, while we know increasingly more about the origins and evolution of Ismaili Shiʿi doctrines and about the Fatimid period, its institutions, economy, society and even its ceremony, there has been little progress in reassessing the place or role of the Fatimids within the broader context of Islam and Islamic history. Part of the reason for this is the dearth of information about the early Ismaili revolutionary movement, which itself has generated a measure of debate among scholars, especially regarding the Qarmati split with the Fatimid cause.[51] More importantly, lack of information about the earliest period of Ismaili Shiʿism has hindered the development of a proper understanding of the milieu in which it evolved, and whether or not it resonated with other trends and currents in Islam at the time.[52] Instead, we are forced to rely on obscure references from contemporary sources and later polemics, resulting in a highly speculative picture of the place of early Ismaili Shiʿism in the intellectual and political climate of the 3rd/9th century, well before its rise to power in North Africa.

Unlike many of these works, the present study does not 'discover' new sources; instead it returns to sources already discovered and discussed and a period already described in order to better understand the significance in its own time of the Fatimid revolution and the state it established. In particular, it reconsiders the North African period of Fatimid history (297–358/909–969) because, unlike the earlier revolutionary period of *satr* or 'concealment' about which little is known, the era of *zuhur* or 'manifestation' and establishment of a Fatimid state produced much comment both inside and outside the Ismaili community, so that we have a wide array of sources. Further, the transition from Shiʿi revolution to a multi-confessional Islamic state tested the doctrinal limits of the Fatimid movement, and so allows us to appreciate the extent to which the Fatimids saw themselves situated within the broader Islamic context. This is evident in the literature from the period of transition or North African period, when the exigiences of the state generated a new discourse in which expressions of law, history, biography, protocol and ceremony reflected the necessary move from opposition to state-building and legitimacy. While in the revolutionary period the Fatimid mission or *daʿwa* could rely on the Shiʿi doctrine of imams in concealment, after the achievement of power the Fatimid *dawla* or state needed new legitimizing narratives, and this resulted in an important re-articulation of the Ismaili doctrine of *imama*, or rule of the Fatimid imams from the *ahl al-bayt*, that was intended to provide a universal basis for Fatimid rule.

The responsibility for constructing these narratives fell on the shoulders of a certain Abu Hanifa, known as al-Qadi al-Nuʿman (d. 363/974), a figure who himself personifies the transitional period of Fatimid history, since he was a North African convert from Sunni Islam and a judge. As a North African convert he represents the success of the Fatimid *daʿwa* in converting local Sunnis, and, as their most prominent judge or *qadi*, al-Nuʿman represents the need of the Fatimid state for a legal system and the expression of its legitimacy among both the Ismailis and non-Ismailis they came to rule. These two aspects of his background provided al-Nuʿman with a particularly vital perspective, and he rose quickly to prominence, serving all four Fatimid imam-caliphs of the North African period, and producing for them an outstanding range of works directed at the many different constituencies that came under Fatimid rule and those beyond their empire.[53] Although most of his work was naturally legal, he also produced other *zahiri* or exoteric works on history, biography, ritual and protocol, as well as works of *haqa'iq* (essential truths) and *ta'wil* (interpretation), constituting the more *batini* (esoteric) of Ismaili sciences or disciplines. These works continue to be important in Ismaili communities and have therefore been preserved and edited, and are used in the numerous studies on Fatimid history and doctrine referred to above. However, little attention has been given to assessing them as part of the Fatimid effort to consolidate power and make the transition from revolution to state, or from a Shiʿi opposition movement to rulers of an Islamic empire.

The following chapters will explore al-Nuʿman's *zahiri* works in order to investigate the reworking of certain Ismaili doctrines into an idiom and form accessible to the diverse elements within and beyond the Fatimid empire. Chapter 1 reviews the events and assesses the results of the Fatimid revolution's success in establishing a state in North Africa in the 4th/10th century, as the background necessary to understanding the circumstances that generated the *zahiri* literature of the North African period. In Chapter 2 the milieu in which al-Nuʿman grew up and which informed his own revisions and inventions for the Fatimids is examined. Chapters 3, 4 and 5 examine the doctrinal modifications he fashioned in three subjects that his *zahiri* works embrace: law, including especially his *Daʿa'im al-Islam* ('Pillars of Islam') and the *Kitab ikhtilaf usul al-madhahib* ('Differences Among the Schools of Law');[54] history and biography, as represented by the *Iftitah al-daʿwa wa-ibtida' al-dawla* ('The Beginning of the Mission and Establishment of the State') and the *Kitab al-majalis wa'l-musayarat* ('The Book of Sessions and Excursions'); and lastly protocol in the *Kitab al-himma fi adab atbaʿ al-a'imma* ('The Book of Etiquette Necessary for the Followers of the Imam').[55]

1

From Revolution to State

By all accounts the Fatimid rise to power was a remarkable phenomenon.[1] It had obscure beginnings in the succession crisis among the Shiʿa following the death of the Imam Jaʿfar al-Sadiq in 148/765, resulting in a movement with a fitful trajectory over a wide and disparate area ranging from North Africa to South Asia, and eventually a successful resolution in the establishment of the Fatimid caliphate in Ifriqiya in 297/909. The succession crisis in the 2nd/8th century, however, did not necessarily or immediately indicate the birth of a new movement or the resulting Fatimid state. Rather, at the time of the crisis, the splintering of the Shiʿi community into several factions seemed only to signal once again the dissipation of Shiʿi resistance to Abbasid rule. As it turned out, this succession crisis led, among other things, to the birth of Ismaili Shiʿism.

The origins of the succession crisis were complex, since Ismaʿil b. Jaʿfar al-Sadiq, who had been designated by his father to succeed him to the imamate despite rumours of his inclination for political activity, was not present when Imam al-Sadiq's heritage was being disputed, while other sons of the deceased imam now laid claims to it. What is more, according to some sources, Ismaʿil had pre-deceased his father, although there are other sources that indicate otherwise.[2] Ismaʿil's full brother ʿAbd Allah and then his half-brother Musa in turn became the focus of the need the Shiʿi community felt for leadership, and different factions of the community argued that the designation had passed to one or the other of them, dividing the Shiʿis into several factions.[3]

These divisions were nothing new in Shiʿism. They had appeared during the time of Muhammad al-Baqir, the fourth generation in descent from the Prophet, whose half-brother Zayd b. ʿAli (d. 122/740) led a revolt against the ailing Umayyad state, because al-Baqir himself had eschewed an activist stance. The revolt did not succeed, but the attempt and what it represented in terms of political struggle gave rise to Zaydi Shiʿism, and its doctrine of the necessity for struggle against unjust rule on behalf of any member of the Prophet's family, or *ahl al-bayt*. Subsequently, untimely deaths or other misfortunes, along with the occasional lack of the necessary qualities in a designated successor, often undermined a smooth succession between recognized descendants of the Prophet and so spawned yet more factions in support of one or other candidate from the *ahl al-bayt*. The necessary secrecy that surrounded different factions provided further cause for confusion, frustration and contesting the succession among the early Shiʿis.

Thus, after the death of Ismaʿil b. Jaʿfar, of the many factions that emerged, one supported the imamate of Ismaʿil (whom some believed had not died), and another that of his son Muhammad. As for the rest, there was a faction that claimed Jaʿfar al-Sadiq himself had not died, one that supported ʿAbd Allah (Ismaʿil's full brother), and two that supported either Musa or Muhammad (Ismaʿil's half-brothers). In the event, many Shiʿa recognized ʿAbd Allah as his father's successor after Ismaʿil, but he died soon after Jaʿfar al-Sadiq. Musa then received support from most of the community and was recognized as their imam. From him descended the line of imams of the Twelver branch of Shiʿism.[4]

The Imami Shiʿis who eventually emerged as the nascent Ismailis were those recognizing as their imam either Ismaʿil b. Jaʿfar al-Sadiq or his son Muhammad b. Ismaʿil. Some of them had previously belonged to the more activist wing of Jaʿfar's followers.[5] Because of such disagreements the nascent Ismaili community emerged as an opposition within the opposition and became susceptible to misrepresentation in Twelver Shiʿi as well as Sunni sources, adding to our confusion as to the nature and activities of the earliest Ismailis.[6]

Consequently, it was in rather obscure circumstances that the Ismaili movement first began to grow. W. Madelung in particular has argued that after the death of Muhammad b. Isma'il (it is assumed sometime after 179/795–796), most of the early Ismailis subscribed to the belief that he had gone into concealment, and that he would reappear as the *mahdi* (or messiah).[7] This at least is the belief that has been ascribed to the Qaramita, who were thought to belong to the Ismaili community by heresiographers of the period.[8] What was to become known as the Qarmati began with the conversion to the Ismaili cause of Hamdan Qarmat and his brother-in-law 'Abdan around 264/878, and eventually became limited to southern Iraq, Bahrayn (then the east coast of the Arabian peninsula) and parts of Iran.[9]

The beliefs of other branches of the Ismaili community (such as those of Sind, Yemen, Egypt and North Africa) are even less clear in this early period. The sources report that Muhammad b. Isma'il was survived by his sons after he fled into hiding in Khuzistan in south-western Persia. One of them, 'Abd Allah, later established himself in Salamiyya, a town in Syria, and led the Ismaili *da'wa* from there in secrecy. After 'Abd Allah, the task of establishing a line of descent becomes trickier: 'Abd Allah was succeeded by his son Ahmad, who was then succeeded either by his son al-Husayn, or by another son Muhammad, and then by 'Abd Allah II (known in non-Ismaili sources as 'Ubayd Allah) who was the son of al-Husayn and the nephew and son-in-law of Muhammad. But whether or not these descendants of Muhammad b. Isma'il were considered to be his successors to the imamate, or initially merely to the status of *hujja* (proof or evidence on earth of a hidden imam), we do know that 'Abd Allah II openly claimed the imamate in 286/899, and ten years later in 297/909 when he was proclaimed the first Fatimid caliph he assumed the title al-Mahdi (by which name he is more commonly known in history, and henceforth he will be referred to as 'Abd Allah al-Mahdi).[10] When he declared himself the imam, the Ismaili *da'wa* split into what were to become the two opposing factions of the dissident Qaramita and the official Fatimid *da'wa*. It is unclear, however, whether in the period of *satr* or concealment, the century between the death of Muhammad b. Isma'il and the succession of 'Abd Allah al-Mahdi (or from about 179–286/795–899), the Ismailis believed that the *da'wa* was active on behalf of Muhammad b. Isma'il, still living in concealment and expected to return in the future, or whether he was believed to be dead and his progeny had succeeded him to the imamate. It is also possible that different groups of the Ismaili community held somewhat different beliefs for quite a while.[11]

In any event, soon after the disappearance or occultation of the last Twelver Shi'i imam, or from 261/875 onwards, the Ismaili *da'wa* spread from its headquarters at Salamiyya in Syria to Iraq, Iran, Bahrayn, Yemen, Sind, Egypt and North Africa, perhaps attesting to the popular appeal of a living imam. This success no doubt engendered power struggles among the Ismaili *da'is* and may have had a part in the Fatimid–Qarmati schism of 286/899, when the Qarmatis, centred in Bahrayn, Iraq and Iran, explicitly rejected the imamate of 'Abd Allah al-Mahdi in favour of belief in the return of Muhammad b. Isma'il. The consequences of this schism were profound, both in terms of al-Mahdi's own personal security in Salamiyya which was now endangered by both the Abbasids and the Qarmatis, as well as the literature and reforms produced by the Fatimids to defend their claims against the Qaramita rejection.[12]

Although al-Mahdi's declaration of himself as imam was received favourably in parts of Syria,[13] the Qaramita of Bahrayn, Iraq and Iran remained implacably hostile to him. Of the remaining, still loyal, areas of *da'wa* activity, the Yemen had been an Ismaili stronghold under the *da'is* 'Ali b. al-Fadl and Abu'l-Qasim b. Hawshab al-Kufi (also known as Mansur al-Yaman) ever since they had been sent there in 266/879–880. From their respective bases of operation in the Yemeni mountains, the *da'wa* spread out and by 293/905–906 almost all the region had been brought under Ismaili control.[14] However, that success was short-lived as Zaydi resurgence under their own imam quickly reduced the Ismaili-held areas. More importantly, between the time that al-Mahdi left Salamiyya in 289/902 and his arrival in Egypt in 291/903–904 (escaping as he was from both the Abbasids and the Qaramita), the Yemen was beginning to become unstable. This was the first indication of ʿAli b. al-Fadl's disloyalty, manifest in 291/903. By 299/911 he had publicly renounced his allegiance to ʿAbd Allah al-Mahdi.[15]

The Ismaili *daʿwa* had also been active in Egypt. Under the *daʿi* Abu ʿAli it was a centre of communications between Yemen and North Africa and Syria, and thus al-Mahdi not surprisingly chose to head towards it. However, Egypt was too important and central a part of the Islamic world for him to elude Abbasid attention there for long, and so the decision was at last made to go to North Africa.[16] Apart from the reasons that drove al-Mahdi away from other areas of *daʿwa* activity, there were also particular reasons that drew him to North Africa. The efforts of the *daʿi* Abu ʿAbd Allah al-Shiʿi had produced a strong base of support among the Kutama Berbers, with whose help he was achieving dramatic conquests, and the region was sufficiently distant from both dissidents and enemies of the Fatimids, such as the Qaramita and the Abbasids.

Abu ʿAbd Allah al-Husayn b. Ahmad b. Zakariyya al-Shiʿi's career is celebrated in the well-known history of the establishment of the Fatimid state in North Africa, al-Qadi al-Nuʿman's *Iftitah al-daʿwa wa-ibtidaʾ al-dawla*. Abu ʿAbd Allah's career began when he and his brother, Abu'l-ʿAbbas, were converted to Ismaili Shiʿism in Kufa by a neighbour, the *daʿi* Abu ʿAli, and when this *daʿi* was transferred to Egypt, both brothers followed him there. While one of them stayed on in Egypt, in 278/892 Abu ʿAbd Allah was dispatched to Yemen to train further under Ibn Hawshab (Mansur al-Yaman).[17] By the following year, 279/893, he had completed his apprenticeship and it was in Mecca en route back to Egypt that he encountered a group of Kutama Berbers on pilgrimage, some of whom were apparently attracted to Shiʿism. Without revealing himself, Abu ʿAbd Allah gained their confidence and accompanied them to Egypt, all the while gathering information. He realized that if he could persuade the Kutama to join the Ismaili *daʿwa*, he would acquire the support of a large tribal confederation whose territory did not come under the control of any of the powers in the region. When they reached Egypt, the Kutama asked Abu ʿAbd Allah to continue on with them to their homeland so that he could further instruct them in Shiʿi doctrine. Since he had received instruction from ʿAbd Allah al-Mahdi to proceed to North Africa, the *daʿi* allowed himself to be persuaded by the Kutama and travelled with them to the mountains of the Lesser Kabylia.[18]

Abu ʿAbd Allah al-Shiʿi arrived in North Africa in 279/893 and for the next 15 years or so, or until the establishment of the Fatimid state in 297/909, he made great progress for the Fatimid cause. His achievements were aided by the fact that his initial audience was receptive to his message; as noted, many of the Kutama were already Shiʿi and thus inclined to accept the Ismaili *daʿwa*. Also their territory, along what is now the coast of eastern Algeria, occupied an area free from the authority of surrounding states such as the Aghlabid centred in Ifriqiya to the east, and smaller states to the west such as the Rustamid in Tahert in central Algeria, and the Midrarids of Sijilmasa and the Idrisids of Fez, now in Morocco.[19] On arriving in Kutama territory Abu ʿAbd Allah first attempted to set himself up in Ikjan[20] (home of the Banu Saktan clan of the Kutama) which was situated just beyond the western Aghlabid boundary fortresses of Mila, Satif and Bilizma. However, he soon had to transfer further south to Tazrut, where he was better protected by the Banu Ghashman clan. For the next ten years (279–289/893–902) the Ismaili *daʿi* consolidated and expanded the territory under his control from his *dar al-hijra* or sanctuary, and began to conquer the fortress towns of the Aghlabids' western hinterland.[21]

Abu ʿAbd Allah's *dar al-hijra* was in many ways an unprecedented phenomenon in North Africa.[22] Although Islam had arrived in many forms and by various means in North Africa, it tended to emanate from the urban areas and garrison towns taken over or set up by Arab Muslim conquerors and immigrants from the Mashriq or the east.[23] So whereas by the 10th century cities like Fez and Qayrawan had become centres of learning and Sunni religious leadership in their own right, the hinterland between these larger urban centres retained a certain ambivalence towards them. It was in these areas that alternative discourses of Islam could be found, whether it was in terms of a non-specific Shiʿism (championing generally the cause of the *ahl al-bayt*) or Kharijism (with its puritanical and egalitarian bent). Abu ʿAbd Allah's *dar al-hijra* represented the propagation of yet another form of Islam in this hinterland, but one that was simultaneously populist and sophisticated enough to pose a real threat to the established centres of religious learning.[24] The novelty of such an experiment is reflected in the anxiety that his presence caused political and religious leaders in the area.

In his *Iftitah*, al-Nuʿman provides us with a brief account of Abu ʿAbd Allah's establishment of the *dar al-hijra*.[25] According to the *qadi*, the Ismaili *daʿi* first carried out a military reorganization of the Berber tribes he had brought to his cause. The Kutama, the Mazata, other tribes and people of the towns were placed in different camps and then deployed as 700 cavalry and 2,000 foot-soldiers against the enemy in their first major engagement, which was over the fortress town of Satif. The resulting victory gave the *daʿi*'s camp so much booty that, according to al-Nuʿman, 20 camels went for a dinar, and the sheep, horses and other booty were far too numerous to be moved back to the *dar al-hijra* in Tazrut.[26] Subsequently, the Kutama were divided into seven groups, each with its own military contingent and commander. These commanders and the *daʿi*s who were sent to each village were considered elders or *mashayikh* (even though some of them were quite young, notes al-Nuʿman), and so replaced or appropriated the role of the traditional tribal leadership.[27] In their hands was entrusted the *ghanima* or the part of the community's wealth that was reserved for the Mahdi to come, while the rest of the tax and tithe money raised was channelled into defence and other requirements of the community.

Because of the military success of Abu ʿAbd Allah's army, continues al-Nuʿman, some people were drawn to his cause as much for religious reasons as for worldly benefit. In an attempt to prevent corruption, therefore, the *daʿi* supervised the portioning of *iqtaʿ* or land grants to his followers or *awliya'*,[28] and began to reform the fledgling society through his own example, as well as through the taking of specific social and legal steps. When members of the community committed an offence, for example, they were banished and isolated from the community of the faithful and from their families until such time as they repented and did good works.[29] When blood had to be taken in revenge, it was done by the kin of the perpetrator so as to avoid feuds between the tribes. In this manner, says al-Nuʿman, the people slowly came around to the high moral standard the *daʿi* set and then became known for it themselves.[30]

Most importantly, within this reorganized community, there was instruction in the faith. When he arrived in North Africa, Abu ʿAbd Allah apparently held regular instructional sessions or *majalis*, to preach the virtues of ʿAli b. Abi Talib (and those of the Ismaili imams from among his descendants) to the Kutama. Those whom he perceived to be taking to his message he would draw into further instruction. From these beginnings Abu ʿAbd Allah developed a core of initiates whom he deemed proficient in doctrinal knowledge, pledged them to secrecy,[31] and eventually entrusted them with the instruction of the community.[32] Sessions in *hikma* (wisdom) or esoteric knowledge were held almost daily, and took up most of the day, comments al-Qadi al-Nuʿman.[33] Moreover, they were open to both men and women. Al-Nuʿman, in fact, makes special reference to the women who not only attended but excelled in learning at these sessions, so much so that some were appointed *daʿis*.[34]

Apart from such comments, al-Nuʿman does not elaborate on what was actually taught in Abu ʿAbd Allah's *majalis*. For this one has to turn to two more or less contemporary sources that shed some light on this role of the early Ismaili *daʿwa* and its curriculum. The first is, in fact, a personal account or memoir of the conversion of a North African to Ismaili Shiʿism, while the second is an idealized account of the process of initiation into the *daʿwa* and of the relationship between *daʿi* and disciple, by the Yemeni *daʿi* Jaʿfar b. Mansur al-Yaman, the son of Mansur al-Yaman and a contemporary of Abu ʿAbd Allah al-Shiʿi.[35] As regards the first account, the *Kitab al-munazarat*, it describes the conversion of Ibn al-Haytham, the son of a prominent family of Qayrawan that had originally come to North Africa from Kufa in the service of an early Abbasid governor.[36]

Ibn al-Haytham's family were Shi'i before the arrival of the Fatimids, although of the less specific Zaydi variety. Evidently they were not alone; Ibn al-Haytham's account of the education he received as a young member of the local elite includes mention of Shi'i as well as Hanafi Sunni and Jewish teachers, and the subjects they taught him, which covered a broad spectrum ranging from the Qur'an and *hadith*s to other religious and literary subjects, and the sciences of the Ancients.[37] The Shi'i and Hanafi teachers Ibn al-Haytham names included the Shi'is Muhammad b. Yahya al-Marwadhi (who became the first Fatimid judge of Qayrawan), Muhammad b. Khalaf, Ibrahim b. Ma'shar (author of a work entitled *Kitab yawm wa-layla*, which became a basis for the subsequent development of Ismaili law),[38] Abu'l-Hasan al-Muttalibi, a Sicilian émigré named Muhammad al-Kufi (later appointed as *khatib* by Abu 'Abd Allah), and prominent Hanafis such as Ibn Abdun, a friend of al-Marwadhi and chief judge under the Aghlabids.[39] Ibn al-Haytham's Jewish teacher was Yahya b. Yusuf al-Khurasani, who taught logic. The mention of these individuals provides us with important evidence on the identities of the local Shi'i *'ulama'*, whose names are largely omitted from the Maliki Sunni sources for this period, creating the impression that Qayrawan was an exclusively Sunni and overwhelmingly Maliki religious centre. The memoir also attests to the fact that the local Shi'is (and Jews) were active members of Qayrawan's scholarly community, and had close ties with the Hanafi Sunnis, even if they were not openly Shi'i, and more unlikely Ismaili Shi'is.[40] Nevertheless, like Ibn al-Haytham, they welcomed the *da'wa* when it arrived, and were eager to convert and to serve the Fatimid state.[41]

The *Kitab al-munazarat* relates Ibn al-Haytham's conversion and his other experiences at the side of Abu 'Abd Allah in those early days of the Fatimid state, in the form of a series of debates, or *munazarat*, that took place between them. These debates themselves represent part of an established tradition and literature of debate in Islamic scholarly circles, usually in the more formal setting of courts, mosques and *madrasa*s, and usually on topics of theology and law, although also as a rhetorical method for elaborating on literary topics.[42] In this case, Ibn al-Haytham's use of the term refers to the equally strong tradition of formal theological debate in the Ismaili *daʿwa* itself, which had quite perfected this mode as its preferred means of instruction. Thanks to Ibn al-Haytham we have evidence for this in the lengthy transcripts he provides of his encounters with Abu ʿAbd Allah, the first of which occurred just after the taking of Qayrawan in 296/909.[43]

The transcript serves to demonstrate Ibn al-Haytham's knowledge and thus also enables us to understand the type of education received by adepts such as himself, and the style of debate the *daʿwa* employed to test and instruct initiates. In this case the *daʿi*, Abu ʿAbd Allah, acts as *agent provocateur*, posing controversial questions in order to test the initiate Ibn al-Haytham, the strength of his convictions and his knowledge of Shiʿism. Their conversation begins in fact with just such a question. When Ibn al-Haytham states that he came seeking knowledge and guidance from the *daʿi*, Abu ʿAbd Allah asks why he has come to an organization which others have accused of killing people, pillaging and seizing booty in war. Ibn al-Haytham replies that the war waged by the *daʿwa* was legal since they were fighting people referred to in the Qur'an as polytheists and wrongdoers.[44] Abu ʿAbd Allah reminds him that those verses referred to the polytheists and the tribe of Quraysh in the Prophet's time. Ibn al-Haytham responds by citing Qur'anic verses referring to those who broke their covenant with God, and argues that those the *daʿwa* fought were guilty of similar offences. When again he is reminded that the reference is to specific groups before and during the Prophet's lifetime,[45] Ibn al-Haytham replies that hypocrites and those that broke their covenant also refer to people later on such as Abu Bakr, who broke his promise to God's Prophet when he deprived the Prophet's daughter Fatima of her inheritance.[46] He who succeeded the Prophet without the consensus of the community,[47] so 'claiming the imamate and leadership ahead of God's friends and taking away the veil of Fatima, the mistress of all the women in creation, belongs among the major sins which cannot be expiated but constitute polytheism that nullifies any merit and which will not be forgiven'.[48] Abu Bakr also waged war on other Muslims during his reign as caliph.[49] Abu ʿAbd Allah then points out that ʿAli b. Abi Talib had also killed people, to which Ibn al-Haytham responds that ʿAli did so only on authorization from God and His Prophet, and adds that, moreover, ʿAli was known for his clemency, for example towards ʿA'isha, the Prophet's wife, even though she had led a rebellion against him.

The conversation then proceeds to other distinctions between Companions of the Prophet like Abu Bakr, on the one hand, and ʿAli b. Abi Talib, on the other, such as: the greater merit of ʿAli because of his ties of blood kinship to the Prophet (which was like the merit of families of previous prophets); the evidence from the *hadith*s about the Prophet's feelings for ʿAli and their close relationship; and ʿAli's well-known and recorded deeds as one of the earliest converts; he was generous to the poor, courageous in defence of Islam, and similar to the associates and right-hand men of previous prophets.[50] Finally, Ibn al-Haytham argues that reason dictates the need for qualified leaders after the Prophet, especially those capable and knowledgeable enough to provide guidance on spiritual, ritual and legal matters not discussed or explained in the Qur'an. That such leaders, like ʿAli, did not immediately succeed the Prophet, continues Ibn al-Haytham, was due to the conspiracies at the time of the Prophet's death that led to the usurpation of his rights by others such as Abu Bakr.

Abu ʿAbd Allah then inquires about those most entitled to leadership after ʿAli b. Abi Talib, and Ibn al-Haytham recites the names of the recognized imams from among his progeny, i.e. Hasan, Husayn, ʿAli Zayn al-ʿAbidin, Muhammad al-Baqir and Jaʿfar al-Sadiq. Abu ʿAbd Allah asks why those and not others such as Muhammad al-Baqir's brother Zayd who also rose up against injustice? Ibn al-Haytham argues that he rose up on behalf of those who wanted someone to take an active stand against oppressors, not as a means of challenging his brother Muhammad al-Baqir's entitlement to the imamate (Ibn al-Haytham thus reveals that he is no longer a Zaydi). When Abu ʿAbd Allah presses him on the succession after Jaʿfar al-Sadiq, Ibn al-Haytham demurs, saying he is confused by the arguments put forth in favour of one or another of his sons (and thus he is not convinced by the position of the Twelver Shiʿis either), which he then proceeds to describe.

At this point Abu ʿAbd Allah, satisfied that Ibn al-Haytham knows enough and is solidly in the Shiʿi camp, invites him to join the Ismaili *daʿwa*, and take the pledge or *mithaq*, and then further instructs him on specific doctrines of Ismaili Shiʿism. This includes a lesson on the significance of the number seven (the number of imams recognized by the Ismailis up to the time of Muhammad b. Ismaʿil b. Jaʿfar al-Sadiq), the infallibility and other characteristics of the true imams, and the need therefore to always obey them. This ends their first session and the initiation of Ibn al-Haytham as he describes it in his memoir.[51]

Ibn al-Haytham's responses to the questions posed by Abu ʿAbd Allah in this session display, among other things, an exceptional familiarity with the events and controversies of the first Islamic state and the context for the revelation of Qur'anic verses. This is largely due, of course, to the nature of the religious training he had received, and the importance of sacred history in it; so not surprisingly he knew the events of the Prophet's life and that of his Companions and the early caliphs in great detail. At the same time, this knowledge is obviously felt to have a real relevance to the political events of his time, indicating the degree to which the political issues of his day were understood or perceived through the lens of controversies in the first Islamic state. The general Shiʿi position on these controversies is, of course, that they occurred as a result of the dubious motives and manoeuvres of those who deprived ʿAli b. Abi Talib of his rightful succession, and thus continued to plague the Muslim community with unjust rule. His own tragically short reign, which only finally occured after having been passed over in favour of less qualified candidates, his assassination and the fact that his descendants had time and again been excluded from power, further lent their cause the aura of a moral alternative in the face of recurring injustice and oppressive rule.

But because historical evidence for the legitimacy of ʿAlid succession proved insufficient in the face of the Sunni community's practical and ideological accommodations, other disciplines and arguments were marshalled to the cause by the Shiʿa, such as allegorical interpretation of Qur'anic verses, philosophical and rational arguments for succession of the *ahl al-bayt*, numerological significance of the acceptable number of descendants, and prognoses for the success of their cause. These are also evident in Ibn al-Haytham's responses and Abu 'Abd Allah's further instruction on the particulars of Ismaili Shiʿism. Despite the use of esoteric interpretation, numerology and other disciplines as supporting arguments, however, the Qur'an and the Traditions of the Prophet remain the basic foundation of Ibn al-Haytham's discourse and of Ismaili Shiʿi doctrine.

This is also evident in the *Kitab al-ʿalim wa'l-ghulam* of Jaʿfar b. Mansur al-Yaman.[52] Like the *Kitab al-munazarat*, the *Kitab al-ʿalim wa'l-ghulam* is the tale of many encounters, debates and conversations, although here between a fictional knower (*ʿalim*) or teacher, and his disciple (the *ghulam*). Unlike the *Kitab al-munazarat*, however, the *Kitab al-ʿalim* recounts a different aspect of the Ismaili *daʿwa*'s message or curriculum, and a different argument for the authority and claims of the imams. In this text, the discussions between master and disciple revolve around the questions of true faith and knowledge, and how both can only be attained by following the imams of the Prophet's family. The arguments conveyed here thus focus more on establishing the spiritual authority of the imams, rather than their political claims as in Ibn al-Haytham's memoir, in large part because the *Kitab al-ʿalim* was written before the public manifestation of the imams and the establishment of the Fatimid state.

The *Kitab al-ʿalim* begins by recalling how a group of the truly faithful expressed their desire to establish a method for searching out true faith so that each 'knower' could properly fulfil his obligation to those seeking knowledge. Then the tale is recounted of one such knower or teacher, who sought to fulfil his obligation to spread the true faith by searching for those seeking knowledge. The teacher travelled far and eventually came to a town where he noticed a group of individuals sincerely arguing about faith. They also noticed him observing them and inquired as to his identity and purpose, about which he remained vague. Nevertheless, they asked him his opinion on their debate and he preached to them so persuasively regarding the need for proper knowledge that a young man among them followed him and beseeched him for guidance. The teacher eventually agreed, on certain conditions: that his student should earn the privilege by upholding the ritual obligations of the faith, that he should wait until his teacher had determined his readiness to receive knowledge, and that he should keep all that he was learning secret from his father.

The disciple kept these conditions until his teacher determined his readiness. He then received the pledge (*mithaq*) from the student and began enlightening him, first by exposing to him the weakness of the premise of his convictions (i.e. agreement with things, either because they are partially true, or as a result of the consensus of others), and then proceeding to an examinination of the foundations of faith, i.e. the nature of God, the significance and symbolism of His creation, the role of His prophets, messengers and other 'friends' (the Shiʿi imams) in both creating awareness of Him, guiding mankind to Him and serving as witnesses of His eternal presence. The teacher then instructed the student on the purpose and meaning of the physical world and worldly existence, not only in terms of its aspects and nature, but also as symbolic of other realities that constitute the inner (*batin*) and innermost (*batin al-batin*) worlds or realities. Thus is established the principle of the exoteric (*zahir*) and esoteric (*batin*), which do and must coexist in order for the full meaning and purpose of things to be known (in terms of faith, the *zahir* or ritual aspects must not be abandoned in the search or acquisition of the *batin* or true knowledge). After arriving at this point, the teacher desired to further his student's progress at the hands of his superior shaykh, and so obtained permission for the student to go to him. The shaykh received and further instructed the student, anointed him as a member of the community of the truly faithful, and then dispatched him to his home, so that he could fulfil his duty to spread this trust and enlighten those around him, among them his father, and other previous teachers whom he now engaged in debate for the purposes of instruction, exposing in the process the limitations of their linguistic and analogical arguments and of accepted knowledge and custom.

This synopsis of the *Kitab al-ʿalim* does not begin to convey the sophistication of the actual text, nor does it fully capture the nature of Jaʿfar b. Mansur's discourse, which involved the use of Qur'anic verses and known *hadiths* as proof-texts for an argument that also employed rational and Neoplatonic philosophy, metahistory, cosmology and numerology to analyse and support the meaning of the former. The *Kitab al-ʿalim* is, in fact, a powerful example of the synthesis of the intellectual trends and currents in Islam at the time, which after its expansion encountered and was challenged by the philosophy of the Ancient world and the traditions of competing monotheisms in its territories. While Sunni Islam eventually abandoned the influence of these traditions on questions of theology and law in favour of a more culturally specific exegesis and an interpretation of texts based on Arabic philology and grammar, the biographies and histories covering the earliest period of Islam, as well as historical accounts and the Traditions of the Prophet, Ismaili Shiʿism used a varity of tools, such as Aristotelian logic, Neoplatonic philosophy and Gnostic tendencies found in the Judeo-Christian tradition, which harmonized with the Qur'anic foundations of faith. At the time the *Kitab al-ʿalim* was composed, however, such intellectual speculation was still part of Sunni Islam's accepted teaching, and was represented in the rationalist tendencies of the Muʿtazili theological school, and the use of analogical reasoning in, for example, the Hanafi legal school. The student featured in the *Kitab al-ʿalim* refers to these in his conversations with his teacher.

Apart from establishing the superiority of Ismaili Shiʿism even to these demanding Sunni intellectual tendencies, the *Kitab al-ʿalim* also seeks to present a recommended mode of instruction. Although not a manual per se, it does outline a distinctive method of engaging students and educating initiates. These are reflected in the conditions laid down by the teacher for the student, such as close adherence to religious ritual, waiting until a sufficient testing period had elapsed, and otherwise maintaining secrecy as to one's true identity and proficiency in proper knowledge until such time as it is safe to reveal both. Abu ʿAbd Allah al-Shiʿi enforced similar conditions in his North African *dar al-hijra*, where initiates were expected to take a pledge of secrecy and gradually proceeded through multiple levels of training in an exclusively Ismaili community. And since the *da'wa*'s curriculum in the *dar al-hijra* probably included concepts similar to those in the *Kitab al-'alim* and political arguments like those in the *Kitab al-munazarat*, it is not surprising that Abu 'Abd Allah's teachings were viewed with considerable apprehension by local Sunni rulers.

The *majalis* of the *dar al-hijra* and the rumours about Abu 'Abd Allah's teaching so impressed or worried his already hostile neighbours that the Arab chatelains of the fortress towns around Ikjan and Tazrut, as well as their Aghlabid overlords and the elites of religious centres such as Qayrawan, considered engaging the *da'i* in a debate with their own *'ulama'* as a way to discredit him. In 280/893, for example, the lord of Mila, Musa b. al-'Abbas, sent word through the Banu Saktan that the *da'i* was invited to engage in a debate with other *'ulama'*. The Banu Saktan, fearing that this was a pretext for a possible ambush or assassination attempt, refused to let him go.[53] But the curiosity and anxiety about Abu 'Abd Allah's teaching persisted. Eventually, the Aghlabid ruler, Ibrahim II, himself sent a messenger to Abu 'Abd Allah to warn him of the consequences if he continued to proselytize. When this did not stop the *da'i*, Ibrahim II, various other lords and some of the non-Ismaili elders of the Kutama approached one Bayan b. Saqlan, a notable of Ikjan, asking him to kill Abu 'Abd Allah or expel him from their territories. Bayan b. Saqlan responded by saying that Abu 'Abd Allah's popularity was too great and again suggested a debate with the local *'ulama'*. But on consideration, Ibrahim II decided that the North African *'ulama'* were not up to challenging the more intellectually sophisticated *mashriqi*, as Abu 'Abd Allah was known.[54]

While Abu 'Abd Allah had clearly impressed his neighbours as a formidable intellectual adversary, so long as he restricted his actions to preaching among the Kutama, his activities did not seem to the Aghlabids to warrant an outright attack. For his part, Abu 'Abd Allah bided his time until an opportunity for expansion presented itself. This was to come ten years or so after he arrived. In the spring of 289/902, Ibrahim II embarked on a military campaign in Sicily, leaving Ifriqiya vulnerable. Abu ʿAbd Allah seized the fortress town of Mila, holding it until the Aghlabid armies returned in the winter of that year to retake it. Unfortunately for them, however, they chose not to pursue Abu ʿAbd Allah, who fled to Tazrut and then to Ikjan in the same year. As a result, when a succession crisis erupted in the Aghlabid dynasty the following year, 290/903,[55] the *daʿi* was able to retake Mila, and then, in 291/904, to seize the fortress town of Satif as well.

It was during this initial period of dramatically successful conquests by Abu ʿAbd Allah, between 289/902 and 291/904, that the Ismaili leader ʿAbd Allah al-Mahdi escaped from Salamiyya in Syria and managed to get as far as Egypt. No doubt encouraged by the expansion of *daʿwa* territory, as well as Aghlabid weakness resulting from their succession crisis and inability to defeat the *daʿi*'s armies, al-Mahdi began to head for the *dar al-hijra* at Ikjan, reaching Tripoli on the Libyan coast by 292/905. There, however, he encountered trouble. Abbasid agents had by this time informed the Aghlabids that he was in Tripoli and so al-Mahdi had to escape quickly and circumvent their territory. Abu'l-ʿAbbas, the brother of Abu ʿAbd Allah, who had accompanied him and whom al-Mahdi had sent ahead to meet the *daʿi*, was not so lucky. He was apprehended in Qayrawan and put in jail there. Meanwhile al-Mahdi was in the far western regions of the Maghrib, where he lived unmolested in the guise of a merchant from 292 to 296/905 to 909.[56]

The Aghlabid succession crisis occurred when Ziyadat-Allah III seized power by assassinating his nephew, who had succeeded Ibrahim II in 290/903. The result of so violent a takeover, however, was to make it difficult to consolidate the power he had gained. Meanwhile Abu ʿAbd Allah was steadily expanding *daʿwa* territory with the taking of Mila in 290/903, Satif in 291/904 and Bilizma in 293/906 and then in a dramatic routing of Aghlabid troops in 292/905, when the *daʿi*'s armies had acquired an impressive amount of booty which was sent to al-Mahdi in Sijilmasa.[57] In 293/906, the Aghlabid armies mutinied, and this resulted in the freeing of prisoners in Qayrawan (among them Abu'l-ʿAbbas).[58]

In the following year, Abu ʿAbd Allah took yet another fortified town further east and much closer to the Aghlabid centre of Qayrawan,[59] prompting Ziyadat-Allah III to belatedly strengthen the defences of the town of Raqqada, just outside Qayrawan, and to assemble an army by financial and other inducements.[60] The army was stationed at another fortified town between Raqqada and Baghaya, al-Urbus (Laribus), where it was ordered to winter in 295/908–909. During this time the Aghlabids watched helplessly as the *daʿi* conducted campaigns that brought almost all the towns from the coast (at Bone or Buna) to the far interior (Tuzur and Nafta) under his control.[61] Finally, in 296/909 the *daʿi* marched on al-Urbus, and after it was conquered the Aghlabid army disbanded, Ziyadat-Allah III prepared to flee and the road to Raqqada and Qayrawan lay open.[62] In the spring of 296/909, Abu ʿAbd Allah marched into Raqqada and proclaimed the foundation of the Fatimid state.

ʿAbd Allah al-Mahdi, however, was still in Sijilmasa, where he had been placed under arrest by its ruler al-Yasaʿ b. Midrar, belatedly reacting to the warnings about al-Mahdi that he had received from the Aghlabids.[63] So Abu ʿAbd Allah had to leave Ifriqiya in the care of his brother, Abu'l-ʿAbbas, while he proceeded to the far Maghrib to rescue his master. When the *daʿi* reached Sijilmasa, his army surrounded the town and demanded al-Mahdi's release. Al-Yasaʿ was persuaded by the merchants of the town to send out another man, one Ibn Bistam whom they disliked, and, as Abu ʿAbd Allah had never actually seen his master, he assumed that Ibn Bistam was al-Mahdi and dismounted in his presence. Ibn Bistam then also dismounted, to Abu ʿAbd Allah's acute embarrassment. Al-Yasaʿ, observing the scene, then sent out al-Mahdi, and this time he was correctly identified by one of the *daʿi*'s company, and after an emotional encounter and a period of rest, al-Mahdi, his son and his entourage were led to Raqqada by Abu ʿAbd Allah and the Kutama, and thus Fatimid rule was fully established.[64]

Although the Fatimid movement had weathered many storms and setbacks, such as the Qarmati schism and Abbasid harrassment, it had nevertheless succeeded in establishing a state in Ifriqiya. Part of the reason for its success was of course Aghlabid weakness, amply demonstrated by Ziyadat-Allah III's prevarication and policies from 293/906 to 296/909, especially his violent rise to power, his inability to comprehend the threat posed by the *da'i* Abu 'Abd Allah, and his belated attempts to fortify and defend his territory.[65] Equally important, however, were the measures taken by Abu 'Abd Allah to persuade the region and its towns to adopt his cause. The North African historian Ibn 'Idhari notes, for example, a public-relations coup that occurred when Abu 'Abd Allah took the town of Tubna, one of the first commercial and urban settlements in his conquests of 293–296/906–909. Abu 'Abd Allah summoned the tax collectors of the town, questioned their practice and determined that collecting the tithe (or *'ushr*) in currency rather than in grain did not conform with Islamic practice, and so it had to be returned to the people, as was also the case with land tax or *kharaj* taken from Muslims.[66] Abu 'Abd Allah exploited such situations by arguing that these taxes were un-Islamic and by repealing them he secured popular support. It not only earned him the gratitude of the townsfolk, but also the reputation of being an upholder of Islamic law and thus a more just overlord than the Aghlabids had been.

As his aim was to conquer rather than simply pillage the border towns west of the Aghlabid capital, it was Abu 'Abd Allah's custom to grant an *aman* or guarantee of safety to those towns that agreed to surrender. Occasionally, however, his troops did not abide by his promise and in some cases looting and killing did occur, creating enough fear in surrounding towns to ensure that surrender was sometimes voluntary. This was the case, for example, with the conquest of Maydara (or Haydara) in 295/908. Abu 'Abd Allah granted the people gathered inside this fortress town an *aman*, but, as he was afflicted with illness, he was unable to supervise its surrender and his troops took advantage of this. As a result, although he tried to bring those responsible for this pillaging to justice, Abu 'Abd Allah warned the people of al-Qasrayn (the next town to surrender) not to open the gates of the town to his army.[67] In this manner his success in taking over territory was swift and spectacular, and the Aghlabids were left with little recourse except to make petulant and futile denunciations of Abu

'Abd Allah and the *da'wa*. An example is the declaration read in the mosques of Ifriqiya after the loss of Tubna and Bilizma in 293/906:

> Salutations from Ziyadat-Allah III, upholder of the *Sunna* of the Prophet, to the inhabitants of Ifriqiya. Know that God guarantees victory and glory to His followers and the defenders of His Messenger's *Sunna*. … Unfortunately, the community of Muslims is now confronted with the San'ani infidel [Abu 'Abd Allah], who has tampered with God's religion and corrupted His Book, made the slaying of Muslims acceptable, the illicit licit – knowing full well the wrong in it – and who has plundered and consumed the wealth of the Muslims. This infidel appeared before the Berber Kutama and other lowly people like them, and made them err. When he called on them to change their religion, they responded, and when he corrupted the Sunna of the Prophet, they obeyed him because of their own ignorance. And so God gave them misfortune and trials, for they are no more than asses and sheep, and therefore they accept whoever flatters them, and follow whoever compliments them. … Among the least of his [Abu 'Abd Allah's] disbelief and ugly lies is the cursing of Abu Bakr and 'Umar, Companions, relations by marriage and successors of the Prophet, as well as 'Uthman, the husband of the Prophet's two daughters, and his followers Talha and Zubayr, and many others amongst the Companions of the Prophet. He has also invented a new law, which is not the law of Islam, and a new Sunna, which is different from that of the Prophet, and has required his followers to conceal this with oaths and vows not to reveal anything until it can be imposed on all Muslims. In the meantime he has made it necessary to wage holy war on Muslims, and for each one of his followers to donate a dinar, which he calls the dinar of the *hijra* [migration], and to donate a dirhem, which he calls the dirhem of *fitra* [?], and he has arrogated to himself the right to the wealth of the community, the destroying of mosques, the shortening of prayer, and the amending of what is considered forbidden in religion and the segregation of his followers from the rest of the Muslim community.[68]

In addition to its hostile tone, what is interesting about this declaration is the familiarity with the Ismaili *da'wa* activity that it displays, far greater than what the Aghlabids had possessed during Ibrahim II's reign. Thanks in part to Abu 'Abd Allah's successes, by this time the *daʿwa*'s message was better known, as were some of the social, legal and fiscal practices of his *dar al-hijra*. Referring to himself as upholder of the *Sunna* or practice of the Prophet, Ziyadat-Allah III in contrast characterizes Abu ʿAbd Allah as the infidel from Sanaʿa, indicating awareness about his apprenticeship in the Yemen, and his Kutama followers as lowly people and sheep, so reflecting and exploiting the anti-Berber sentiment of the Arab towns. More significantly, Ziyadat-Allah III criticizes the laws and policies of Abu ʿAbd Allah and his *dar al-hijra* as un-Islamic innovations, whether because of the alleged cursing of the Companions of the Prophet, or because Abu ʿAbd Allah allegedly promulgated a different law (referring no doubt to the reorganization of the Kutama's tribal society and the repealing of Aghlabid taxes), followed a different *Sunna*, amended accepted rituals, levied special tithes and segregated his followers from others, destroyed mosques and waged war on fellow Muslims.

Unfortunately for Ziyadat-Allah III, as al-Qadi al-Nuʿman notes, support for the Aghlabids had been seriously eroded by this time, and such insults and peevish accusations only served to remind people of the difference between the corrupt Aghlabids and the egalitarian and austere community of Abu ʿAbd Allah's *dar al-hijra*. To al-Nuʿman's mind it was not surprising that people did not rush to support the last Aghlabid, and that he was eventually forced to flee Ifriqiya when Abu ʿAbd Allah's armies marched into Raqqada and established Fatimid rule.

By the time al-Mahdi arrived in Raqqada in Rabiʿ I 297/January 910, the groundwork had been laid for his assumption of power. His entry into Raqqada is described as one of great pomp and circumstance even by Sunni historians (such as Ibn ʿIdhari and Ibn al-Athir), whose accounts indicate not only the chagrin of the Sunnis but also the impression that was left of the importance of the Fatimid experience, even at a remove of several centuries. Their telling of the story, while consistent in its disapproval of the Shiʿi nature of the Fatimid regime, nevertheless credits it with a uniquely impressive victory.

Ibn al-Athir, author of the universal history *al-Kamil fi'l-ta'rikh*,[69] describes the entry of Abu ʿAbd Allah into Raqqada and

Qayrawan in 296/908 as follows:

> The *fuqaha'* [jurists] and notables of the city went to meet Abu 'Abd Allah, and they greeted him and congratulated him on the victory. He responded warmly and promised them protection, and this pleased them and made them happy. They cursed Ziyadat-Allah [the Aghlabid] and remembered his misdeeds, and Abu 'Abd Allah said to them: 'How powerful, invincible, and arrogant this [Aghlabid] state was, and how much was destroyed in its defence! And yet God's will cannot be deflected or opposed!' They took to these words and returned to Qayrawan.[70]

And then on the Mahdi's accession, Ibn al-Athir comments:

> And when the Mahdi appeared, he remained in Sijilmasa for forty days and then left for Ifriqiya. He obtained money from Ikjan, and taking it along with him as cargo, he arrived in Raqqada toward the end of Rabi' II, in the year 297. Thus ended the kingdom of the Banu Aghlab and the kingdom of the Banu Midrar … which had lasted 130 years in Sijilmasa, and the kingdom of the Banu Rustum in Tahert which had lasted 160 years. … The Mahdi now possessed all of this, and as he approached Raqqada, he was met by its people and the people of Qayrawan [as he rode]; with Abu 'Abd Allah, and the chiefs of the Kutama, and his son and heir, the people greeted him and he responded warmly.[71]

Ibn al-Athir's description registers both the triumphant entry of Abu 'Abd Allah and amazement at the dramatic sweep of the Fatimid victory, which destroyed and replaced so many other long-standing North African states. Ibn 'Idhari, the well-known North African historian of the 7th–8th/13th–14th centuries, emphasizes the spectacle of al-Mahdi's entry into Raqqada and his assumption of power in his *Bayan al-mughrib fi akhbar al-maghrib*:[72]

> In this year, 'Abd Allah [al-Mahdi] arrived in Raqqada, with his son Abu'l-Qasim, and Ja'far al-Hajib, and Abu'l-Hasan Tayyib b. Isma'il known as al-Hadin. They were met by the *fuqaha'* and notables of Qayrawan who blessed him and congratulated him and showed him their happiness at his accession, and asked him for the renewal of his protection of them. He said to them, 'You and your children are protected.' … He entered the city of Raqqada wearing a dark

> silk robe and turban, seated on a bay horse, with his son Abu'l-Qasim behind him, wearing a saffron-coloured robe and turban, on a sorrel horse, and with Abu 'Abd Allah [al-Shi'i] in front of him ['Abd Allah], wearing a crimson robe and linen cape, turban and Alexandrian head kerchief, on a dark bay horse, and in his hand a kerchief with which he wiped the sweat and dust from his face; the people flocked to welcome them. 'Abd Allah alighted [from his horse] at the castle known as al-Sahn, and his son at the castle of Abu'l-Fath. 'Abd Allah was proclaimed the Mahdi.

The sense of triumph and stateliness is also evident in the tone and content of declarations issued by Abu 'Abd Allah al-Shi'i at the time of his conquest of Qayrawan and the rescue of al-Mahdi at Sijilmasa. The texts of these declarations are often reproduced in al-Qadi al-Nu'man's *Iftitah*.[73] The declarations or letters were distributed to the various urban centres of the new state, to be read out to the people, and so were received as statements of proof of the inevitable and divinely aided victory of the Fatimid *da'wa*. The rhetoric exemplifies the revolutionary fervour of the campaigns led by Abu 'Abd Allah in its condemnation of Aghlabid oppression and immorality, and assertion of the just cause and rights of the family of the Prophet.

In his letter and *aman*, or guarantee of safety, after entering Raqqada in 296/909, for example, Abu 'Abd Allah al-Shi'i begins with an exhortation to thank God for granting victory to His friends (*awliya'*) and the supporters of truth against wrongdoers who did not heed His warning and were therefore left to perdition and destruction. He goes on to state that he was still, by the grace of God, defending His religion and seeking to uphold the good and forbid evil, and striving to revive the truth that was suppressed by the oppressors, and fighting the enemies of God who reneged on and usurped the rights of the Prophet's family. And he argues that the Banu Aghlab and their supporters had to be attacked and pursued in order to make them repent and to return them to the truth.

As for their associates who had cooperated in wrongdoing, oppressing God's servants, and rebelling and transgressing, and by deceit taking money reserved for God, and enslaving His servants, continues Abu 'Abd Allah, they would not be able to hide or receive God's protection. For this reason he argues, he had no choice but to confront the Aghlabid with his armies at al-Urbus, and when it became clear that God would grant victory to His friends, the coward Ziyadat-Allah fled, abandoning his family and wealth. This was at least to the advantage of the Muslims, for it spared their blood and ended his oppression of them, Abu 'Abd Allah points out. He adds that he spared the women of Ziyadat-Allah's household from dishonour, and proffered his guarantee of safety to the people of Qayrawan and Raqqada when they approached him, and this same guarantee applied to all other towns provided that their people recognized what a blessing it was for them to have been saved from tyranny, and that they submitted to and obeyed those who had saved them.[74]

Of course, the facts of the *da'wa*'s victories provided a measure of credibility to the charges of corruption and oppression that Abu 'Abd Allah levelled against the Aghlabids and their vassals. Certainly, they further invigorated and convinced its members of the righteousness and inevitability of their cause. Given such conviction, the establishment of the Fatimid state and Ismaili Shi'i rule in Ifriqiya was not a gradual process. Instead, the enthusiasm that sustained the Fatimid revolution informed the initial period of al-Mahdi's reign and its policies. The most immediate changes to be expected were having the first Friday sermon or *khutba* read in the name of 'the Servant of God and His deputy, the one who upholds the good of His servants, 'Abd Allah Abu Muhammad, the Rightly Guided Imam, the Commander of the Faithful'; changing the call to prayer or *adhan* to the Shi'i specification (with the addition of 'come to the best of works'); being proclaimed and received as the new ruler or caliph; receiving delegations, and so on.[75]

There was also the business of setting up a new administration. This involved some radical departures from the past regime (although of necessity some continuity as well). The seven tribes of the Kutama, through whose efforts the conquest of North Africa had been possible, were rewarded with the control and governorship of the provinces of Ifriqiya, and their leaders dispatched to rule them in the style of royal governors.[76] This dispensation rewarded the Kutama, and moreover kept them from disturbing the urban centres of Ifriqiya and alienating their mostly Arab residents. Administration of the urban centres, however, required a different approach. Here members of the Ismaili *daʿwa* were strategically placed with the aim of creating a counterbalance to the necessary reliance on former Aghlabid administrators in new and old branches of government.[77] As a revolutionary organization, the *daʿwa* could be relied upon to provide fidelity and loyalty, but not the expertise essential to running affairs of state. Thus, while the running of the *bayt al-mal* or treasury went to the *daʿi* Abu Jaʿfar al-Khazari, the *diwan al-kharaj* (bureau of land tax) and the post (*barid*) went to a defector from the Aghlabid regime, Ibn al-Qadim, and the mint (*sikka*) went to another former Aghlabid administrator, Ibn al-Qamudi.[78] The governorships of Qayrawan and al-Qasr al-Qadim (a suburb) went to two Arab brothers, the Ibn Khinzir, and the supervision of the market of Qayrawan to another Arab, Ibn Abi Minhal.[79] Court personnel were also a mix of old and new: al-Mahdi's four chamberlains were old servants, while his court poet and physician were former members of the Aghlabid court.[80]

The necessarily makeshift nature of some of the new regime's appointments also extended to the composition of the various branches of government. While the *diwan*s for land tax, post and stipends (or *ʿata'*, which paid the salaries of the old Arab *jund* or standing army) were retained, others were abolished (such as the position of vizier and its corollary, the chancery or *diwan al-insha'*, both replaced simply by a secretary to al-Mahdi).[81] At the same time, new bureaus were established to meet the needs of the transition from revolution to state, such as the *diwan al-kashf* (bureau of investigation) and another to deal with lingering issues such as reclamation of plundered property, reflecting the new regime's desire to consolidate its position and its promise of a new order.[82] According to Ibn ʿIdhari, '[al-Mahdi] ordered the excising (*tuqliʿ*) from the mosques, cisterns, fortresses and bridges, of the names of all those who had built them, and he wrote his name on them',[83] although actual evidence of the excision of Aghlabid names from mosques and other monuments in Qayrawan is scarce.[84]

The new order was also reflected, perhaps more painfully, in the initial missteps and mishaps of Fatimid religious policy. During the revolutionary period, Abu ʿAbd Allah's *dar al-hijra* had consisted largely, if not exclusively, of converts to Ismaili Shiʿism and the Fatimid cause. The very success of the revolutionary movement, however, made the continuation of such a policy impractical if not impossible, and yet the new regime lacked a method or programme for organizing the affairs of the now mixed community of Sunnis and Shiʿis under its authority. As a result, in the early years of the Fatimid state, its religious policy appeared sometimes inconsistent and heavy handed, thus incurring the hostility of the local Sunni community. This included a Hanafi minority who had previously enjoyed the support of and positions in the Aghlabid administration. The otherwise predominantly Maliki *ʿulamaʾ* viewed Fatimid rule as an unmitigated disaster. For these *ʿulamaʾ*, the Fatimid rise to power represented both a worrying change of rule and role. Whereas under the occasionally Hanafi-leaning Sunni regime of the Aghlabids, the Malikis had dominated the intellectual scene in Qayrawan and constituted a pious opposition to the state's lapses of judgement, the establishment of the Fatimid state made it impossible for them to adopt even a pose of tolerant dissent, given their antipathy towards ʿAlid succession. Moreover, as an imam, the Fatimid caliph had in theory also replaced them as the source of religious authority and legal instruction, thus depriving them of their traditional role in society as well as their means of living. Consequently, Maliki accounts paint an unrelentingly grim picture of the early Fatimid period and its religious policy.[85]

According to Maliki sources, the Fatimid *daʿwa* ruthlessly imposed Ismaili Shiʿism on a captive Sunni population, and persecuted and killed *ʿulamaʾ* who resisted the Shiʿi modifications to religious rites.[86] But Ibn al-Haytham's *Kitab al-munazarat* exposes a far more complex situation, where in those early years of the Fatimid state its religious policy was actually often driven by the concerns of the local pre-Fatimid Shiʿi *ʿulamaʾ*. As previously noted, Shiʿism had already made inroads in North Africa long before the advent of Abu ʿAbd Allah.[87] According to al-Nuʿman, some form of Shiʿism had been propagated earlier on by *daʿis* such as Abu Sufyan and al-Hulwani, resulting in the emergence of Shiʿi scholars who were later to teach Ibn al-Haytham. The fortunes of these individuals improved dramatically with the establishment of the Fatimid state.[88] Because he cites names, Ibn al-Haytham's memoir enables us to correct the selective memory of the Maliki community and its writings, and to establish exactly who was active in the early months of Fatimid rule. As is clear from his memoir, the first Fatimids' lack of personnel experienced in administering a mixed community forced them to rely on the local Twelver Shiʿis to fill religious and other offices, to negotiate relations between them and local non-Shiʿi *ʿulama'*, as well as to establish ritual and other guidelines. In the course of doing so, it appears that the local Shiʿis and their allies found opportunities to pursue old vendettas against their enemies, and so exacerbated tensions within the local community.

For example, when Abu ʿAbd Allah took Qayrawan in 296/909, some of the local Shiʿis argued that an Ismaili judge or *qadi* should be appointed to the town. One of them, Abu'l-Hasan al-Muttalibi, had already acquired al-Mahdi's approval on the issue and so, although not all of the *daʿwa* were agreed, Abu ʿAbd Allah could not ignore the request. When he put it to the local Shiʿis, and in particular to Ibn al-Haytham, the latter deferred in favour of his senior colleague, al-Marwadhi. Thus al-Marwadhi became the first Fatimid chief *qadi* of Qayrawan. It was this al-Marwadhi who was responsible for implementing Ismaili Shiʿi changes to ritual and law in Qayrawan and in Fatimid-held territory generally, such as the instituting of the Shiʿi *adhan* or call to prayer and the abolition of noisy expressions of grief at funerals. Subsequently he forbade the issuing of any ruling on the basis of the Maliki or Hanafi *madhhabs* (schools of law), and prohibited the teaching of the Sunni rite. As a result, there was an increase in Maliki resentment towards the Fatimids, and towards al-Marwadhi in particular. His removal from office and then his death in 303/915 were remarked upon with satisfaction by the Maliki community.[89]

Anti-Fatimid sentiment further intensified, and not only because of the modifications to ritual. When Abu 'Abd Allah al-Shi'i placed Qayrawan in the hands of his brother, Abu'l-'Abbas, while he went to rescue al-Mahdi in Sijilmasa, the pursuit of an old vendetta caused even deeper wounds. Apparently, in the period shortly before the Fatimid takeover, a Maliki, one Ibrahim b. Muhammad al-Dabbi (known as Ibn al-Birdhawn), who was skilled at disputation, had offended a prominent Hanafi by the name of Muhammad b. al-Kala'i, for which he had already received a flogging. Once the Fatimid takeover had occurred, this same Ibn al-Kala'i denounced Ibn al-Birdhawn along with another Maliki, Abu Bakr b. al-Hudhayl, to the Fatimid governor Ibn Abi Khinzir, for saying that Mu'awiya was more entitled to the caliphate than 'Ali b. Abi Talib. The matter became serious and the governor, forced to take action, had both men put to death in late 297/909. When Abu 'Abd Allah al-Shi'i was informed of these events, he was apparently much dismayed, knowing this would only add to the hostility of the Sunnis.[90] In the annals of Maliki martyriology, however, they were vaunted as the first in an allegedly long line of Malikis persecuted by the Fatimids.[91]

At the same time, as relations between the local Shi'i and Maliki *'ulama'* were deteriorating owing to a lack of a clear policy on religious affairs, there also emerged a growing opposition within the ranks of the state's supporters. The Kutama were increasingly finding their position in the new Fatimid order unsatisfactory. Although their positions in the Fatimid state conferred prestige and a certain amount of power, they were ultimately restricted to a rather peripheral existence as local governors, which neither satisfied their desire for autonomy nor their nomadic traditions of plundering the sedentary population. This caused much friction, as is evident in the periodic clashes between the Kutama and those under their authority, further destabilizing Fatimid rule.[92]

The resentment of the Kutama soon won sympathy from Abu 'Abd Allah al-Shi'i, who was himself frustrated at the loss of his personal authority and power once al-Mahdi assumed rule. Abu 'Abd Allah's tragic fall from grace and eventual execution are recounted by al-Qadi al-Nu'man in his *Iftitah*, and commented upon in other studies.[93] And yet it remains unclear how and why Abu 'Abd Allah found himself at the centre of a plot to remove al-Mahdi after he had reigned for only a year. Anti-Ismaili sources argue, of course, that Abu 'Abd Allah realized that al-Mahdi was an imposter and had failed to live up to the prophecies concerning his manifestation and rule.[94] As for Ismaili sources such as the *Iftitah*,[95] Abu 'Abd Allah's defection is presented as the result of the influence of some of the disgruntled Kutama, as well as his brother Abu'l-'Abbas who, greedy for power, convinced his brother to avenge himself for having been set aside by al-Mahdi, saying, 'We did not give up the house that we strove all our lives to build, only so that someone else could inhabit it and leave us standing at the door'.[96] So Abu 'Abd Allah agreed to join the plot, and al-Mahdi, having got wind of it through an informer, had both brothers executed in 298/911. It was a tragic end to a brilliant career, but one that was perhaps inevitable, for as long as Abu 'Abd Allah served as a focus for opposition al-Mahdi could not count on his loyalty and hope to gain full control over the Kutama.

Although the *Iftitah* and Ismaili tradition in general rehabilitated Abu 'Abd Allah as a once faithful servant wilfully misled by those around him, the resentment of his Kutama supporters did not immediately disappear with his death.[97] On the contrary, it was manifested the following year in various fracas involving rampaging Kutama, and in the episode of the false *mahdi* which took place in 299/912. The latter involved a youth from the Banu Mawatnit of the Kutama, who was presented as the awaited *mahdi*, and in whose name several towns were taken in the area around Abu 'Abd Allah's original *dar al-hijra* in the Lesser Kabylia.[98] Al-Mahdi responded by declaring al-Qa'im as his successor, and sending him out to put down the rebels and establish control over the Kutama once and for all. Nevertheless, although control over the Kutama was soon regained,[99] the events of the first two years of his rule clearly indicated to al-Mahdi that the time had arrived to reconsider his policies.

In terms of immediate changes, the most apparent was the search for a more secure capital. Al-Mahdi had already begun to search for a site for his capital in 299/912, and even though construction of the city of Mahdiyya (as the new capital was called) did not begin until 303/916 and was not completed until 308/921, when finished it was stunningly impregnable. The most remarkable feature was the massive wall surrounding the peninsula on which the city was built, with a single gateway on a narrow isthmus connecting it to the mainland. Inside this wall, after passing through the half-ton iron gates, was a complex of administrative buildings and royal residences whose plan was to be echoed later in the layout of the royal city of al-Qahira (Cairo) in Egypt.[100]

This enceinte was perfectly designed to serve the Fatimids as a place of refuge from revolts such as that of Abu Yazid, the Khariji rebel whose uprising in the time of al-Mahdi's successors threatened Fatimid rule up to the very walls of Mahdiyya. It also served as a base for expansion north into the Mediterranean and west into Egypt. Symbolically it most obviously reflected a retreat from the heady days of early Fatimid rule, when the success of the revolution had obscured the fact that the Fatimids ruled as leaders of a minority religious group over a Sunni majority. Already in the reign of al-Mahdi this had brought the Fatimids to the brink of disaster, both because of Sunni hostility, manifested in Maliki resistance and martyriography, and because of dissent within the Fatimid *daʿwa*, expressed in Abu ʿAbd Allah's treason and Kutama revolts.

Subsequently, while al-Mahdi and his successors al-Qa'im (r. 322–334/934–946) and al-Mansur (334–341/946–953) survived these and other threats, and succeeded in consolidating and expanding Fatimid territory in North Africa, the lessons of the early years of Fatimid rule indicated that they could not rely entirely on their Kutama army or on many newly converted members of the *daʿwa* whose allegiance to the Fatimids was weak or opportunistic. They could now depend on them even less when seeking to ensure the obedience, by military or ideological means, of their overwhelmingly non-Ismaili subjects. Nor could they assume that either Maliki opposition or Khariji resistance, such as that of Abu Yazid, would eventually diminish. The

Fatimids, therefore, endeavoured to forge a different approach, based on a more accommodating and pluralistic religious policy. By the reign of al-Muʿizz (341–365/953–975), when the Fatimids had brought Egypt under their control, this issue had become all the more critical.

Official Fatimid policy, especially from the time of the Imam-caliph al-Mansur, began to seek to strike a balance between the propagation of the doctrines of Ismaili Shiʿism, and ensuring that some form of acceptance of the Fatimid state could be guaranteed from its non-Ismaili subjects. This tendency resulted in an increasingly latitudinarian official policy regarding the appointment of judges and the permitting of Sunni ritual and law, thus institutionalizing the principle of religious freedom.[101] At the same time, moving towards a more ideologically discursive stance, the Fatimids began to further develop a *zahiri* or public discourse acceptable to the Sunni majority, to function alongside the *batini* or esoteric canon that continued to be disseminated to the Ismaili community. The architect of this two-tiered approach was al-Qadi al-Nuʿman, whose own development, career and works will be examined in the following chapter.

2

From *Batin* to *Zahir*

In order to understand al-Qadi al-Nuʿman's role in devising a *zahiri* discourse or a viable state religious policy and legitimizing discourse for the Fatimids, one must return to the early Fatimid period to further explore the environment and attitudes that ultimately shaped him. As has been noted, the first years after the establishment of the Fatimid state were turbulent, not only because Fatimid ideology had not yet accommodated itself to the realities of power, but also because it created ripples of discontent among both supporters and detractors of the regime. Some supporters of the Fatimid regime, including a faction of the *daʿwa*, suffered from disappointed expectations, both political and doctrinal. The doctrinal expectations that attended the *zuhur* or manifestation of the Fatimid imam concerned his function in the Ismaili beliefs of the pre-Fatimid revolutionary period. During that time, the imams lived in *satr* or concealment, and since their identity and whereabouts were a closely guarded secret known only to a few members of the *daʿwa*, certain beliefs had come to surround their eventual manifestation, which involved some notion of messianism and a radical break with the past.

In this regard Ismaili Shiʿism was no different from many other forms of Shiʿi Islam. The basic Shiʿi belief that the Prophet was succeeded by ʿAli b. Abi Talib and his progeny in the leadership of the Muslim community encountered the sort of problems that dynastic projects often confront, that is, the competing claims of rival descendents of ʿAli and/or the rupture of a line of succession due to the untimely deaths of some of these individuals. The absence of a clearly designated successor would often present a quandary for their supporters. This was often dealt with through the subtleties of the concept of *ghayba* or occultation. If an imam died or disappeared without leaving a successor, he was considered to be in hiding by his supporters, until such time as conditions were favourable for him to reappear as the *mahdi* or saviour, heralding the final and just era of human history. The concept of *ghayba* thus enabled the followers of a particular imam to project their expectations of and for him into the future, as well as to preserve and reinforce their own identity as a distinct group within the Muslim community. But since Shiʿism could not by definition exist without a living imam, the doctrine of *ghayba* became a means of immortalizing those men and perpetuating their cause.[1]

Ismaili Shiʿism was likewise beset with certain problems, including the disappearance of Ismaʿil's son Muhammad, which, however, achieved a different resolution. Ismaʿil's supporters, maintaining as they did that he had been designated successor to the previous imam, Jaʿfar al-Sadiq, remained loyal to his or his son's cause despite these obstacles. Nevertheless, during the period of *satr* or concealment (which started with Muhammad b. Ismaʿil's disappearance), questions did arise as to whether the son had designated a successor, and, if so, when and where his successors would make themselves known. Those who doubted or denied Muhammad b. Ismaʿil's death and awaited his return, it has been argued, ultimately coalesced around the Qarmati movement. But those who maintained that Muhammad b. Ismaʿil had indeed died and had been succeeded in the imamate remained faithful to his presumed but concealed successors, causing speculation as to the successor imam's identity and when he would make himself known to his followers.

These speculations influenced early Ismaili thought of the pre-Fatimid period, and while it expressed itself in the general Shiʿi repertoire of beliefs concerning the return or manifestation of a hidden imam as the *mahdi*, it evolved considerably beyond the simple messianism of other early forms of Shiʿism. As illustrated by Jaʿfar b. Mansur al-Yaman in his *Kitab al-ʿalim waʾl-ghulam*,

Ismaili Shiʿism emphasized the necessity of the imam's spiritual guidance by arguing that the outer or *zahir* meaning of scripture, which varied with every prophet and the particular revelation he communicated, was accompanied by the inner or *batin* meaning which contained the eternal truths or *haqa'iq* of God's word. The latter was communicated to a select few by each prophet's deputy or *wasi* (imam), through the mechanism of *ta'wil* or allegorical interpretation,[2] and just as prophets were needed in order to reveal the scripture, their deputies or imams were needed to reveal the unchanging inner truth of scripture. And so while individual prophets ushered in different eras in human history, every one of those eras also had its series of imams, and according to early Ismaili thought these eras constituted seven cycles culminating with the manifestation of their imam as the *mahdi* or *qa'im* (the 'riser' or 'resurrector'), who in ushering in the seventh and final era would reveal not a new law or scripture to the public, but rather the inner truths or *haqa'iq* that would prevail in the final and just era of human history.[3] Thus the imam's manifestation was necessary, inevitable and to some degree predictable, and would result in the salvation of humankind.

The first Fatimid Imam-caliph, ʿAbd Allah al-Mahdi, had to confront these beliefs and expectations at several points, but most acutely when he assumed power in 297/910. Earlier, questions about his lineage or claimed descent from Muhammad b. Ismaʿil, and about his status as imam, had given rise to the Qarmati schism and their resistance in the east. Now he also had to contend with the expectations of those who, having accepted his imamate during the period of *satr*, anticipated the eschatological changes which they believed to be forthcoming with his manifestation as the *mahdi*. While such messianic expectations had lent conviction and determination to his supporters during the revolutionary or *satr* period, they were bound to be disappointed once al-Mahdi took power. Not only did his physical appearance not conform to certain local prophecies concerning the manifestation of the imam,[4] but there was the more important issue of his presumed eschatological or messianic role as the *mahdi*-saviour, a belief that many anticipated literally and which urgently needed adjustment.

To this end he first attempted to postpone the expectations surrounding his role as the *mahdi* by proclaiming himself 'the rightly guided imam' (*al-imam al-mahdi bi'llah*), as opposed to 'the Mahdi', while his son Abu'l-Qasim, who bore the proper name Muhammad b. ʿAbd Allah (as did the Prophet), was given the title al-Qa'im ('he who presides over the resurrection') when al-Mahdi proclaimed him his successor.[5] To the uninitiated these titles probably differed little from each other, but to the eschatology-minded among the Ismailis they signified the deferral of messianic expectations to the son.[6] Secondly, al-Mahdi retained his legitimacy as the inheritor of the ʿAlid legacy and asserted this by publishing his genealogical credentials to those branches of the *daʿwa* beyond North Africa whose loyalty needed to be maintained.[7] Lastly, al-Mahdi attempted to consolidate his control over the local North African *daʿwa* through the removal of Abu ʿAbd Allah al-Shiʿi in 298/911, apparently because of his involvement in an attempted coup, and also by dealing firmly with controversial doctrinal dissidents, especially among the Kutama Berbers.[8] These subtle changes in designation, genealogical disclosures and the elimination of political and religious opposition helped al-Mahdi to diffuse messianic expectations and consolidate control over his constituency at home and abroad. However, the majority of the population under Fatimid rule in North Africa was not of al-Mahdi's religious constituency, and for this larger community of predominantly Sunni persuasion the issue was not so much his real genealogy and identity (and therefore the messianic expectations attending his appearance), but rather the nature of Shiʿi rule altogether. The task before al-Mahdi was, therefore, to promote the universal rather than particular aspects of Ismaili Shiʿism. This meant a more inclusive policy on religious and legal matters to accommodate the legitimate needs and interests of the majority Sunni community.

Consequently, even as the Sunni majority were subjected to new ritual and legal guidelines implemented by the local Shiʿi *ʿulama'* and Ismaili *daʿis*, efforts were made to engage them in dialogue and discussion as early as the time of Abu ʿAbd Allah's takeover of Qayrawan and Raqqada in 296/909. The dialogue most obviously took the form of *munazarat* with the Sunni *'ulama'*, first convened by Abu 'Abd Allah al-Shi'i as part of the Fatimid effort at outreach.[9] Accounts of these debates vary widely, depending on whether the source is Ismaili or Maliki Sunni. Al-Nu'man provides a brief reference to these debates when he recounts that Abu 'Abd Allah rejoiced when his brother Abu'l-'Abbas joined him in Raqqada in 296/909, and comments:

> Muhammad [Abu'l-'Abbas] was older than him [Abu 'Abd Allah], and was sharper of mind and better versed in the religious sciences, even as Abu 'Abd Allah was more forbearing and pious. … When Abu'l-'Abbas arrived, the *shuyukh* of Qayrawan came to pay respects and congratulate Abu 'Abd Allah on his arrival, and when they saw Abu 'Abd Allah's reverence for his brother, Abu'l-'Abbas grew in their estimation. [Soon] Abu'l-'Abbas began preaching to the people and he gathered the *fuqaha'* of Qayrawan and debated with them on the issue of *imama* and all that constituted differences between them and the *ahl al-bayt* on matters of law, and he impressed them in this and they marvelled at his perspicacity.[10]

This mention does not reveal much about what was debated, with whom in particular and why. For this, one has to turn to the more detailed account of the debates provided in Ibn al-Haytham's *Kitab al-munazarat.*[11] As noted earlier this work deals primarily with Ibn al-Haytham's conversion to Ismaili Shi'ism through his conversations with Abu 'Abd Allah and other members of the *da'wa*. In the process, Ibn al-Haytham also recalls that the debates often took place between the Ismaili *da'is* and the Sunni *'ulama'*, sometimes at the invitation of Abu 'Abd Allah himself.[12] On one such occasion, the debate was between Abu 'Abd Allah and Sa'id b. al-Haddad (known as Abu 'Uthman), a prominent Maliki, and some others.[13]

The discussion began when Abu 'Abd Allah recalled the Prophet's declaration at Ghadir Khumm that whosoever considered him *mawla* (master) should consider 'Ali likewise after him. Abu 'Abd Allah turned to Abu 'Uthman and asked, 'Do you consider 'Ali your *mawla*?' Abu 'Uthman replied yes, he considered 'Ali his *mawla* ('friend', a play on the word) just as he was *mawla* (friend) of ʿAli. Ibn al-Haytham jumped in objecting, and asked, 'So then you would also say that the Prophet is your *mawla* in the same way as you are his *mawla*? And that you are dearer (*awla*, another form of the word) to the Prophet than himself, just as he is dearer to you than yourself.[14] And you say this even though both terms refer exclusively to the Prophet, and even though ʿUmar himself acknowledged ʿAli as his *mawla* (master) at Ghadir Khumm?!' At this point Abu ʿUthman conceded and appealed to Abu ʿAbd Allah not to harm the people of Qayrawan. Abu ʿAbd Allah reassured him, saying, 'There is no compulsion in faith' (citing the Qur'an 2:256), then turned to Ibn al-Haytham and commented, 'You may call them and debate with them and prove the truth to them; as for me, I will follow the saying attributed to Shuʿayb (Jethro), "When one group among you believes, and another doesn't, await God's judgement, for He is the best of judges"' (Qur'an 7:87). Ibn al-Haytham then adds that Abu ʿUthman wrote a false account of these debates which he, Ibn al-Haytham, refuted.[15]

Even if Ibn al-Haytham's account of this dialogue is clearly in favour of Ismaili Shiʿism, which he had recently embraced, it reveals at the same time the nature of the dialogue between the *daʿwa* and the local *ʿulama'*. Significantly, the emphasis of the debate is on the principle of ʿAlid succession, rather than the person of al-Mahdi himself, and in asserting the legitimacy of ʿAlid rule the Shiʿis refer back to the *hadith*s and Qur'anic proofs commonly associated with the event at Ghadir Khumm. In other words, rather than referring to the messianic arguments of the *satr* period, the debate here is grounded in a historical discourse that was shared, if contested, with Sunni Islam.

This is, paradoxically, far more evident in the Maliki accounts of the debates that took place on the issue of *imama*. Ismaili accounts of the *daʿwa*'s encounters with the Sunnis and especially the Maliki community are, as in the case of Ibn al-Haytham, quite favourable towards the Fatimids. As records of a triumphant movement, the Ismaili sources exhibit considerable interest in the outlook and opinions of their vanquished Maliki opponents, but only insofar as they are an aid to establishing the superiority of the *daʿwa*'s arguments. On the Maliki side, however, one source in particular stands out for this very reason. Muhammad b. al-Harith b. Asad al-Khushani (d. 371/981), in his *Kitab tabaqat ʿulamaʾ Ifriqiya*, fortunately preserves more evidence on the topics and strategies that the Ismaili *daʿwa* employed to win the acceptance of Maliki *fuqahaʾ*, precisely because the author himself was hostile to Fatimid rule. As a Maliki, al-Khushani sought to present the Fatimid *daʿwa* activity and state policy as systematically oppressive. In doing so, he provides information on the content of the Fatimid *daʿwa* and indicates the divisions among the Sunni *ʿulamaʾ* of Qayrawan which the *daʿwa* caused. A case in point is the lengthy transcript of the four sessions of debates that took place between Saʿid b. al-Haddad (Abu ʿUthman) and Abu'l-ʿAbbas.[16]

Al-Khushani's transcript of these debates is under the biographical entry for Abu ʿUthman (or again, Saʿid b. al-Haddad), whom al-Khushani characterizes as a man 'well versed in theology (*kalam*), debate and disputation (*jadal* and *munazara*)'.[17] The first session between Abu ʿUthman and Abu'l-ʿAbbas occurs when Abu ʿUthman is summoned to the old Aghlabid palace near Raqqada to speak to Abu'l-ʿAbbas. The debate begins with the issue of *qiyas* or analogical reasoning, whose use Abu ʿUthman supports with a proof-text from the Qur'an which permits the substitution of one thing for another, and in which the authority for determining what is to be substituted is granted to 'those of justice among you (*dhu'l-ʿadl*)'.[18] Someone mentions ʿAli b. Abi Talib as the person intended in the phrase 'those of justice', and Abu'l-ʿAbbas tries to exploit this opening by repeating the *hadith*, 'ʿAli is the most preferable among you', intending to establish the excellence of ʿAli over other Companions of the Prophet like ʿUmar b. al-Khattab. Abu ʿUthman counters with a *hadith* about ʿUmar b. al-Khattab's superiority in religion, but Abu'l-ʿAbbas reminds him of ʿAli's heroism at the Battle of Khaybar.[19] Abu'l-ʿAbbas additionally notes that Malikis omit mention of such bravery because they despise ʿAli b. Abi Talib.[20] Abu ʿUthman denies this, yet he refuses to utter the honorific 'May God's blessings be upon him', arguing that the word *sala* in this expression means praying for God's blessings, and one can only exhort people to pray in this way for the Prophet. When then asked by Abu'l-'Abbas whether or not he considered 'Ali his *mawla* (master) after the *hadith* about Ghadir Khumm, again, as in Ibn al-Haytham's account, Abu 'Uthman resorts to wordplay and states, ''Ali is my *mawla* in the sense that I am his *mawla*.' A last attempt by Abu'l-'Abbas to produce proof of 'Ali's superiority over other Companions, after the *hadith* in which 'Ali is likened to Moses' brother Aaron, ends the session on an inconclusive note. Abu 'Uthman then requests tolerant treatment of the non-Ismaili *'ulama'*, to which Abu'l-'Abbas responds with the Qur'anic verse 7:87 on Shu'ayb as in Ibn al-Haytham's account.[21]

The second session begins with a question about the sources of law (*usul al-fiqh*) and the definition of acceptable *hadith*s about the Prophet, posed to both the Malikis and the Hanafis present. When the question is directed at Abu 'Uthman, he argues that the establishment of acceptable *hadith*s depends on the reliability of the transmitters, according to the methodology of *jarh wa-ta'dil*, the disciplines which had evolved to investigate the trustworthiness of transmitters. Abu'l-'Abbas notes that often such transmitters convey contradictory *hadith*s, suggesting the need for a transcendent authority. He cites a verse from the Qur'an in support of this, regarding a successor Book: 'Say, bring a Book from God which is a better guide than either of them that I may follow it. Do this if you are truthful' (28:49). The Shi'is understand this verse as a reference to the need for the guidance of an imam to interpret the Book. Abu 'Uthman, however, understanding the verse literally, reacts strongly and says, 'God has forbidden what you are saying … for He wanted to deny that they could come with a Book that was a better guide. … He said, "If the whole of mankind and the jinn were to gather together to produce the like of this Qur'an, they could not produce the like thereof"' (17:88). Fearing the repercussions of Abu 'Uthman's outburst his companions hurry him out and, unlike the previous session, this one ends on a frantic note. Abu'l-'Abbas's interpretation of the Qur'anic verse, here in an attempt to assert the need for an imam to explain and guide the community on the basis of the Qur'an, is portrayed as blasphemy and elicits an indignant literalist rebuttal from the Malikis.[22]

The record of the third session begins when Abu ʿUthman comes in during a discussion between Abu'l-ʿAbbas and a Hanafi, in which the Shiʿi is asking the Hanafi whether or not the teacher must by definition be more knowledgeable than the student. The Hanafi agrees and the discussion continues until Abu ʿUthman realizes where it is going. He says, 'I understood what he [Abu'l-ʿAbbas] was getting at, for he was trying to undermine Abu Bakr al-Siddiq ['the trustworthy'], by bringing up the case when Abu Bakr had questioned ʿAli about a grandmother's share in an inheritance. So I rose and said, "The Prophet said, 'Many are the transmitters of *fiqh* to those better at *fiqh*, and many are the transmitters of *fiqh* who are not themselves *fuqaha*' "; thus the teacher is not always more knowledgeable than the student.' Abu ʿUthman then adds that in any case, God invests some people with the natural ability to apprehend both the universal and the particular in the Qur'an. He launches into a long monologue on this subject, attempting to prove that no hierarchy of knowledge exists among either peoples or prophets, and in the process prevents Abu'l-ʿAbbas from returning to the issue of the first caliph, Abu Bakr, and his inadequacies, especially as it concerned his ability to provide religious guidance to the community.[23]

The record of the fourth and last session that took place between Abu ʿUthman and Abu'l-ʿAbbas begins with a curious statement. Abu ʿUthman says, 'This session between us was one in which I felt he [Abu'l-ʿAbbas] and I were closest in position to each other, as if in his debate with me he was someone from a different *madhhab* [school of law].' The debate itself was about the issue of *fadil* and *mafdul* [superior and inferior], an argument that was often deployed by Sunnis to justify the rule of the first three caliphs. When Abu'l-ʿAbbas questions Abu ʿUthman about his *madhhab*'s position on whether or not the inferior can ever supplant the superior, he responds with the verse 2:247: 'Their prophet [Samuel] said to them, "God has appointed Talut [Saul] as king over you." They [the people] said, "How can he exercise authority over us when we are more deserving than he to exercise authority …?" He said, "God has chosen him above you and has increased in him knowledge and power." ' Abu ʿUthman argues that this is proof that the *mafdul* (in this case Saul) can sometimes supplant the *fadil* (Samuel). Abu'l-ʿAbbas counters with the argument that Saul was only appointed over Samuel with the knowledge and *idhn* (permission) of the prophet himself. Abu ʿUthman rejects this argument and then points to other examples from the experience of the Companions which uphold his understanding of this verse, such as the Prophet's appointment of ʿAmr b. al-ʿAs to the command of an army, in which capacity he led the prayer and held a rank superior to that of worthier Companions such as Abu Bakr and ʿUmar. Abu'l-ʿAbbas objects to the implications of these historical examples, saying, 'We don't hold as you do that the community can agree and put over itself an imam, for the imam has to be selected by God and His Prophet', otherwise he obtains no respect. Abu ʿUthman responds with the Sunni argument that neither God nor His Prophet clearly indicated a successor, and then outlines all the implications of its influence for *usul al-fiqh*: the necessity of *ijmaʿ*, or consensus of the scholars, and *ijtihad*, or an independent legal judgement. Abu'l-ʿAbbas makes one last attempt, and Abu ʿUthman ends with some rather disparaging remarks about him, bringing to a close the transcript of the sessions between Abu'l-ʿAbbas and Abu ʿUthman.[24]

Al-Khushani's account of these four debates is obviously an attempt to undermine the tenets of Ismaili Shiʿism, but in the process the account also illustrates the discursive styles and arguments the *daʿwa* employed when dealing with the Sunni *ʿulama'*, and in greater detail than do the Ismaili sources. In the first debate, which Ibn al-Haytham's memoir also covers, Abu'l-ʿAbbas's effort to posit the ultimate legal and political authority of ʿAli relies on favourable and commonly accepted *hadith*s, while on the Sunni side the authority of the Companions is defended with countervailing *hadith*s from the Prophet, as well as wordplay when a *hadith* in ʿAli b. Abi Talib's favour is too well established to be dismissed. Although in al-Khushani's account Abu'l-ʿAbbas appears to be challenged by Abu ʿUthman, the narrative thread of his argument is as follows: *qiyas* or analogical reasoning is faulty, and 'Ali's judgement is preferable to all others, and hence the Prophet indicated that he was to be considered the *mawla* of the Muslims after him. Abu'l-'Abbas thus argues the Shi'i position from a Traditionist standpoint. The second and third sessions or debates culminate in a heated rebuttal by Abu 'Uthman, apparently because he is troubled by the *ta'wil* or allegorical reading of the Qur'anic text that Abu'l-'Abbas injects from time to time into their discussion. Equally problematic for him is the presence of the Hanafis, who appear to be susceptible to the arguments of the Shi'is. The transcript of both of these debates begins with a diversionary tactic on the part of Abu 'Uthman to sabotage consensus among the Shi'is and Hanafis. It is only in the fourth debate that the issue of *imama* comes up explicitly, in the context of superior and inferior, which both parties implicitly agree refers to 'Ali b. Abi Talib and the Companions respectively. The disagreement lies, of course, in whether or not the inferior (i.e. the Companions) can have authority over the superior (i.e. 'Ali b. Abi Talib), as Saul did over Samuel. Abu 'Uthman argues for the legitimate authority of inferiors, on the basis of Qur'an 2:247 and historical examples from the Prophet's time. Significantly, al-Kushani fails to present a counter-argument from Abu'l-'Abbas, which he probably did and it was probably one that could have involved the designation of 'Ali at Ghadir Khumm.

All in all, al-Kushani's account gives us important information on issues contested by the local Sunni *'ulama'*, the degree to which these caused divisions within the Sunni community itself and something of the *modus operandi* of the Fatimid *da'wa* vis-à-vis the non-Ismaili Muslims. As for the Sunni opposition, what was clearly at stake was more than just a difference of opinion regarding the relative merits of the Companions versus 'Ali b. Abi Talib, the use of *qiyas* and interpretation of the Qur'an. The assertion of the knowledge, qualifications and legitimacy of the Companions, the upholding of *qiyas*, insistence on a literal reading of the Qur'an and other issues raised by the Malikis represent both a defence of Sunni tradition and an affirmation of their own authority as scholars and sources of religious guidance. Both were threatened by the Ismaili *da'wa*'s ascendancy and its promotion of a canon that asserted the supreme religious authority of the Ismaili imams and the legitimacy of their ʿAlid succession. Thus Maliki sources exhibit a particular venom towards the Fatimids and their *daʿwa*, reflected in Abu ʿUthman's attitude and responses in the *munazarat* of the early Fatimid period.

Abu ʿUthman's ire is most evident when the Shiʿis occasionally resort to *ta'wil*, which again was not simply threatening to the Malikis on theological and legal grounds. It was also an area of agreement between Shiʿis and Hanafis, whose intellectual and Muʿtazili tendencies led to an allegorical interpretation of the Qur'an similar to *ta'wil*. The debates thus exacerbated the fundamental divisions within the ranks of the Sunnis of Qayrawan. The presence of Hanafis, in fact, reflects an important shift in policy on the part of the late Aghlabids. Although Qayrawan had early on acquired strong Maliki affiliations, it became the seat of doctrinal diversity even within the Sunni camp. The Aghlabid rulers followed the policies of their Abbasid overlords in religious matters, and consequently religious officials of Muʿtazili and Hanafi affiliation were often appointed. Nevertheless, with the resurgence of Sunni orthodoxy after the decline of the Abbasid *mihna*, Malikism became the *madhhab* of the Aghlabid state, and this state of affairs lasted until the advent of Abu ʿAbd Allah al-Shiʿi and the growing threat of Ismaili Shiʿism. During the short reign of Abu'l-ʿAbbas ʿAbd Allah II b. Ibrahim (289–290/902–903) in particular, an effort was made to counteract the appeal of Shiʿism with the promotion of Hanafism and Muʿtazili theology once again.[25] In fact, al-Qadi al-Nuʿman reports in his *Iftitah* that this penultimate Aghlabid followed the Hanafi *madhhab* himself and professed the doctrine of the created Qur'an, which earned him the hostility of the Sunni masses.[26]

ʿAbd Allah II's policy of promoting Hanafis in an attempt to undermine the appeal of Shiʿism in his domains ultimately backfired, earning him the wrath of the Malikis, and creating a foothold for Shiʿism in Qayrawan itself, as is evidenced by the mention of Shiʿis and their easy interaction with Hanafis in Ibn al-Haytham's *Kitab al-munazarat*. Al-Khushani's entries also provide evidence of several Hanafi *ʿulama'* who converted to Ismaili Shiʿism before and during the establishment of the Fatimid state. In al-Khushani's descriptions of these converts, six were originally Maliki, one Shafiʿi, and the remaining 11 were adherents of the Hanafi or Iraqi *madhhab* as it was known at the time. The Shafiʿi convert, ʿAbd al-Malik b. Muhammad al-Dabbi, was the brother of Ibrahim (Ibn al-Birdhawn) who was sentenced to death by al-Marwadhi, the *qadi* of Qayrawan;[27] and one of the Malikis, Muhammad b. Hayyan, was in fact the father of al-Qadi al-Nuʿman.[28]

As for the Hanafis, they included the *qadi*s Ishaq b. Abi Minhal and his brother Abu ʿAli who converted on the arrival of the Ismaili *daʿwa* in Ifriqiya (this prominent family included another brother who remained a Hanafi).[29] Ishaq was appointed *qadi* of Sicily and then of Qayrawan, and in his turn, while *qadi* of Qayrawan, appointed the former Hanafis Jaʿfar b. Ahmad b. Wahb to the *mazalim* (appeals court) and Ahmad b. Bahr to the *mazalim* and then as *qadi* of Tripoli. One Abu Muhammad b. Shahran also converted from the Hanafi *madhhab* when the *daʿwa* arrived in Qayrawan and was appointed secretary of the *qadi al-qudat* al-Marwadhi. Another convert, Zurara b. Ahmad, who frequented both Malikis and Hanafis and distinguished himself in the use of *ra'y* (personal opinion) and by his knowledge of the differences between legal schools, was appointed *qadi* of Mahdiyya and became, according to al-Khushani, one of the fanatical Shiʿis.[30]

The conversion of so many Hanafis indicates their willingness to assimilate into the new Fatimid order, as well as the obvious benefits they derived from so doing. Their conversion was probably motivated in part by necessity, inasmuch as their previous Aghlabid patrons had been replaced by the Fatimids, but probably also out of a sense of doctrinal affinity, reflected in their appointment as judicial officials. As such they no doubt exerted an important influence in the formation of an Ismaili *madhhab*. In all events, the Hanafis' conversion greatly angered the Maliki *ʿulama'*, as is clear from al-Khushani's transcript of the debates between Abu'l-ʿAbbas and Abu ʿUthman, and his disparaging comments about the Hanafi converts.

The debates most importantly reveal something of the Ismaili *daʿwa*'s changing relations with the majority Sunni community. It is clear that the encounters between the two involved something of a hermeneutic shift for the *daʿwa*, which found it necessary to structure its inquiry around issues and questions of *usul al-fiqh* and the history of the first Islamic state, as distinct from the more spiritual and esoteric concerns reflected in, say, the *Kitab al-ʿalim wa'l-ghulam* of Jaʿfar b. Mansur al-Yaman. The need to engage the Sunnis on their own *zahiri* or exoteric terms, and at the least establish a way of rendering acceptable the political authority of the Fatimid state, if not to convert their Sunni interlocutors, resulted in recourse to a shared discourse characterized by theological and legal argumentation. Thus, although the information from Ibn al-Haytham and al-Khushani does not tell us anything about al-Qadi al-Nuʿman per se, it does indicate how those debates and the diverse intellectual traditions of the North African Sunni community helped to shape subsequent Fatimid religious policy and al-Nuʿman's role in it. This emphasis in Fatimid forms of representation also generated something of a renaissance in Malikism.[31]

Al-Qadi Abu Hanifa al-Nuʿman b. Muhammad b. Mansur b. Ahmad b. Hayyun al-Tamimi came from a Maliki Sunni family, as we have learned from al-Khushani. His father had converted to Ismaili Shiʿism before the establishment of the Fatimid state in 296/909. Al-Nuʿman himself joined the service of the Fatimids in 313/925, and so he must have been quite young at the time of his father's conversion. Yet al-Khushani states that al-Nuʿman's father had practised *taqiyya* or dissimulation, suggesting that al-Nuʿman may not have been brought up as an Ismaili. Nevertheless, he clearly identified himself as such at the time he joined the service of al-Mahdi in 313/925, when he was employed as a secretary charged with reporting news about the court to the imam. He was also a copyist of books for al-Mahdi's grandson and the future third Fatimid imam-caliph, al-Mansur. When al-Mansur acceded to the throne in 334/946, al-Nuʿman was appointed judge of Tripoli, and then supreme judge or *qadi al-qudat* of the

Fatimid territories. His jurisdiction included the new capital of Mansuriyya in 337/948, as well as the old capital of Mahdiyya and Qayrawan. Under al-Mansur's successor, al-Muʿizz (who came to power in 341/953), al-Nuʿman was further charged with supervising the *mazalim*, and 'matters related to the royal entourage, ... the various classes of the caliph's bondsmen, [and] the soldiery stationed in the capital. ... In addition to this he was also authorised by the caliph to hold the *majalis al-hikma* (sessions of wisdom) every Friday following the noon prayers, in the royal palace to instruct the Ismaili congregation in the religious sciences of the *daʿwa*, especially the *batini* (esoteric) sciences.'[32] Al-Nuʿman accompanied al-Muʿizz to Egypt in 363/973, and died a year later in the new Fatimid capital. His sons and other relatives continued to hold important positions in the Fatimid state: two of his sons, two grandsons and a great grandson were either appointed supreme judge or achieved high rank in the *daʿwa*,[33] and his works were read and recited by them and other *daʿis* in the *majalis al-hikma* that took place at al-Azhar and elsewhere in Cairo and Egypt.[34]

Despite al-Nuʿman's importance to the Fatimids, this is the extent of our biographical information on him.[35] As a result, there has been some confusion regarding his religious affiliation and training. Medieval biographical dictionaries, such as Ibn Khallikan's *Wafayat al-aʿyan*, suggest that al-Nuʿman converted from Maliki Sunnism to Twelver Shiʿism, an assertion found in many other sources.[36] The authors of Twelver Shiʿi biographical works of the same period claim al-Qadi al-Nuʿman as their co-religionist, and attempt to explain away his close association with the Fatimids by claiming that he practised *taqiyya* throughout his career. The genesis of these claims has been traced to Twelver Shiʿi scholars in Cairo during the 6th/12th century. But early Twelver Shiʿi biographers, such as al-Najashi (d. 450/1058) and Abu Jaʿfar Muhammad al-Tusi (d. 460/1067), did not comment on or make a similar claim about his Twelver identity and thus his appropriation by this branch of Shiʿism occurred relatively late.[37]

There has similarly been confusion over al-Nuʿman's status as a scholar. Unlike most *ʿulama'*, for whom biographical dictionaries supply information on teachers, students and their works, virtually nothing definite is known about al-Nuʿman's training or teachers. His prominence derived from his association with the Fatimid imams themselves and thus, beyond the fact that his father converted to Ismaili Shiʿism, the process by which al-Nuʿman acquired the education and qualifications that made him most valuable to the Fatimids remains a mystery. Because of this some later scholars and members of the Ismaili community considered al-Qadi al-Nuʿman a *daʿi*, and, as such, someone whose training in a secretive organization like the *daʿwa* would not have been recorded. And the absence of chains of transmission in many of his legal works was explained in terms of his proximity to the imam as *hujja* (proof), or a similar high-ranking member of the *daʿwa*.[38]

Other Ismaili sources, however, accord him a status subordinate to the *daʿis*. An example is the apocryphal story about al-Nuʿman's relationship to Jaʿfar b. Mansur al-Yaman, recounted in the *ʿUyun al-akhbar* of Idris ʿImad al-Din (d. 872/1468). According to the *ʿUyun*, al-Nuʿman once fell sick in the time of al-Muʿizz and was visited by members of the Ismaili community and *daʿwa*, who paid their respects, all except for Jaʿfar b. Mansur. When al-Muʿizz asked al-Nuʿman who had visited him during his illness, al-Nuʿman responded only that Jaʿfar b. Mansur had not. Al-Muʿizz then proceeded to speak about Jaʿfar and requested that certain books be brought to him. Opening one of them, he asked al-Nuʿman to peruse it and then asked for his opinion on it. Al-Nuʿman, thinking it was the work of the imam himself, responded that he could not. Al-Muʿizz then said to him, 'This is the work of your master Jaʿfar,' and so when the *qadi* recovered his health he immediately set out for the *daʿi*'s house and, when led into his presence, prostrated himself in recognition of Jaʿfar's higher status.[39]

Regardless of the inconclusive evidence on al-Nuʿman's training and real vocation, his importance to the Fatimids of the North African period is clear from his close relationship with them and the many works they commissioned from him. Like other local converts he was extremely useful to the Fatimid regime because of their need to bridge the gap between the Ismaili state and its non-Ismaili subjects with a new policy, legal system, protocol and court history. The problem was that all these had to be created anew, and in such a manner as to be particularly defensible against criticism from their Sunni subjects. Considering the immediate need for ritual and legal guidelines, the first work al-Mahdi commissioned from al-Nuʿman was the *Kitab al-idah*, a large compendium of *hadith*s on the authority of the *ahl al-bayt*.[40] With the exception of a small surviving fragment on prayer, this work is lost, but that fragment reveals that in the absence of a specifically Ismaili Shiʿi law, al-Nuʿman turned to other Shiʿi traditions, some of them local and many from the North African scholarly Shiʿi curriculum noted in Ibn al-Haytham's *Kitab al-munazarat*. The surviving fragment incorporates the traditions of a local Musawi Shiʿi school, whose founder al-Nuʿman quotes as a source,[41] as well as traditions common to Zaydi and Twelver Shiʿism.[42] Building on these beginnings in the time of al-Mahdi, al-Nuʿman continued to formulate his scholarship, and by the time of al-Muʿizz he had fully developed a distinctive Ismaili Shiʿi synthesis of law.

A picture of al-Nuʿman's works and contribution was first derived from extant medieval bibliographical and biographical sources. Of all the listings for al-Qadi al-Nuʿman, the two most comprehensive are the entries in the *Fihrist*[43] of al-Majdu (d. 1183/1769) and the section dealing with the life and merits of al-Nuʿman in Idris's *ʿUyun al-akhbar*, both Ismaʿili sources. Sunni sources such as Ibn Khallikan's *Wafayat* provide only an abbreviated and somewhat inaccurate listing of al-Nuʿman's works (he mentions only six), based on the *Fihrist* of Ibn Nadim (377/987). Ibn Hajar al-ʿAsqalani (d. 852/1449), while providing a lengthy account of al-Nuʿman's life in his *Rafʿ al-ʿisr*, provides no information whatsoever on his works.[44]

What emerged as a list from al-Majduʿ, Idris and Ibn Khallikan combined to constitute the first published lists by modern scholars as found in W. Ivanow's *A Guide to Ismaʿili Literature* (1933) and A.A.A. Fyzee's 'Qadi an-Nuʿman, the Fatimid Jurist and Author' (1934). I. Poonawala, in his *Biobibliography of Ismaʿili Literature*

(1977), has since added to or amended these early lists in the light of newly available material and works. The resulting list, based on a far greater number of biographical sources than Fyzee's or Ivanow's, puts al-Nuʿman's total output at 60 works, although of these, 11 have an uncertain attribution to al-Nuʿman.[45]

Dating al-Nuʿman's works, however, is difficult unless there is some indication in prefatory remarks or introductions, or internal evidence of the time when they were composed. It is likely that most of his works were written prior to the conquest of Egypt and many during the four years between the conquest (358/969) and al-Muʿizz's departure for his new capital (362/973). According to the *ʿUyun* of Idris ʿImad al-Din,[46] in al-Mahdi's time al-Nuʿman finished, in addition to the *Kitab al-idah*, two abridgements of it, the *Kitab al-akhbar* (which consisted of 300 folios, from the original 3,000, without chains of transmission), and the *Mukhtasar al-idah* ('Summary of the *idah*').[47] Apparently he also composed the *Kitab maʿalim al-Mahdi*, which was a work either on the teachings of or prophecies concerning al-Mahdi, now lost.[48] During al-Qa'im's reign (322–334/934–946), al-Nuʿman produced the *Urjuzat al mukhtara*, a *qasida* or poem in defence of the Fatimid imams' claims to authority, and a *qasida* on *fiqh*, the *Urjuzat al-muntakhaba*.[49] These verse compositions were abridgements of the earlier works, composed for ease of memorization and dissemination. In addition he also produced the *Kitab al-iqtisar*, a short handbook of *hadith*s ascribed to the *ahl al-bayt*.[50]

By the time of al-Mansur's reign (334–341/946–953), al-Nuʿman had attained the rank of *qadi* of Tripoli and then was appointed *qadi al-qudat* or supreme *qadi* of the Fatimid domains, and at this time composed a work on the Qur'an, which he mentions in a later work.[51] When al-Muʿizz acceded to the throne in 341/953, al-Qadi al-Nuʿman reached the zenith of his career as not only supreme judge of the Fatimid domains, but also the head of the *mazalim* and in charge of the *majalis al-hikma*. He was also the imam's friend and confidant. This close relationship was important in many respects, although mostly in terms of the collaborative nature of the works al-Nuʿman composed at that time which are mentioned in, for example, his *Kitab al-majalis wa'l-musa-*

yarat. Al-Nuʿman recalls here that al-Muʿizz commissioned from him a work on the history of the Fatimid state (most probably the *Iftitah)*, and a work on the virtues of the Banu Hashim (the clan of the Prophet) and the shortcomings of the Banu Umayya (the clan of the Umayyads) entitled the *Kitab al-manaqib wa'l-mathalib.*[52] He notes that he collected all the information that could be obtained on both subjects in two huge volumes, broken down into numerous sections, according to al-Muʿizz's instructions. On finishing the volumes, al-Nuʿman submitted them to al-Muʿizz, who reviewed, improved upon and finally approved them.[53] The imam was thus involved at every step of the process, from suggesting subject matter and organizing material to reviewing and editing the work and specifying its uses.

Apart from the above works whose dates can be established from internal evidence, the remaining known works of al-Qadi al-Nuʿman have been listed and organized in Poonawala's *Biobibliography* according to presumed (in the case of lost works) or actual subject matter. Under the *Biobibliography*'s heading of *fiqh*, many of the entries deal with the duties and obligations of the *mu'min* (faithful) towards the imam, in contrast to, for example, Twelver Shiʿi works which often discuss *imama* in works on *usul al-din* or in the context of theology.[54] Treating *imama* as an integral part of legal or *fiqh* works here reflects the concern for the binding authority of a living and ruling imam.[55] Many of al-Nuʿman's *fiqh* works are summaries of the earlier *Kitab al-idah*, such as the *Kitab al-akhbar*, the *Mukhtasar al-idah*, the *Urjuzat al-muntakhaba*, the *Kitab al-iqtisar* and the *Mukhtasar al-athar.*[56] The *Daʿa'im al-Islam*, written in the time of al-Muʿizz, is the last of this series of legal works and is considered the definitive Ismaili legal work of al-Nuʿman.

Under 'history', the *Biobibliography* lists the following works: the *Urjuzat dhat al-minan* (a biography in verse of al-Muʿizz),[57] the *Iftitah al-daʿwa*, the *Kitab al-manaqib li ahl bayt Rasul-Allah al-nujaba' wa'l-mathalib li bani ʿUmayya al-luʿana'* (referred to as *Kitab al-manaqib wa'l-mathalib*), the *Sharh al-akhbar* (a collection of *hadith*s concerning the imams from the time of ʿAli b. Abi Talib),[58] and the *Kitab al-majalis wa'l-musayarat* (a collection of narratives about the Fatimids, and especially al-Muʿizz). There is also an *urjuza* or verse composition on Abu Yazid, the Khariji rebel, entitled *Dhat al-mihan* (the companion to the *Urjuzat dhat al-minan* mentioned above).[59]

In addition to jurisprudence and history, al-Nuʿman composed other works that are classified as 'polemics and refutations' in the *Biobibliography*. Among these works are various refutations or 'ripostes' (*al-radd ʿala*) in the form of *rasa'il* or 'letters' to scholars of the Sunni schools of law, and leading polemicists, such as al-ʿUtaqi,[60] Ibn Qutayba,[61] Ibn Surayj al-Baghdadi,[62] as well as the eponyms of the schools of law, al-Shafiʿi, Malik and Abu Hanifa,[63] indicating the extent of the concern and attention the Fatimids devoted to Sunni tradition (as opposed to competing forms of Shiʿism, which are noticeably absent from the list of reponses), especially those most strongly represented in their North African and later on in their Egyptian territories.

There are also the works that the *Biobibliography* lists under 'Qur'an and *ta'wil*' that include the following: *Kitab fi ma rafadathu'l-ʿamma min kitab Allah* ('What Has Been Rejected from God's Book'),[64] the *Nahj al-sabil ila maʿrifat ʿilm al-ta'wil* ('The Straight Path to Knowledge of *Ta'wil*'),[65] *Asas al-ta'wil* ('The Bases of *Ta'wil*'),[66] *Kayfiyyat al-salat ʿala al-nabi* ('How to Pray and Bless the Prophet'),[67] *Ta'wil al-daʿa'im*,[68] *Ta'wil al-ru'ya*,[69] and the *Ta'wil al-shariʿa* (the *ta'wil* of the *Daʿa'im*, dreams and Shariʿa, respectively).[70] None of these works deal with *imama* per se, but they do support the imam's claim to ultimate authority as a source of knowledge. Also they indicate al-Nuʿman's proficiency, if not specialization, in the esoteric sciences of *ta'wil*, and thus his usefulness in transmitting and expounding Ismaili *ta'wil* of diverse subjects, including the ritual prayer and other religious practices.

And finally, under 'miscellaneous' are listed the following works dealing with the imam's role and attributes or wisdom: the *Kitab al-himma fi adab atbaʿ al-a'imma* ('The Importance of Correct Protocol for the Followers of the Imam'),[71] *Kitab al-tawhid* (or *al-Tawhid wa'l-imama min khutab amir al-mu'minin*, 'The Book of Unity'),[72] *Manamat al-a'imma* ('The Dreams of the

Imams'),[73] and other works, some juridical, some exegetical, and a collection of responsa to various jurists on legal matters.

It is obvious from this overview that apart from the remarkable diversity of his works, genres and topics, al-Nu'man was prolific, especially during the reign of al-Mu'izz, who, as we have seen, took a close personal interest in his writings. Clearly during a long career which spanned the reigns of all four Fatimids of the North African period, al-Nu'man's legal thinking developed along with the Fatimid state and its religious policy. The culmination in al-Mu'izz's time is the Ismaili synthesis in al-Nu'man's most important legal work, the *Da'a'im*, the defence of that synthesis against Sunni legal *hadith*s in his many ripostes, the development of a historical narrative for the Fatimid state, biographies of the imams, and arguments for the superiority of their knowledge in his works on *ta'wil*, and even a protocol for the state and its subjects. The guiding role of the Fatimid imams in many of his works, moreover, indicates their desire for a *zahiri* or exoteric discourse that would be acceptable to the many different audiences – Ismaili, Twelver Shi'i and Sunni – they had to address, and the unique role al-Nu'man was qualified to play in articulating such a discouse, as an individual who himself personified Ismaili Shi'i success in a Sunni context.

Three of al-Qadi al-Nu'man's works in particular will be examined next: the *Da'a'im al-Islam* (and, relatedly, the *Ikhtilaf usul al-madhahib*), the *Kitab al-majalis wa'l-musayarat* (as compared to the *Iftitah*) and the *Kitab al-himma fi adab atba' al-a'imma*. These three works represent three genres of literature that are quintessentially *zahiri* in nature; that is, the *Da'a'im*, which is an example of *fiqh*, the *Majalis*, which is a compilation of *hadith*s (or reports about/history of the imams), and the *Kitab al-himma*, a manual of duties and conventions of obedience to the imam. Taken together they provide an insight into the means by which Shi'i Ismaili doctrines were translated into a working framework in a Sunni setting, or how formerly *batini* issues came to be addressed in a *zahiri* context.

3

The *Zahiri* Framework

The *Da'a'im al-Islam* of al-Qadi al-Nu'man may have been the culmination of the development of an Ismaili *fiqh*, yet at the same time that Ismaili *fiqh* was in the making, significant developments in the evolution of Sunni as well as Twelver Shi'i *fiqh* were taking place, also in response to changing political and social circumstances. These changing circumstances were for the most part derived from the expansion and consolidation of Islam in the previous centuries, which had generated questions about the legitimacy of the Islamic empire and a debate over the state's jurisdiction – in other words, not only who should rule but also on what basis. Given that, ideally, the Islamic state had a role that was both political and religious, efforts were made to establish the sources from which religious guidance should be provided, especially in the face of the new and often unforeseen administrative challenges that expansion had created.

In the early Islamic period (or roughly until the 2nd/8th centuries) religious guidance, including the elaboration of a code and practice of law, was derived primarily from and based on the Qur'an. However, the emergence of a multitude of issues on which the Qur'anic text did not provide explicit guidance required a resort to the *ra'y* or independent judgement of judges and governors dispersed throughout the empire, or to that of the caliph himself. But by the early Abbasid period (from 132/750), there was an increasing unease among those who came to be considered the Sunni scholarly and religious classes about the heterogeneity of precedents that this policy had produced. They increasingly sought to systematize and justify the sources for law, leading eventually to a methodology that acknowledged that the authority of the Qur'an and the *Sunna* or customary practice of the Prophet stood over and above any immediate or local tradition, and limited independent judgement to *qiyas* (analogical reasoning) and the *ijmaʿ* (consensus) of religious scholars.[1] The need to standardize and normatize, in other words, resulted in a more circumscribed corpus of acceptable law in Sunni Islam by the 4th/10th century (even while it produced a burgeoning of disciplines related to establishing a Prophetic *Sunna*, for example), and, paradoxically, in the transfer away from the state of the responsibility for the law in favour of the religious classes.

The concern with *usul al-fiqh*, or sources of law, that had come to predominate in Sunni Islam was clearly in evidence in the debates of the early Fatimid period that were recorded by Ibn al-Haytham in his *Kitab al-munazarat*, and al-Khushani in his *Tabaqat*. As we have seen, the emphasis in the debates was not only on the question of succession to the Prophet in leadership of the community, but also on the question of acceptable sources for the law. That the Sunni (especially Maliki) side put forth arguments which emphasized a literal reading of the Qur'an, the validity of *qiyas* and use of the *Sunna* is not surprising given the developments noted above. And in responding to such arguments, the Ismaili *daʿwa*, not surprisingly, likewise utilized a Traditionist discourse with emphasis on the Qur'an. Of course, regarding the use of *qiyas*, the Fatimid *daʿwa* proposed instead the superior qualifications of an imam (descended from the Prophet and therefore most likely to reliably continue his practice) over that of so many *ʿulama'* (who in any case disagreed with each other) to provide an elucidation of the Qur'an and *Sunna* that was responsive to changing needs.

As for Twelver Shiʿism, it had emerged after the death of Jaʿfar al-Sadiq in 148/765 as the cause of his descendants through his other son Musa al-Kazim (d. 183/799), a line that continued for four more generations until the death of the eleventh imam, al-Hasan al-ʿAskari in 260/874, and the *ghayba* or occultation of the twelfth imam, Muhammad al-Mahdi (b. 255/869). Owing to the relative longevity of this line of imams and their avoidance of political involvement, their cause was able to survive at the heart of the Abbasid empire. However, the death of al-Hasan al-ʿAskari and the disappearance of his son put the Twelver Shiʿi community in the predictable dilemma of many Shiʿi sects, that is, the absence of a manifest imam and thus the possible obsolescence of his cause. The occultation of the twelfth imam in the late 3rd/9th century was therefore initially assumed to be temporary; it was believed that he continued to guide his community through deputies who received his instructions sent from his place of hiding. After the death of his last deputy, however, his disappearance was recognized as permanent, and thus began the period of the Greater Occultation in Twelver Shiʿism (from 329/940).[2] It is noteworthy that the Greater Occultation of Muhammad al-Mahdi coincided with the manifestation of Fatimid rule in North Africa.[3]

By the time of the Greater Occultation in the mid-4th/10th century, the Twelver Shiʿi doctrine of *ghayba* was incorporated in what came to be referred to as the 'four books' (*al-kutub al-arbaʿa*), Twelver Shiʿism's most authoritative early works on law and doctrine.[4] The authors of these works include Abu Jaʿfar Muhammad b. Yaʿqub al-Kulayni (d. 329/941),[5] and Abu Jaʿfar Muhammad b. Abu'l-Hasan ʿAli b. Husayn b. Musa al-Qummi al-Saduq (known as Ibn Babawayh, d. 381/992).[6] Two of their works, the *Kafi* of al-Kulayni[7] and the *Risalat al-iʿtiqadat* of Ibn Babawayh,[8] provide useful points of comparison with the contemporary *Daʿaʾim al-Islam* of al-Qadi al-Nuʿman, as an indication of the differences between Twelver and Ismaili Shiʿi doctrines of *imama*.

Just as Ismaili Shiʿism responded to the Sunni difference of opinion regarding *imama* by emphasizing their arguments regarding it and presenting a historical justification for the ʿAlid succession, one can suppose that developments within Twelver Shiʿism were on some level taken into consideration in the shaping of Ismaili thought and vice-versa. Not only did both forms of Shiʿism share a fundamental belief in *imama* (in this case, belief in the succession of the ʿAlid imams via Husayn, up to Jaʿfar al-Sadiq), but both were also emerging as major Shiʿi communities at this time. While the Fatimids were consolidating their political success in North Africa in the 4th/10th century, Twelver Shiʿism had become a major community in the east and representative of Shiʿi sentiments there. But their development as distinctive communities followed divergent paths: on the one hand, the attainment of power and rule by a living imam in the Fatimid case, and the disappearance or Greater Occultation of the Twelver Shiʿi imam on the other. Both camps responded to these events with the production of doctrinal and legal works which sought, in arguing either for the universal legitimacy of a manifest imam or the viability of the occultation of the imam, to establish a definitive understanding of *imama* and thus an authoritative Shiʿi dogma. This implied that there was some rivalry between the two forms of Shiʿism which, in turn, indicates the existence of an equally implicit dialogue, or at least a strategic elaboration of doctrine.

Ultimately Ismaili Shiʿism charts a distinctive course vis-à-vis both Twelver and Sunni forms of Islam, insofar as the systematic elaboration of its doctrines occurs as a result of the manifestation of an imam, and of an Ismaili *fiqh* and *madhhab* in consequence of the establishment of his rule. Unlike Twelver Shiʿism where *fiqh* developed in lieu of the imam and in absence of power, and Sunni Islam where *fiqh* developed in opposition to power, Ismaili *fiqh* evolved in response to the acquisition of power, a state of affairs that challenges conventional notions about the strictly autonomous development of an Islamic legal tradition. At the beginning of Fatimid rule, however, the path to this end was not clear. As in the case of the Abbasids, the transition from revolution to state prompted some necessary and critical changes to Fatimid policy and politics. In addition to the unremitting hostility of the Sunni, especially the Maliki, *ʿulama'* and the rebellious Khariji Berbers of the western Mahgrib, the early Fatimids had to contend with internal dissent and opposition within their *daʿwa*. As already noted, this culminated in the execution of Abu ʿAbd Allah al-Shiʿi and his brother Abu'l-ʿAbbas in 298/911, and was followed by the purge of extremist and antinomian *daʿis* in the year 309/921. Despite these problems, al-Mahdi's religious policy remained in many ways that of the revolutionary period, the era of Abu ʿAbd Allah's *dar al-hijra*. While he did not abstain from appointing Sunnis to administrative positions, he continued to rely exclusively on Shiʿis for religious offices, including not only the imams (that is to say, the prayer leaders) of mosques, but also *qadis*, *muftis* (those who delivered religious opinions), public witnesses, and those who were allowed to draw up legal contracts and documents.[9] At the same time, instruction in Sunni *madhahib* was officially prohibited, presumably to encourage conversion to Ismaili Shiʿism. Subjecting the Sunni *ʿulama'* to these restrictions (similar to those previously imposed by the Aghlabids on the Shiʿis) resulted in growing resentment towards the Fatimid state.

By the time of al-Qa'im,[10] this resentment had found an outlet in another revolt, that of Abu Yazid, and because of this he had little time to reassess Fatimid religious policy and so continued his father's policy, reinstating most of the administrators appointed by al-Mahdi.[11] Abu Yazid Makhlad b. Kaydad, a Khariji schoolteacher of humble origins, managed to galvanize the opposition to the Fatimid regime and launch a major rebellion that almost destroyed the Fatimid state. By 332/944, Abu Yazid had managed to take several strategic towns in the old area of Abu ʿAbd Allah's *dar al-hijra*. After taking al-Urbus, Abu Yazid proceeded to Raqqada and Qayrawan, where his Berber followers looted the city. By the end of the year he blockaded Mahdiyya, where al-Qa'im was residing, but his erratic behaviour and the desertion of some of his troops led to his retreat and a pursuit by the Fatimid armies. The future caliph al-Mansur then proceeded with an army to Qayrawan where he engaged Abu Yazid and his troops in battle and, to the relief of the Qayrawanis, defeated him. But before pursuing Abu Yazid further, al-Mansur consolidated the support of Qayrawan by appointing a Maliki judge (Ahmad b. Bahr) to replace the Ismaili judge who had been killed by Abu Yazid. At the same time, and to further reconciliation, he distributed the booty taken from Abu Yazid's army as alms, withheld taxes for a year and began construction of a new capital (Mansuriyya) in the vicinity of Qayrawan. These measures succeeded in consolidating support for al-Mansur, and in the following year (336/947) he finally cornered Abu Yazid in the Hodna mountains and took him prisoner (he died soon after his capture), at which point al-Mansur publicly announced his succession to al-Qa'im.[12]

Following the defeat of Abu Yazid, and perhaps as a result of it, al-Mansur actively pursued the support of his Sunni subjects. This he did in a number of ways, such as leading the prayer on major occasions in Qayrawan and otherwise engaging the population in festivals of his own devising. For example, in 340/941 al-Mansur held a festival on the occasion of his sons' circumcision, which was accompanied by the circumcision of 1,000 young boys from Qayrawan and those of the Kutama.[13] More importantly, he initiated a radical departure in policy, allowing for the appointment of Maliki judges in predominantly Maliki towns, while jurisdiction in Ismaili towns such as Mansuriyya and Mahdiyya went to Ismaili judges like al-Qadi al-Nuʿman (who had at this time also been appointed supreme judge for all Fatimid territories). Nevertheless, al-Mansur's policy of rapprochement and bipartisan administration still had its problems. For example, in the last year of his reign, the Sunni judge of Barqa refused to follow the caliph's instructions on the correct time for ending the month of Ramadan. This brought him into open conflict with the local Kutami governor and threatened to split the festivities of the Sunni and Ismaili communities of the town, and was only resolved with the arrest and execution of the offending *qadi*.[14]

Al-Muʿizz continued his father's policy of inclusive religious administration and actively engaging the public, both Sunni and Shiʿi, when he came to power in 341/953. In addition to leading the prayer on main feast days and every Friday during Ramadan,[15] he held public banquets on important holidays.[16] As in al-Mansur's time, the occasion of al-Muizz's sons' circumcision was accompanied by the circumcision of all the youths in the realm, and to accommodate which tented pavilions were erected in the capital, with entertainment and gifts for the boys and their families.[17] The policy of conciliation and accommodation was obviously designed to make allowance for the establishment of a *modus vivendi* with the Sunni population. So long as certain legal and ritual guidelines, such as the call to prayer, were performed in the Shiʿi manner, the Sunnis were allowed to go their own ritual and legal way. In 349/960, for example, he issued instructions through al-Qadi al-Nuʿman to the Maliki judge of Qayrawan, ʿAbd Allah b. Hashim, introducing certain modifications to prayer and funerary rituals (such as the Shiʿi call to prayer and prohibition of excessive mourning by women at funeral processions) to enable Ismailis to pray together with Sunnis. By so doing al-Muʿizz was apparently seeking to discourage the emergence of separate communal practices for Sunnis and Ismailis, which would have increased division between the two communities.[18] The new latitudinarianism or more tolerant outlook as a matter of policy allowed for the consolidation of power after Abu Yazid's revolt, and the stability that resulted in turn allowed for expansion as far as Egypt in the time of al-Muʿizz.[19] The conquest of Egypt in 358/969 launched another chapter in Fatimid history, one that involved the realization of an empire large enough to approximate to the pan-Islamic state which the Fatimids aspired to rule.[20] Apart from its usefulness as a policy, the ideological accommodation of other communities with the purpose of establishing a consensus for the legitimacy of the Fatimid state found its expression in al-Qadi al-Nuʿman's *Daʿaʾim al-Islam*.

As for dissidents within the Ismaili community, al-Muʿizz likewise made attempts at rapprochement. This is not only evident in the close attention he gave to the doctrinal and legal works of al-Qadi al-Nuʿman, but also in his concern with the activities of Ismailis beyond North Africa. According to al-Nuʿman's *Majalis*, al-Muʿizz regularly received news of, or delegations from, the *daʿwa* in the east, who often came seeking instruction and advice on doctrinal and other matters.[21] More often than not, al-Muʿizz judged them extremist because of their propagation of a modified Qarmati doctrine. They still called for the return of Muhammad b. Ismaʿil as *mahdi*, but with the addition that until his return the community would be led by *khulafa'* or deputies (meaning the Fatimids). Clearly, such a doctrine was highly problematic, for while it acknowledged the Fatimids, it ascribed a non-ʿAlid ancestry to them and demoted them to the role of mere caliphs as opposed to imams. Al-Muʿizz therefore took great pains to correct this impression in the numerous sections in the *Majalis* devoted to the affairs of the eastern *daʿwa*. After his arrival in Egypt, moreover, al-Muʿizz allegedly sent a letter to the Qarmati *daʿwa*, which sought to both correct this doctrine and appeal to the Qaramita to join forces with the Fatimids.[22] He also communicated directly with a newly established *dar al-hijra* in Sind (in modern-day Pakistan) where the efforts of a *daʿi* sent from Yemen by Ibn al-Hawshab had succeeded in establishing an Ismaili community. In his letter to the the *daʿi*'s successor, Jalam b. Shayban, al-Muiʿzz refutes the myth that the Fatimids were descended from Maymun al-Qaddah, a shadowy figure of uncertain identity whom anti-Fatimid accounts claimed was the ancestor of the Fatimids.[23] In the same letter al-Muʿizz also deplores some Hindu practices retained by the newly converted Indian converts.[24]

A resurgence of belief in the return of Muhammad b. Ismaʿil in this new form was not altogether surprising, given the profundity of the schism in the Ismaili *daʿwa* between the Fatimids and the Qarmatis, and subsequently al-Mahdi's postponement of messianic expectations. Thus in the official literature of al-Muʿizz's period, for example the *batini* works of al-Qadi al-Nuʿman and Jaʿfar b. Mansur al-Yaman,[25] we find a reconfirmation of the imamate of the Fatimids, even as it is argued that the *qa'im* (or *mahdi*) would appear at some future date.[26] As we have seen, some Qarmatis sought to reconcile their abiding belief in the *mahdi*-ship of Muhammad b. Ismaʿil with the rise and success of the Fatimid state, and even communicated with al-Muʿizz, but they would only recognize the Fatimids at the expense of their status as imams.

There were others in the eastern *daʿwa*, however, who allowed for the imamate of the Fatimids, as in the case of the important Iranian *daʿi* and philosopher al-Sijistani.[27] Like his predecessors the *daʿis* Abu Hatim al-Razi (d. 322/934) and al-Nasafi (d. 332/943), al-Sijistani had originally preached the Qarmati doctrine which held that Muhammad b. Ismaʿil had disappeared and before his return the community would be led by deputies who were neither his descendents nor imams. However, by the time of al-Muʿizz and in his *Ithbat al-nubuʾat*,[28] al-Sijistani had reformed this doctrine to include a continuous cycle of imams before the return of Muhammad b. Ismaʿil. Because of his intellectual efforts, Iran continued to produce loyal servants for the later Fatimids such as the *daʿi*s Hamid al-Din al-Kirmani (d. after 411/1021) who was active during the reign of al-Hakim (disappeared in 411/1021), al-Muʾayyad fiʾl-Din al-Shirazi (d. 470/1078) who supervised the *daʿwa* in the east from Cairo for al-Mustansir (d. 487/1094), and Nasir-i Khusraw (d. after 465/1073), also active during the time of al-Mustansir.[29]

On the whole, the attention al-Muʿizz gave to the eastern communities led to the rehabilitation of some of these communities (such as that of northern Iran), if not all of them (such as the Qaramita of Bahrayn, who continued to reject the legitimacy of the Fatimids). More importantly, they indicate al-Muʿizz's attempts to accommodate, wherever possible, divergent expectations within his own community. This dialogue with both Sunni Islam and competing tendencies within Ismaili Shiʿism is reflected in most of al-Qadi al-Nuʿman's works, whether *batini* or *zahiri*. And while any comprehensive study of the articulation of Ismaili Shiʿi doctrines of this period would have to take all such works into consideration, this study focuses on al-Nuʿman's *Daʿaʾim* and its book or chapter on *walaya*, representing as it does the culmination of the development of al-Nuʿman's legal thought, and reflecting the transition from Shiʿi revolution to a major Islamic state.

The *Daʿaʾim al-Islam* ('Pillars of Islam') has been characterized as a 'well-organized dogmatic presentation of the tenets of Ismaili positive Law',[30] and consists of two *ajzaʾ* or volumes. Fyzee noted that 'the contents of the *Pillars* show that it is a work midway between the style of *fiqh* books and *hadith* literature', meaning that both legal argumentation and Prophetic *hadith*s are incorporated into the text.[31] The *hadith*s cited, however, do not have the chains of transmission or *isnad*s that normally accompany Sunni compilations of *hadith*s, in part because they are transmitted on the authority of the ruling imam, and also because the

Da'a'im is a handbook. The first *juz'* or volume deals with the acts of worship, or *'ibadat*, consisting of *walaya* (obedience to the imams), *al-tahara* (ritual purity), *al-salat* (prayer, including a subsection on burial procedures), *al-zakat* (alms), *al-sawm* (fasting), *al-hajj* (pilgrimage) and *jihad* (including a political treatise on rulership). The second volume, more properly on jurisprudence, or *mu'amalat*, includes 25 'books' on legal issues ranging from contracts to dietary prescriptions, marriage and *hudud*, or punishments. As mentioned above, the 'book' on inheritance incorporates the principles of *wasaya* or bequest, upon which the legitimacy of the imams is in part based, and so *imama* is again invoked in this context.

As regards the dating of the *Da'a'im*, a report states that al-Mu'izz commissioned this work after a meeting with al-Qadi al-Nu'man and a group of *da'is*, during which was discussed the issue of heterodoxy in Islam. Al-Mu'izz cited *hadith*s of the Prophet to the effect that the community should follow the ways of those who came before, and that in times of *bida'* or innovation it was incumbent upon an *'alim* or religious scholar to make knowledge manifest. Then, turning to al-Qadi al-Nu'man, al-Mu'izz continued saying, 'It is you, O Nu'man, who is meant by this saying in this age,' and ordered him to compose the *Da'a'im*.[32] While this passage confirms that the *Da'a'im* dates from al-Mu'izz's reign, scholars have assigned approximate dates of 347/958 or 349/960 on the basis of internal evidence (which additionally indicates that it was completed when preparations were getting under way for the conquest of Egypt).[33]

The first volume includes a brief statement on the purpose of the *Da'a'im*, which resulted from the existence of the multitude of *madhahib* that permitted the forbidden and forbade the permitted to the faithful. Consequently, as al-Nu'man notes, the *Da'a'im* was written to establish the true faith of the Prophet and the *ahl al-bayt*, in accordance with the Prophet's saying on the necessity of the learned to manifest their knowledge in times of innovation.[34] The learned here, of course, are the followers of the imam, the friends of God (*awliya'*), who are to return the community to the true faith through adherence to the 'established Traditions on the authority of the imams of the house of the Prophet, from among the Traditions over which there has been disagreement'.[35] According to al-Nu'man then, the *Da'a'im* was written in response to the dissemination of many false *hadith*s and erroneous attitudes in Sunni Islam, which despite its claim to uphold the *Sunna* of the Prophet, failed to do so because of the deficient knowledge of, and disagreements between, its *'ulama'*. By contrast the *Da'a'im*, in also limiting its *usul* or acceptable sources for law to the Qur'an and the *Sunna* of the Prophet, achieves greater accuracy because it relies exclusively on the superior knowledge of the *ahl al-bayt*.[36]

Al-Qadi al-Nu'man opens the 'book' on *walaya* with a discussion of *iman* (faith or conviction), in which he employs Qur'anic verses, *hadith*s and theological and legal argument to create a distinction between *iman* and *islam*, or mere submission.[37] The distinction between the two involves the issue of *imama* or belief in the succession of the Prophet's descendants, and thus this preliminary discussion aims at situating *imama* in the realm of true belief, and therefore among the *fara'id al-din* (obligatory religious acts). It also sets the stage for a subsequent discussion of *imama* as a historically contested institution and the defence of rightful claimants. A definition of *iman* is provided on the authority of the Imam Ja'far al-Sadiq, the foremost religious scholar and transmitter of *hadith*s in Shi'i law.[38] According to him, faith consists of intention (*niyya*) as well as acts and professions of faith, a position that contrasts with what the Murji'a[39] and the majority (*al-jama'a*) allegedly believed. The Murji'a claim they are satisfied with a purely verbal profession of faith, while the majority contend that the profession of faith combined with adherence to the *fara'id* or acts of faith (not including obedience to the imam, of course) is sufficient.[40] But how, asked Ja'far al-Sadiq, can the Murji'a claim that profession of faith is enough when they themselves have agreed that if a person does not perform acts that God has made obligatory, he has become an unbeliever (*kafir*) whose blood can legally be shed, just as happened after the Prophet with those who were referred to as the *ahl al-ridda* (apostates who were likened to those mentioned in the Qur'an 41:6–7: 'Woe to the idolators who do not give poor-due')?

As for the majority, their assertion that profession and action are sufficient is equally flawed, continues Ja'far al-Sadiq. Acts such as prayer, fasting, pilgrimage and so on are not sufficient unless accompanied by the proper intention. As the Prophet said, good works have to be performed with the right intention, for one will receive reward only for what one intends. A person who emigrates for the sake of God and His Prophet will be held to have emigrated for their sake, and he who emigrates for the sake of a woman he wants to marry, or for worldly gain, will receive accordingly.[41] Thus, al-Nu'man states, faith (*iman*) is the declaration that there is no god but God, who is one and without partner, that Muhammad is His servant and messenger, that Heaven, Hell and the Resurrection are truths, that the Day of Judgement will come, and that faith is belief in God's prophets, messengers and imams, and acknowledgement of the imam of the age, and belief in him and submission to his will, and the performance of the acts required by God, and avoidance of the forbidden, and obedience to the imam and acceptance of what comes from him.

In short, true faith consists as much in profession and act as it does in an earnest desire (intention) to obey God, which in turn requires obedience to the imams. At the same time, al-Nu'man reports on the authority of Ja'far al-Sadiq that faith exists in 'conditions, degrees, levels and stages', and thus can decrease and/or increase. This statement leads to a discussion of not only what is incumbent upon the individual believer, in terms of prescriptions and proscriptions, but also of the ranking of the faithful according to time and their success in achieving perfection of faith.

Ja'far al-Sadiq begins by explaining to a questioner that no act is preferable to any other, for God has assigned to all of man's parts obligatory acts of faith, and to each organ duties that it alone must perform and be held responsible for. These taken together determine the extent to which a believer is in fact faithful, and the degree to which his faith is perfect or imperfect. The duties incumbent upon the heart (considered the seat of the intellect) are, of course, the most important, for it commands the other organs and enables them to perform the acts incumbent upon them.[42]

Yet, even in the perfection of faith there are degrees, and these depend on historical time. The earliest to convert to Islam have precedence over those who came later, even if the later believers excelled in the performance of religious acts. ʿAli b. Abi Talib outstrips all in terms of precedence as the second person (after the Prophet's first wife, Khadija) to convert to Islam, and he is followed by the *muhajirun* (those who emigrated with the Prophet from Mecca), and then the *ansar* (those who supported the Prophet in Medina). As God said, 'Those who take precedence were the first among the *muhajirun* and the *ansar* and those who followed them in goodness, for God was pleased with them as they were with Him' (9:100). Likewise, the prophets have also been ranked: 'For We have given preference to some prophets over others' (17:55). Nevertheless, and subsequent to the Prophet's time, precedence depends on perfection of faith, and this, Jaʿfar al-Sadiq reiterates, consists not only of profession and good works but also of conviction and belief.[43]

After defining and describing faith, al-Nuʿman arrives at the discussion of the difference between faith (*iman*) and mere submission (*islam*).[44] God said, 'The Arabs (Bedouin) said, "We have faith (*amanna*)". Say to them: "You do not have faith, you should say 'We have submitted (*aslamna*)', for faith has not entered your hearts"' (49:14).[45] This indicates that faith is one thing, says al-Qadi al-Nuʿman, and mere submission another, unlike what some among the majority have alleged. As Jaʿfar al-Sadiq explained, *iman* includes *islam*, whereas *islam* does not include *iman*, for *islam* is the external (*zahir*) and *iman* the inward (*batin*), in the heart. *Islam* is what regulates marriage, inheritance and prevents bloodshed (in other words, the laws and prescriptions that regulate the affairs of the community), whereas *iman* is in the heart (and is therefore faith and conviction). Jaʿfar al-Sadiq's father, the Imam Muhammad al-Baqir, had illustrated this by drawing two concentric circles, the outer one signifying *islam* and the inner one signifying *iman*. And likewise, ʿAli b. Abi Talib had in his time defined *iman* as both affirmation as well as knowledge, whereas *islam* is merely affirmation.[46]

The point of this discussion is not only to make the basic

distinction between inner faith and outward submission (which exists in Islamic discourse generally), but also to make the corollary distinction between the true believers and the mere *muslim*. That is, whoever God has granted knowledge of Himself, His Prophet and the imam to, is the *mu'min* or true believer, explains al-Nu'man, for God plants this knowledge in the heart of the believer, and without this one cannot be guided. 'Those who are ignorant should come to us,' said 'Ali b. Abi Talib, 'and heed God's word, "Ask the people of remembrance if you know not"' (21:7). And when 'Ali was asked what must one do in order to be a *mu'min*, he replied that one must know and obey God, His Prophet and the imam, the proof and witness of God on earth. As for those who do not follow the imam, they are only believers in name (the *'amma*), whose pursuit of good works (according to the outward Shari'a) will be rewarded accordingly. This distinction between *mu'min* and *muslim*, while bestowing privilege on the followers of the imam (the Shi'is) does not at the same time condemn the non-Shi'i majority. The distinction is not one between an unequivocal belief and disbelief,[47] so much as one between *zahir* and *batin*, the *'amma* and the *khassa* (select community).

Al-Nu'man's argument in favour of *imama* in the *Da'a'im* is ultimately rooted in certain Qur'anic verses, which are considered testimony of, or divine evidence for, the Shi'i claim that the rights of 'Ali b. Abi Talib and his descendants to leadership of the community were usurped. While many of these verses occur in other Shi'i compilations on *imama*, al-Nu'man's presentation does not include verses which other forms of Shi'ism more creatively interpret as referring to the imams. The verse most commonly quoted by all, however, is 4:59: 'Obey God and His Messenger, and those among you who are in authority,' in which the expression 'those in authority' (*ulu al-amr*) is understood to refer directly to the imams from the *ahl al-bayt*. In the *Da'a'im* it forms the theme of the subsection about *walaya* to the imams (*dhikr wilayat al-a'imma min ahl al-bayt rasul allah*),[48] in which a 'discussion' takes place between the Imam Muhammad al-Baqir and an unidentified party, over the divine provisions and precedents for *imama*. Within the narrative framework of this 'discussion' are listed many other Qur'anic verses which also articulate the characteristics and qualifications of the imams.

So, for example, the imams are the ones who have a share in sovereignty and are envied (4:54); the members of the family of Abraham who have been given the Book and wisdom and a great kingdom (4:54); the ones who will be admitted to plenteous shade (4:57); the ones to whom leadership has been entrusted (4:59); those who pray and give alms (5:55); the truthful ones (*al-sadiqin*, 9:119); the believers (9:105); the just community (*ummatan wasatan*, 2:143) whom God has witnessed and who have been given knowledge (29:49); the witnesses of God who have knowledge of the Book (13:43); the people of remembrance (43:44); the guides (13:7); those of sound knowledge (3:7); and those pre-eminent in good deeds (35:32). These verses allude to the characteristics or attributes of the imams (their pre-eminence in good deeds, prayer, giving alms, sound in knowledge, etc), and indicate their right to rule by virtue of divine selection (as witnesses among the people, inheritors of a great kingdom, etc), and testify to a lineage that returns to the beginnings of monotheist history (the time of Abraham).

The listing of verses or evidence of divine provision for *imama* is then followed by a lengthy critique of the majority's understanding of who those holding authority or *ulu al-amr* should be. Al-Qadi al-Nu'man dismisses the two definitions of *ulu al-amr* posited by the Sunni majority: the more literal reading is that this phrase refers to military commanders, or to the *'ulama'*, the religious scholars.[49] As to the first, he argues that it is absurd to suggest that all believers, including the imams, should obey mere military commanders as the authority after God and the Prophet, for they bring no qualification to the task except the ability to command an army. And as for the second reading, which assumes that leadership of the community belongs to those who have the most knowledge, even if one were to define them as the *'ulama'*, they are as a group in disagreement with each other. So for someone to obey one *'alim* would be to disobey another, and thus this definition is also absurd. Moreover, if one were to interpret 'those in authority' to mean the learned, they would naturally be the imams who are the most learned people of the community. This last is confirmed by a *hadith* from the Imam Ja'far al-Sadiq, who was asked by two brothers about verse 4:59, and he replied that 'those in authority' refers to the *'ulama'*. The brothers left, but then realized that they did not know who these *'ulama'* were, and so returned and were told that they are the imams. Several other *hadith*s from Ja'far al-Sadiq, 'Ali b. Abi Talib and Abu Dharr al-Ghiffari[50] are recorded that reiterate the identification of *ulu al-amr* with the imams, as well as two *hadith*s from the Prophet (identifying the imams with the inhabitants of the 'summits' (*a'raf*) between Heaven and Hell).[51]

In addition to the provisions for and references to *imama* in the Qur'an, there are also those verses that provide historical material in favour of al-Nu'man's defence. These verses refer to previous prophets, their successors and their communities, whose experience is constructed as a historical precedent to be reproduced in the case of the Prophet and his community. That is, the notion of succession to prophets by imams is read into the text of monotheist history, and especially into the case of Abraham.[52] Al-Qadi al-Nu'man leads into this second type of argument for *imama* in the *Da'a'im* subsection that begins with a discussion of the verse 33:56: 'God and His angels bless the Prophet. O believers, bless him also, and greet him well.'[53] When the Prophet was asked by some of his followers how he wanted them to greet him, he responded that they should greet him and his family (*Al*) in the same fashion as Abraham and his family were greeted (blessed). His instructions to them on this matter were like his instructions on the other obligatory acts, which were revealed but not elaborated on in the Qur'an. The majority, argues al-Qadi al-Nu'man, undermine the pre-eminence of the Prophet's family by claiming that the *Al* (family) of the Prophet refers to all Muslims, the *umma* or community of believers, and not to the *ahl al-bayt* exclusively.[54]

This subversion of meaning by the Sunni majority is taken up in a lengthy *hadith* attributed to Ja'far al-Sadiq, which is set again in the form of a dialogue between the imam and an unidentified party. Within this framework, the imam reasserts the distinction between the *Al* of the Prophet on the one hand and the general community on the other. The distinction derives chiefly from Qur'anic references to Abraham (and his progeny), as well as to other Biblical prophets mentioned in the Qur'an.[55] When asked whether or not the majority are correct in saying that the *Al* of Muhammad is the community of believers, the imam responds that to a degree they are right, for there are some believers who uphold the Qur'an and are therefore to be considered as the family of the Prophet, not by virtue of kinship but by virtue of their obedience to the Prophet and his family. They are meant by the verse 5:51, 'For whoever befriends them among you, is of them', and 14:36, in which Abraham says of his followers, 'He who follows me is truly of me.' Nevertheless, says Ja'far al-Sadiq, it is only the family of the Prophet that God has purified (33:33), and so, although in some sense true believers are to be considered as belonging to the 'family' of the Prophet, there are proofs in the Qur'an that clearly indicate God's preference for his actual family. One such proof is (3:33–34): 'God had chosen Adam and Noah and the families of Abraham and 'Imran in preference to others. They were descendants of one another.' Thus 'family' here refers to the people of one's house. This demonstrates the inaccuracy of the majority's position, which equates the family of the Prophet with his community in general.

The imam continues to explain that the term *umma* can, likewise, refer to the Prophet's actual family and/or community of followers. Although those to whom the Prophet was sent constitute the *umma* of the Prophet, there is evidence that indicates that God sometimes uses *umma* to signify only the descendants of the Prophet. For example, in 2:127–128, 'When Abraham was erecting the foundations of his house with Isma'il, (he prayed), "Accept this from us our Lord … and make us submit to Your will, and make our progeny a community (*umma*) submissive to you."'[56] This was confirmed in a *hadith* from the Prophet in which he declared, 'I am the prayer of my father Abraham, and who follows this community that God described in His Book is of it, and who denies their pre-eminence, he is of the community to which the

Prophet Muhammad was sent but which rejected him.'[57] Lastly, there is 2:143: 'We have appointed you a just community (*ummatan wasatan*)', which clearly refers to those among the progeny of Abraham who are preferred by God, and to whom obedience is therefore necessary.

Just as prophethood was granted to the progeny of Isaac and then to the progeny of Isma'il through Abraham, so the imamate was granted to 'Ali b. Abi Talib's son Hasan and then to his brother Husayn. This was according to God's word, 'And the foremost in race are the foremost' (56:10). That Husayn's successors were his progeny rather than Hasan's was then based on verse 8:75, 'Those related by blood are closer to one another, according to the Book of God.'[58] In short, continues al-Nu'man, God has said that not all Muslims are equal, and that the family of the Prophet has pre-eminence in deeds and therefore the preference of God (and, in turn, those who follow the family of the Prophet are considered pre-eminent). Moreover God had, in this fashion, previously distinguished between the progeny of His prophets and their communities, and designated leaders for these communities from the descendants of His prophets. The same should follow for His last prophet. The necessity of *imama* is an established precedent evidenced by the progress of monotheist history.

The third argument for *imama*, after Qur'anic provisions and the precedent of monotheist history, is the historical evidence for the specific designation of 'Ali b. Abi Talib as the successor of the Prophet. The event at Ghadir Khumm is naturally the cornerstone of this evidence, although other indicators of 'Ali's selection are also provided. Al-Qadi al-Nu'man opens the discussion with a *hadith* from Muhammad al-Baqir in which the imam is asked to explain the occasion for the revelation of 5:55: 'Your friends can only be God and His Messenger, and those who have faith, who establish worship, pay the poor-due and bow down.' The imam explains that this verse refers to the many things God made obligatory but did not explain, and which, therefore, were left to the Prophet to explain and establish. This is why the explanation of obligatory acts such as pilgrimage and what and how much is to be paid in poor tax (*zakat*) are actually found in the *Sunna*, even though the requirement is laid down in the Qur'an. And because the need for such explanations continued, the Prophet knew that he had to leave the community in the hands of a reliable authority such as 'Ali b. Abi Talib. For this reason he intended to announce the succession of 'Ali, and yet he feared the reaction of the community. So he hesitated until after the Farewell Pilgrimage, when God revealed: 'O Messenger! Make known that which has been revealed to you from your Lord, for if you do not, you will not have conveyed His message. And God will protect you' (5:67).

Thus it was on the day of Ghadir Khumm that the Prophet made known the succession of 'Ali. And then God revealed: 'This day I have perfected your religion for you and have chosen for you as religion al-Islam' (5:3).[59] On that day the Prophet proclaimed to the assembled Muslims that those who considered him their *mawla* (master) had to consider 'Ali their *mawla* after him, and that just as devotion was due to him, so it was due to 'Ali, for this was what God had commanded. Although the majority have tried to deny the significance of this designation, continues al-Qadi al-Nu'man, many of them have nevertheless acknowledged the reference to 'Ali of 5:55: 'Your friends can only be God and His Messenger, and those who pay the poor-due and bow down', who famously had thrown his ring (as alms) to a beggar who was standing by him as he was praying.[60] Yet there are those of the majority who, despite this verse and the declaration at Ghadir Khumm, deny 'Ali's right to succession. A longer variant of the declaration at Ghadir Khumm is provided, in which the Prophet additionally likens 'Ali's relationship to him to that of Aaron to Moses. And so, al-Nu'man asks, what clearer proof is there concerning the *walaya* or viceregency of 'Ali?

In addition to the events of Ghadir Khumm, and 'Ali b. Abi Talib's well-known and universally recognized virtues (such as his exemplary regard for the poor), there are also other proofs or instances when 'Ali b. Abi Talib stood out or was singled out for special recognition. For example, al-Qadi al-Nu'man incorporates in his argument a series of *hadith*s from 'Ali, such as the occasion for the revelation of 26:214: 'Warn your clan of near kin.'

This was a gathering of the Banu 'Abd al-Muttalib (the descendants of the Prophet's grandfather) that the Prophet had arranged in order to request the support of his kinsmen for his cause. After sharing a meal, the Prophet addressed his male kin, saying, 'If you follow me, you shall inherit the earth, for God has never sent a messenger without providing for him a deputy, or vizier, so which of you will volunteer to be my deputy?' All of his kinsmen in turn remained silent, except for 'Ali who exclaimed that he would follow the Prophet of God. Abu Lahab, chief of the clan, derided the arrogance and folly of his nephew 'Ali for presuming that he had such a degree of power and importance, especially over the elders of the clan.[61] Also, when the Prophet ordered that all the doors of the houses adjoining his mosque in Medina be closed except 'Ali's (in order to obtain a measure of privacy for his family), and when Companions such as Abu Bakr and 'Umar complained, the Prophet replied that God had commanded him to purify his house in this manner, acting as Moses had done with Aaron. And 'Ali says that Gabriel had commanded the Prophet to let him rather than Abu Bakr read the first seven verses of *Surat al-bara'a* to the Meccans.[62] These Prophetic *hadiths* and the presentation of the event at Ghadir Khumm are common to both the Sunni and Shi'i sources. Ghadir Khumm features in the Sunni account of the Prophet's life, as does the declaration he made about 'Ali (as we have seen from the debates of the early Fatimid period). As for the *hadiths* which speak of 'Ali's loyalty to the Prophet, his other virtues and the preferential treatment he received from the Prophet, they also feature in Sunni tradition, although again the significance assigned to them differs from that in Shi'i accounts.

As a corollary to the discussion of the designation of 'Ali b. Abi Talib, there is also the issue of his descendants and the mode of their succession from him as imams. As noted above, the *Da'a'im* establishes the succession of Hasan by Husayn through a standard Shi'i reference to verses 56:10 and 8:75. Subsequent succession in Twelver and Ismaili tradition is based on an explicit act of designation or *nass*, as it was at Ghadir Khumm. However, al-Nu'man's listing of the succession of the imams stops at Ja'far al-Sadiq, the last imam shared with Twelver Shiʿism. Beyond that, he merely states that imams continued to succeed one another, avoiding names of those specifically Ismaili imams of the *satr* period after Jaʿfar al-Sadiq. This omission is highly significant for several reasons. Al-Sadiq's contribution and the recognition of him as a religious authority in his own time transcended Shiʿism. By virtue of his outstanding religious learning and knowledge of *hadith*s (on the authority of the *ahl al-bayt*), Jaʿfar al-Sadiq established a reputation among the Sunni scholars of his day, as he did among his own circle and within Shiʿi legal tradition. Al-Nuʿman's reliance on the teachings of al-Baqir and al-Sadiq thus aided the acceptance of the *Daʿaʾim* in Twelver Shiʿi legal tradition (to the extent that al-Nuʿman himself was appropriated by it, as previously noted), and even won the respect of Sunnis (so that al-Nuʿman appears in Sunni biographical dictionaries as well). And by avoiding the contentious issue of succession to Jaʿfar al-Sadiq, al-Nuʿman left matters open in such a way that it was still possible that the Fatimid imams, on some level, could be accepted by the Twelver Shiʿi community, which at the time was experiencing a crisis over the occultation of their own last imam.

Al-Qadi al-Nuʿman follows up the issue of ʿAli's succession to the Prophet with further arguments against the *jamaʿa* or Sunni majority. Having re-presented the historical evidence for ʿAli b. Abi Talib's succession, al-Nuʿman now addresses the succession of Abu Bakr, ʿUmar and ʿUthman, and the position of the Sunnis generally speaking, as it seems he had done in a previous work composed in the time of al-Mansur.[63] Four specific attitudes are delineated within the general position of the *jamaʿa*: those of the Murjiʾa, the Muʿtazilis[64] and the Kharijis,[65] on the one hand, and that of the rest of the Sunnis on the other. Al-Nuʿman presents the Murjiʾa as believing that the imam should ideally be the most qualified and knowledgeable member of the community, in order that he may rule on the basis of the Qurʾan and *Sunna*, and provide *ijtihad* (independent judgement) when necessary. Thus if he rules unjustly, he loses authority over the community, and should be replaced. As for the Muʿtazilis, al-Nuʿman argues, they claim that the Prophet had commanded the community to choose a successor, and in this manner Abu Bakr was installed as his successor. The Kharijis, on the other hand, will neither acknowledge nor deny any evidence presented for the Prophet's choice of successor; their position is that the imam should simply be able to pronounce judgement and execute punishment. Thus the imam's authority is limited to enforcement of the law. And as for the rest of the majority, they argue that the election of Abu Bakr constituted an acceptable precedent, even if they disagreed over the criteria for election.[66] For some of them, the designation of Abu Bakr to lead the prayer at the time of the Prophet's death in Medina was sufficient proof of his preference over others.

Al-Qadi al-Nu'man's refutation begins with the examination of the issue of election. He argues that the various positions held by the non-Shi'i groups all concur on the absence of explicit Prophetic designation. This was to him both untrue and legally unsound since, as opposed to an act for which there is a witness, the absence of something cannot be asserted. The testimony of the act of the Prophet's designation of 'Ali on the day of Ghadir Khumm thus overrides all arguments for the absence of explicit designation. Moreover, if the Prophet had intended the people to select their leader (as the Mu'tazilis argue), he would have gathered them together and had them do so in his own time. Of course, this would not only have been unfeasible (for the people would never have been able to unanimously agree on one individual above all the rest), but it would also have been futile, for the leader who receives his mandate from the people (as the Murji'a proposed) would be ruled by them instead of ruling over them.

In any case, continues al-Qadi al-Nu'man, God reveals in the Qur'an (5:3) that he has perfected his religion, and this could only be by the appointment of imams to succeed the Prophet. Even the majority agree that the perfection of religion entails the succession of an imam. Yet, if one were to accept the basis of the Prophet's preference for Abu Bakr as some of the majority have argued, on what basis is the appointment of 'Umar by Abu Bakr, and of 'Uthman by 'Umar, made valid? The instance of Abu Bakr leading the prayer does not legitimately constitute an indication of his designation as successor to the Prophet, for Abu Bakr led the prayer only when ʿAli b. Abi Talib was absent. Otherwise it was always ʿAli who led the prayer (except when the Prophet himself did so). Moreover, Abu Bakr and ʿUmar were themselves on numerous occasions led in prayer by others such as ʿAmr b. al-ʿAs and ʿUsama b. Zayd.[67] Thus, if leading the prayer was the basis on which succession was to be decided, then those appointed by Abu Bakr to lead the prayer should have been more entitled to succeed him than ʿUmar and ʿUthman.[68]

Al-Nuʿman then provides a résumé of the weaknesses of the various positions taken by the Sunnis. The position of the Murji'a is tantamount to claiming that the imam be chosen by the people themselves (in which case the people would presumably be empowered to select not only their imams but also their prophets). The Muʿtazilis wrongly attribute the principle of election to the Prophet, and the position of the Kharijis is absurd since they cannot refute that of which they claim to have no knowledge. For these reasons, it cannot but be agreed that the right to succession lies with the *ahl al-bayt*, and this is how, says al-Qadi al-Nuʿman, the Prophet designated ʿAli b. Abi Talib, who then designated Hasan, who then designated Husayn, and so on. And as previous prophets had chosen their imams, so it should not be denied to the Prophet to do the same, especially as he was the Seal of the Prophets, thus leaving the community in greater need of guidance by an imam after him. The discussion ends with the invocation of various Qur'anic verses concerning the designation of previous prophets and imams, and those whose doubt had not diminished even in the face of God's numerous portents.[69]

By this point, al-Nuʿman's effort to establish the rightful succession of the *ahl al-bayt* has explored the Qur'anic mandate for the imams and invoked the evidence of the explicit designation of ʿAli b. Abi Talib at Ghadir Khumm. In this presentation, explicit designation follows monotheist experience and history, and is sanctioned by divine revelation. Alternative methods of nomination and succession posited by the Sunni majority are thus tantamount to *bidʿa* or innovation. And attributing the selection of Abu Bakr to the Prophet is even more absurd, especially in the light of ʿAli's designation, who even by their dubious criteria would far excel any of the Companions in qualification.

The following three sections of the *Da'a'im* deal essentially with the issues of extremism (*ghuluww*), dissimulation (*taqiyya*) and the concept of love for the Prophet's family (*mawadda*), which define the relationship of the followers to their imams.[70] The section dealing with extremism begins with a restatement of the necessity of obedience to the living imam, and a categorical denial of the allegations that the imams receive divine revelations or that they possess knowledge of the 'unknown' or *'ilm al-ghayb*, which is known only to God. Nor are they deities or prophets, but merely select mortals who are creatures of God, states al-Nu'man. He continues with a denunciation of the susceptibility of some followers to temptation by Satan, and those who were thus led to disobey the imam. Some were tempted to embellish the attributes of the imams, and still others to dismiss obligatory acts. As Ja'far al-Sadiq reminded one of his followers, this burden must be borne heavily, 'for the world is a prison for the faithful and a paradise for the unbelievers'. Yet, rewards will accrue to the followers who adhere to the word of their imams.[71]

Al Nu'man then recalls the problems faced by 'Ali b. Abi Talib in his time, such as the opposition of 'A'isha, Talha and Zubayr, the defection of the Kharijis during the arbitration at Siffin in 40/661, and the excesses of the Saba'iyya, the followers of one 'Abd Allah b. Saba', who proclaimed 'Ali's divinity. Similarily, the Imam Muhammad al-Baqir had to denounce extremists such as al-Mughira b. Sa'id, who claimed to be able to resurrect the dead, and attributed divinity to the imam, among other things.[72] And Ja'far al-Sadiq had in his time to deal with the Khattabiyya, whose leader, Abu'l-Khattab, had also ascribed divinity to the imam, and claimed prophecy for himself, and moreover engaged in all manner of unacceptable things, to which Ja'far later responded: 'What we permit is on the basis of God's Book, and what we forbid also.'[73] Several *hadith*s attributed to Ja'far al-Sadiq follow, in which the imam rejects deification, possession of special books, or knowledge of the unknown, as well as a lengthy one in which the observance of the Shari'a is dealt with. Those who would argue that knowledge (*ma'rifa*) of God and His imam excuses them from performing obligatory acts, they are nothing more than unbelievers, says Jaʿfar al-Sadiq, for the outer (*zahir*) and the inner (*batin*) of all that is prescribed are equally binding and obligatory on the followers of the imam.[74] There is then a brief mention of similar experiences with extremists who were encountered by the Fatimids al-Mahdi, al-Qa'im and al-Mansur, who are explicitly, and significantly, first referred to in this context.[75]

Of course, one of the means by which extremism is avoided is strict obedience to the imam, and a discussion of this is the preamble to the next section on the counsel of the imams. This section deals primarily with *taqiyya* or dissimulation, with which act the followers of the imam both protect the imam and attract other people to his cause. It begins with a *hadith* from ʿAli in which he defines his party (*shiʿa*) as those who perform obligatory acts so vigorously that they have the look of ascetics.[76] This is followed by several other *hadith*s which equate the necessity for obedience to the imam with the necessity for the performing of obligatory acts. For example, Jaʿfar al-Sadiq, when he heard that some of his followers had fallen short in performance of obligatory acts, said that they could not be saved from hellfire even by the intercession of the Prophet. And he said to them, 'Obey us and perform that which God has commanded, for only through us is there salvation, and this is the reason we are the gates of Heaven (*bab*), the proof of God (*hujja*), the guides, the secret (*nafathat sirrihi*) and the repositories of His knowledge (*mustawdaʿ ʿilmihi*).'[77] At the same time, obedience to the imam not only involves performance of good works, but also obliges his followers to conceal his secret (*kitman*). Thus Jaʿfar al-Sadiq said to a group of his followers who asked him for advice that they should obey God, return the *amanat* (religious due) to the imams, remain friendly with those who are friends, and be silent missionaries among the people. When asked how they could spread the mission silently, Jaʿfar replied that the performance of good works is the most effective way to accrue goodwill for the imams.[78] The *hadith*s that follow reiterate this obligation to conceal the secret of the imams. As Jaʿfar al-Sadiq said to another group of followers, 'None shall belong to this party except he who guards his tongue.'[79] In fact, Ja'far al-Sadiq added elsewhere that God will reward those who conceal the imams' secret, for as his father, Muhammad al-Baqir, had declared, *taqiyya* was part of his religion.[80] And admonitions are dealt out to those who obeyed the imams in every way, except in keeping silent.[81]

The necessity for keeping silent is explained by al-Qadi al-Nu'man again on the authority of Ja'far al-Sadiq, by saying that only some people have been given the intelligence and inclination to follow the imams. Thus it is futile to attempt to persuade all the people do so, and preferable to appear before them as exemplary in works and acts. For example, he said to a group of followers that God has created those who love the imams, and those who despise them, and there was nothing they, the faithful, could do to increase or decrease their numbers; so they should avoid speaking to the ignorant about things they could never understand.[82] Finally, the followers of the imams are to be recognized by their good works: their love for their neighbours, concern for the sick and poor, their zeal in performing prayers and fasts, their unity of voice, their trustworthiness, their obedience to authority, silence, and disassociation from evil.[83] In all other respects they are indistinguishable from the rest despite their presence in all the far corners of the earth.[84] As these instructions and *hadith*s assert, the *zahir* is as important as the *batin*, and the *khassa* (truly faithful) have to be careful in their relations with the *'amma* (ordinary Muslims), so as not to antagonize them. Beyond that, Ja'far al-Sadiq said, 'Do not disagree with the people over your religion, for disagreement is unhealthy for the heart, and God said to His Prophet, "You guide not whom you love, but God guides whom He wishes" ... for the people take from the people, whereas you (the faithful) take from God, His Prophet, 'Ali and us.'[85]

Mawadda or love for the Prophet's family is another characteristic of the followers of the imam.[86] The *Da'a'im*'s treatment of it is addressed first to the general or Sunni audience whose understanding of the Qur'anic verse 42:23 is refuted in a *hadith* from Muhammad al-Baqir. The verse, 'Say, I (the Prophet) ask of you (the people) no fee except love of kin (*urba*)', is the textual proof of the preference for the Prophet's family, the *ahl al-bayt*, in Shi'i tradition. Muhammad al-Baqir reviews the interpretation of 42:23 by both the Sunnis and the Shi'is, all of whom he refers to simply as four schools. The first school (the Shi'is) interpret 'kin' correctly as the *ahl al-bayt*. Even according to Ibn 'Abbas, the Prophet's uncle and a source of transmission in the Sunni tradition, the definition of 'kin' is the progeny of 'Ali and Fatima in particular.[87] The second school argues that verse 42:23 is reversed by 34:47, 'Say, whatever reward I asked of you is yours', but al-Baqir points out that these two verses do not in fact negate each other, for in return for the 'fee' given to the *ahl al-bayt*, their followers will get their 'reward'. Then, of course, there is the interpretation of the majority or the Sunni *jama'a*, who claim that 'kin' refers to the tribe of Quraysh, for the Prophet was eventually related to all the Quraysh through blood. However, al-Nu'man adds, this is an absurd interpretation, for among the Quraysh were those who did not accept the Prophet (Abu Lahab, for instance). And lastly, al-Nu'man criticizes the interpretation of Hasan al-Basri that 'kin' refers to all those who submit to God, a position that was repudiated by Ja'far al-Sadiq.[88]

The second half of the section consists of various incidents wherein the imams, in following the example of the Prophet, ask of their followers nothing more than love of God and His Messenger, and themselves show nothing but love and mercy to their followers. Thus, for example, when a follower approaches Muhammad al-Baqir with cracked and bruised feet, the imam asks him how this came about. He responds that he had walked to reach the imam's residence, and that he did so out of love for the *ahl al-bayt*. Al-Baqir, visibly moved, responds, 'For what is faith but love?' On another occasion the imam relates an incident between the Prophet and a bedouin who came to ask for acceptance from him. Al-Baqir comments: 'When the people had cause for alarm, you took refuge with us, as we had taken refuge with the Prophet; so rejoice, for God will not judge you (the followers of the imams and the people) equally; no by God, they (the people) will receive no mercy.'[89]

The final two sections of the *Da'a'im*'s chapter on *walaya* deal with the important issue of the knowledge of the imams. The first of the two sections on knowledge presents *hadith*s extolling the necessity and virtue of its acquisition, indicated primarily in Qur'anic verses 16:43 and 21:7: 'Ask the People of Remembrance if you know not'.[90] Prophetic *hadith*s, as well as *hadith*s from the imams, are here recounted in which the community is encouraged to seek knowledge, and the knowledgeable are encouraged to disseminate it.[91] Other examples of *hadith*s further identify those from whom knowledge should be acquired, namely the *ahl al-bayt*. Ja'far al-Sadiq said that the *ahl al-bayt* were like Noah's ark: he who boards it is saved and he who does not perishes.[92] And, from the Prophet, he said that knowledge will be transmitted by his upright successors (the imams), who will thereby refute corruption of it by the ignorant, the misattributions of the wrongdoers and the interpretations of the extremists.[93] The next section on knowledge continues with the case for the overriding authority of the imams in the transmission of knowledge. Al-Qadi al-Nu'man begins with the statement that knowledge should only be transmitted from the imams of the Prophet's family, and not from the ignorant to whom the majority adhere, for their knowledge is mere opinion and reasoning by analogy (*qiyas*). Just as their leaders usurped the right to temporal authority from the imams, their *'ulama'* have usurped the role of the imams in the transmission of knowledge and have steeped the community in ignorance; and for this they have even been admired by the majority.[94]

This statement is followed by the account of numerous instances where 'Umar b. al-Khattab proved himself insufficiently knowledgeable or simply ignorant. For example, he was corrected by a woman in the crowd he was addressing about dowries, and implicated himself in the fraud of his own succession by expressing disagreement with Abu Bakr's succession. He was also corrected by 'Ali regarding the duration of pregnancy, and again by 'Ali regarding the legality and ethics of stoning a pregnant woman for adultery.[95] And yet, al-Nu'man exclaims, the people consider such ignorance a sign of his virtue. As for the other Companions and early Muslims such as 'Uthman, Mu'awiya and 'Amr b. al-'As, these are likewise considered as acceptable sources of knowledge by the majority, although their ignorance is well documented, and their murderous disagreements and questionable allegiance to the Prophet are well known. Surely God did not intend that the community be led and guided so; their unacceptability is so evident that it does not need proof, concludes al-Qadi al-Nuʿman.[96]

With regard to 'those whose opinions were upheld in later times', such as Abu Hanifa, Malik and al-Shafiʿi, again numerous examples are provided of the weakness of their legal principles and decisions. Abu Hanifa's disciples revealed their insecurity about their master's opinions, Malik was notorious for his inconsistency, and al-Shafiʿi forbade blind imitation (*taqlid*) of the opinions of his peers, and yet, because he did not establish the means by which a distinction between opinions could be made, he only succeeded in perpetuating a more arbitrary *taqlid* of opinions.[97] Al-Nuʿman dismisses the use of *qiyas* (analogy) in the Hanafi *madhhab*, the arbitrariness of *ʿurf* (customary Medinan practice) in the Maliki *madhhab*, and the failure of al-Shafiʿi to establish valid and reliable *usul al-fiqh*. Their efforts and opinions, he argues, have only amounted to confusion and innovation within the community, and the reliance on untrustworthy and ignorant authorities. This is why the Prophet required strict obedience and warned against innovation, and why God revealed in verse 39:55, 'Follow the best of that which your Lord has sent down.'[98]

In the remainder of the section, several examples of *hadith*s are related on the weakness of the *fiqh* of the Sunnis, which highlight their tendency to contradict themselves or be proved ignorant by the imams and their followers. For example, al-Nuʿman recalls one of Jaʿfar al-Sadiq's encounters with Abu Hanifa, during which he proved the unreliability of *qiyas* as a means of deriving opinions. The imam asks Abu Hanifa what his sources of knowledge are, and he responds that they are the Qur'an, the *Sunna* and *qiyas*. Referring to the latter, the imam recalls the infamous analogy of Iblis or Satan that resulted in disaster: Iblis fell from grace because he refused to prostrate himself before Adam as God had ordered, arguing that, as he was made of fire, he was superior to

Adam, who was only made of clay. Then the imam demonstrates the problem with the use of *qiyas* in other cases: it would entail arguing that urine is purer than semen, if established through analogy with the laws of ablution (which require ritual cleansing after the sexual act but not after urinating), and claiming that fasting is more important than prayer if based on the prohibitions applying to the performance of religious obligations by menstruating women (who are exempted from prayer, but allowed to fast).[99] In two lengthy *hadith*s that follow, a well-known follower of Abu Hanifa, Ibn Abi Layla, winds up acknowledging the higher authority of ʿAli b. Abi Talib's opinions vis-à-vis those of the other Companions.[100] And then follow several more *hadith*s on the subject of Jaʿfar al-Sadiq's encounters with Abu Hanifa, to which al-Nuʿman adds as postscript that the imam had taken so much trouble with Abu Hanifa because he and his followers were the closest to the Shiʿis among the majority.[101]

By way of conclusion, there are more *hadith*s from ʿAli and other imams which lay the blame for the community's ignorance on those individuals who claimed to represent and speak for the majority.[102] Lastly, al-Nuʿman states:

> We have exposed the persistence of ignorance among the people, and the frequency of their wrongdoing, and the weakness of their Traditions and reliance upon them, for their use of personal opinion and analogical reasoning is without knowledge or information about the Prophet and his example, and in defiance of the imam to whom submission is obligatory. And we have described the qualities of the imams from the Prophet's family, and what God has required regarding submission to their authority and command. … In this [we have provided] sufficient proof and example.[103]

Al-Nuʿman's concern with establishing the knowledge of the imams as a source of law is also reflected in another important work of the same period as the *Daʿaʾim*, the *Kitab ikhtilaf usul al-madhahib*. Written sometime after 343/954, it further elaborates his critique of *ijmaʿ* (consensus) and *qiyas* (analogy) as sources of law, the two principles by which Sunnis established what constituted acceptable Prophetic *hadith*s, and how these *hadith*s and the Qur'an were to be interpreted. These principles were thought to have been established by al-Shafi'i (d. 204/819) in his *Risala*, from whose time onwards Prophetic *hadith*s increasingly replaced individual opinion or *ra'y* as the most important tool for interpreting the Qur'an and deriving substantive law.[104] And now, some 150 years later, al-Nu'man addresses the problem of relying on the consensus of so many scholars to establish Prophetic *hadith*s, and on analogy for interpreting the Qur'an and the *hadith*s, in his *Ikhtilaf*.[105] In doing so, he seeks to establish the superiority of Ismaili *usul*, that is to say the Qur'an, the *hadith*s of the Prophet on the authority of the *ahl al-bayt*, and interpretations made by the ruling imams. He proceeds towards this end primarily by focusing on Sunni *usul*, and methodically reviews the problems with opinion (*ra'y*), imitation (*taqlid*), consensus (*ijma'*), analogy (*qiyas*), discretionary rulings for the good of the community (*istihsan*), and individual reasoning (*ijtihad*); in other words the range of possible justifications and guiding principles, of both primary and secondary importance, used in the Sunni legal schools up to his time.

As Lokhandwala points out, the 'attitude of the Ismailis towards the Sunna of the Prophet spared them from the laborious occupation of working out methods and manners of determining the credibility of the narrations or listing their own separate authorities for such narrations as the Sunni and other Shi'i schools had done'.[106] The issue was not just one of convenience, however. Ismaili *usul* were ultimately guided by different principles and premises. Unlike Sunni legal schools, which increasingly granted Prophetic *hadith*s a privileged status (and likewise to their compilers, historians, biographers, philologists, etc), Ismaili *usul* attempts to restore the primacy of the Qur'an as a source of guidance. That is to say, if the Qur'an is the sum total and seal of divine revelation, then it must contain all that humankind needs. But a literal reading of it, based largely on a philological and historical reading of it through *tafsir*, often yields insufficient guidance on all matters. For this reason there is a need for *ta'wil* or allegorical interpretation, which, if exercised properly and authorized by the imam, becomes a means for teasing out all its possible meanings and ramifications. The analysis of the Qur'anic text by means of *ta'wil* thus permits a greater elasticity and responsiveness to changes in time and place. It also is truer to the meta-historical and homilitic nature of the Qur'anic discourse. And for these reasons Shi'i legal tradition, and Ismaili *fiqh* in particular, relies heavily on *ta'wil* in its elaboration of law.

When Sunni jurists asserted the importance of Prophetic *hadith*s as a canonical source of law, they also created a seemingly endless debate about the means for their verification. This gave rise not only to polemical debates among these scholars, the utilization of *hadith*s in certain political agendas, and a vast industry of corollary sciences (with their practitioners) that emerged in the service of establishing a canonical collection, but also resulted in the unsatisfactory situation where contradictory or dubious *hadith*s were nevertheless considered orthodox. This, in turn, has preoccupied much modern scholarship, and generated various positions on the authenticity or historical accuracy of the *hadith* corpus. Not surprisingly, al-Nu'man's legal works often begin with caveats regarding the need to establish proper knowledge or acceptable *hadith*s. And equally unsurprising is his and other Shi'is' insistence on limiting *hadith*s to only those transmitted on the authority of the *ahl al-bayt*.

Similarly, with regard to the imam's ruling, this third of the Ismaili Shi'i *usul* helps to avoid endless and unhelpful disagreements by establishing the transcendent authority of one individual imam in each generation who inherits the received wisdom of his predecessors on the interpretation of the Qur'an and the *Sunna* of the Prophet. In other words, and as opposed to the many methods the Sunnis devised to arrive at acceptable *hadith*s and interpretations, reliance on the traditions of the *ahl al-bayt* and the interpretations of imams obviated the need for much, apparently futile, discussion and debate in the elaborations of the Ismaili Shi'i *madhhab*. At the same time, in terms developed by Twelver Shi'ism, limiting acceptable *hadith*s to those established by the time of Ja'far al-Sadiq obviated the need to produce literature justifying the occultation of subsequent imams. Al-Kulayni's *al-Kafi* and Ibn Babawayh's *Risalat al-i'tiqadat* both reflect the lengths to which Twelver Shi'ism had to go in order to resolve the disappearance of their last imam. As previously noted, both authors contributed to the 'four books' of early Twelver Shiʿism, and were contemporaries of al-Nuʿman. Al-Kulayni's *Kafi* was composed shortly before the *Daʿa'im* (or before the mid-4th/10th century), and in it al-Kulayni compiled *hadith*s then accepted by and circulating among the Twelver Shiʿis. The *Kafi* thus serves as an interesting counterpoint to the *Daʿa'im*, the latter reflecting, as it did, the culmination of a process of distillation and refinement of legal traditions and theory for Ismaili Shiʿism. In the more amorphous collection of the *Kafi*, on the other hand, one can find evidence of a range of Shiʿi attitudes, enabling us to understand the areas of agreement and difference between the Ismaili and Twelver forms of Shiʿism.

As regards the doctrine of the imamate, the *Kafi* incorporates the discussion of *imama* in its *usul* section, or in the section entitled *kitab al-hujja* of the first volume of the *Usul min al-kafi*.[107] This is explained in the prologue to the *Kafi*, where al-Kulayni deplores the increasing ignorance of the community and the necessity, therefore, of compiling a work that would aid those who seek to uphold the good and forbid wrongdoing in the community. This cannot be achieved without the knowledge supplied by the imam, who, despite his absence, must continue to guide the *ʿulama'*.[108] In order to do so, there must be 'a comprehensive book, in which is compiled all the disciplines of religious science, sufficient enough for the learned, and a reference for those who seek guidance, so that from it can be acquired all that he who wants religious knowledge desires, and thus act accordingly and in the true tradition of the *sadiqin* [i.e. the imams] … and this will lead to the fulfilment of God's commands and the *Sunna* of the Prophet.'[109] In other words, the *Kafi* stands as proxy for the knowledge of the absent imam, in contrast to the *Daʿa'im* which serves as a textual reflection of the universal authority of the living imam.

Recognition of the imams is nevertheless obligatory, because 'the servant will not be a *muʿmin* unless he acknowledges [*yaʿrif*] God, His Prophet and all of the imams, including the imam of his time, to whom he is required to submit and defer'.[110] Furthermore, and from Jaʿfar al-Sadiq: 'We are the ones to whom God made obedience obligatory. Only knowledge [*maʿrifa*] of us will be acceptable, and those who are ignorant of us will not be excused. He who knows us is a *mu'min* [believer] and he who rejects us is a *kafir* [unbeliever], and he who neither knows us nor rejects us is misled [*dall*] until he returns to the guidance that was made obligatory by God.'[111] Thus recognition is the due of the imams as ultimate sources of knowledge, and the envied referred to in God's words, 'Are they so envious of those whom God has given of His bounty?' (4:54).

The bulk of evidence marshalled by al-Kulayni to support the necessity for obedience to the imams, however, consists of *hadiths* which highlight the role of the imam as *hujja* or 'proof' of God on earth (hence *kitab al-hujja*). For example, a *hadith* from Muhammad al-Baqir says: 'By God, since the death of Adam, God has not left the earth without an imam, through whom He guides people to God, and who is His proof [*hujja*] to His servants. There will always be on earth an imam, who is the proof of God to His servants.'[112] In another *hadith* from al-Baqir: 'We are the warehouse of God's knowledge, and the interpreters of God's revelation [*wahi*], and the manifest proof between heaven and earth.' And from Jaʿfar al-Sadiq: 'The legatees [*awsiya'*] are the gates [*abwab*] of God, through whom and without whom there would be no knowledge of God, and through them God has provided evidence [of Himself] to his creation.'[113] Furthermore, the imams are the 'light of God', as emphasized by Muhammad al-Baqir when he was asked about the verse, 'Believe in God and His Messenger and the light that has been sent down to you' (64:8). He said, 'The light is the imams from the family of Muhammad, down to the Day of Judgement. They are the light of God that was sent down, and they are the light in the heavens and on earth, and ... the light of the imams that is in the hearts of the believers is greater than the light of the midday sun ... and God conceals their light to whom he wishes and so darkens their hearts.'[114]

While there is much congruence between the *Daʿa'im* and the *Kafi* on the essential principles of *imama* as outlined above and established since the time of Muhammad al-Baqir and Jaʿfar al-

Sadiq, the nature and scope of knowledge attributed to the imams in the *Kafi* far exceeds anything found in the *Daʿaʾim*. This tendency derives from their role as *muhaddath*, someone who is able to receive direct divine guidance, although not revelation, through various means.[115] Although the Prophet's knowledge was the sum total of all that of his predecessors, the imams not only inherited this knowledge but also other abilities. There are numerous *hadith*s incorporated in the *Kafi* which claim that the imams have supernatural abilities, such as the ability to receive divine guidance through dreams, the ability to foretell events and possess knowledge beyond all other prophets, and so on. The imams are the ones who have inherited the knowledge of all previous prophets and their *awsiya*';[116] they have knowledge of all the languages in which God has revealed His word;[117] they know the Hidden Name of God;[118] they possess the science of cosmic knowledge (*ʿilm al-jafr* and *jamiʿa*) and the book (*mushaf*) of prophecies given to Fatima by the Prophet;[119] they receive instructions on *laylat al-qadr*;[120] they have knowledge of the unknown;[121] they will know when and how they will die;[122] they know the future and the past, and so forth.

These and similar references to the supernatural powers of the imams and their performance of miracles are obviously very different from the *Daʿaʾim* where they appear only occasionally. Whereas the main concern of the *Daʿaʾim* is to establish the imam's leadership of the community in this world, in the *Kafi* he occupies an elevated station in the spiritual topography of Heaven and presides over the judgement of souls in the next world. For Twelver Shiʿis such references assist in establishing the eschatological authority of their imams in occultation and ultimately portray a shift towards a largely soteriological understanding of *imama*. We may suppose additionally that since the Twelver community had postponed expectations of the rule of their imams, Twelver Shiʿi tradition was more inclined to exaggerate claims on their behalf without any fear of accountability.

Historical arguments likewise occur in a slightly different context in the *Kafi*. Whereas in the *Daʿaʾim* monotheist history sets a precedent, in the *Kafi* the importance of past prophets is not so much their experience as their transmission of qualities and attributes which reach their perfection in the imams of Muhammad's family. Thus numerous *hadith*s recount the imams' possession of the relics and knowledge of previous prophets. The relics, such as the tablets of Moses, the ring of Solomon, the shirt of Adam, the arms of the Prophet and so on, endow the imams with special abilities and status,[123] and the inherited knowledge of earlier prophets underwrites the imams' primary role as sources for the transmission of correct knowledge.

As for Ghadir Khumm, it forms only a part of the discussion of 'Ali's succession to the Prophet in the *Kafi*.[124] For example, in a lengthy *hadith* from Ja'far al-Sadiq, God told Jesus to inform his followers that one from the progeny of Abraham's son Isma'il would come after him and he would be called Ahmad, and after him those who would possess the Great Name and the Book, from which everything would be known.[125] And when God required Muhammad to declare his successor, he replied that as the Arabs had no previous experience with prophets or scripture or succession, he was unsure how they would react. So God revealed, 'Be patient … and grieve not …' (16:127), and '… say, Peace, for they shall soon come to know,' (43:89) as encouragement, after which the Prophet recounted the qualities of 'Ali, and hypocrisy appeared in the hearts of the community. Thereafter God revealed, 'And surely, We know that your heart is distressed at what they say' (15:97). The Prophet had previously allied with members of the community and supported them, and imposed nothing on them until he received the following verse, in which God encouraged him to redouble his efforts: 'So when you are free, nominate' (94:7); the Prophet proclaimed 'Ali's *walaya* three times in front of the people.[126] God also ordered that the *ahl al-bayt* should receive what is their due: 'And give to the near of kin his due' (17:26). Another verse cited in the *Kafi* refers to the loving kindness (*mawadda*) due to the imams (42:23), and *hadith*s are quoted that attribute to 'Ali secret knowledge that was taught to him by the Prophet.[127]

The relative insignificance given to Ghadir Khumm in this sort of discussion of 'Ali's merits has ultimately to do with the fact that for Twelver Shiʿis succession of their imams came to be seen as divinely foreordained even before the advent of Islam, and thus does not entirely depend on historically explicit designation. Moreover, possession of relics and insignia (such as the Prophet's arms, the sword of ʿAli, Dhu'l-fiqar and the *mushaf* of Fatima) also indicate succession, and for this reason those who were descended from Hasan b. ʿAli or other members or branches of the *ahl al-bayt* (including the Zaydi imams and the Abbasid contenders) are regarded as imposters.[128] Most importantly, the Twelver Shiʿi emphasis on foreordination helped to circumvent Ismaili claims for the succession of Ismaʿil b. Jaʿfar and his son, Muhammad b. Ismaʿil. According to this view, if Ismaʿil predeceased his father as the Twelvers claim, this must be part of the divine plan that resulted in the truer succession of Musa al-Kazim and the line of Twelver Shiʿi imams.

Ibn Babawayh's *Risalat al-iʿtiqadat* provides another example of the Twelver Shiʿi doctrine of *imama*. Most probably composed between 355/966 and 381/991, the *Risala* can be dated slightly later than both the *Daʿa'im* and the *Kafi*. The discussion of *imama* in the *Risala* follows a discussion of theological matters, and involves a statement on the nature, identity and role of the imams in the Twelver Shiʿi line. Ibn Babawayh states that there were 124,000 prophets and an equal number of *awsiya'* (successors as imams), and that of these prophets five held a superior position: Noah, Abraham, Moses, Jesus and Muhammad.[129] The most excellent of them was Muhammad, and so therefore are his progeny.[130] The imams of his progeny are listed and culminate in Muhammad al-Muntazar, who is the *hujja*, the *qa'im* (upholder) of God's command, the *sahib al-zaman* (master of the age) and the *khalifa* or deputy of God on earth, even though he is absent (*gha'ib*) from the community.[131] Like his predecessors, he is also the *bab* (the gate to God), *sabil* (the path to God), *dalil* (the guide) and the repository of knowledge. He is also pure, immune from sin, perfect in knowledge and possesses the power to perform miracles. The earth cannot exist without him, and belief in him is obligatory even if he does not return until the end of time, for he is the only one who can establish a just society. He will be known on his return as the

Mahdi and Jesus will be seen praying behind him.[132]

Moreover, when Isma'il asked his father Ja'far al-Sadiq about the fate of sinners among their followers, the imam replied that their fate will be determined in line with verse 39:60 ('And on the Day of Judgement, will you not see those who lied against God? Their faces will be blackened, for is not Hell the abode for the arrogant?') which refers to those who falsely claim to be imams, even though they are of 'Alid and Fatimid descent.[133] Other chapters deal with groups from whom the Twelver community should disassociate. There are primarily two: the *ghuluww* or extremists who attribute powers of creation to the Prophet and the imams, or claim the occultation of any but the last imam from the Twelver line; and the oppressors, among whom are those who falsely claim to be imams themselves. For the Prophet identified all twelve imams after him until the *qa'im* or *mahdi*, and as he himself said, disobedience towards them was like disobeying himself and God.[134]

Thus, whereas al-Kulayni's *Kafi* reveals the range of beliefs regarding the imams in Twelver Shi'i tradition, Ibn Babawayh's *Risala* makes explicit who those imams are. Both elaborate a very different understanding of the imam's role compared to the *Da'a'im*. The occultation of the twelfth imam not only enabled them to emphasize but also to amplify the supernatural qualities of the imams. As for the *Da'a'im*, which sought to establish the political authority of the Fatimids, it distanced itself from exaggerated claims for the imams and messianic expectations which could not be realized. So even where there is convergence in the essential principles of the doctrine of *imama*, supported by interpretations of the Qur'an and the use of *hadith*s from al-Baqir and al-Sadiq, the claims made for the imams through these tools differ fundamentally between the *Kafi* and *Risala* on the one hand, and the *Da'a'im* on the other. Ultimately the *Da'a'im*'s focus on the legitimacy of 'Alid succession (and, by extension, that of the Fatimids) is made through arguments that could be historically and doctrinally defended to a larger audience, including the Sunnis. The next chapter will explore how these arguments are reflected and elaborated in the historical works of al-Qadi al-Nu'man.

4

Zahiri Paradigms

As he did with the formation of an Ismaili system of law, so al-Qadi al-Nuʿman did with Ismaili historiography – he charted a course between Sunni and Shiʿi literary and historiographical traditions, modifying and developing from them important Ismaili contributions to Islamic historiography. Two examples of these are the *Iftitah* (*al-daʿwa wa-ibtida' al-dawla*) and the *Majalis wa'l-musayarat*, the former resembling the *futuh* or conquest literature of Sunni tradition, and the latter deriving from the *akhbar* or hagiographical tradition regarding the imams in Twelver Shiʿi literature. By the 4th/10th century, literary and historiographical traditions in both communities had arrived at fundamentally differing approaches to commemorating and recording their respective communal memories.

Sunni historiographical tradition is canvassed and analysed in Khalidi's *Arabic Historical Thought in the Classical Period*.[1] Towards classifying and understanding the variety and prodigious volume of historical writing produced by Islamic societies from the 2nd/8th to the 9th/15th centuries, Khalidi argues that 'the net must be cast wide, to include not only the historians themselves, but the various conceptual frameworks within which they operated. Once these "epistemic canopies" were determined, it was also important to show how these were, in turn, implanted in social and political developments.'[2] He identifies four of these canopies, one leading to the other, but all inevitably overlapping. They are *hadith* or 'tradition-writing', *adab* or belles-lettres, *hikma* or the 'scientific' writing of history (not to be confused with the Shiʿi sense of *hikma* or esoteric knowledge), and *siyasa* or political and administrative history. In focusing on guiding principles, form and method, and in taking into consideration political agendas and group interests in the evolution of an Islamic historiographical tradition, Khalidi reveals the complexity behind previous notions of the simple transition from oral to written culture (or from *hadith* to history proper), and allows for the consideration of a broader range of works as historical.

Although Khalidi's study is limited to Sunni sources, it also provides a useful scheme for understanding the value of al-Qadi al-Nuʿman's historiography which, with the exception of the *Iftitah*, has often and otherwise eluded classification and therefore appropriate analysis. As Khalidi observes, it was more the political concerns of the mid-Umayyad period, or the succession crises and civil war in ʿAbd al-Malik's time, rather than a simple shift from oral to written culture brought on by the expansion of Islam, that first prompted the systematic collection of *hadith*s. In other words, the need for recording and collecting *hadith*s arose from Umayyad attempts to justify their policies through the wider circulation that written *hadith*s afforded, and at the same time embroiled the newly created specialists in *hadith* collection in specific political agendas. These, in turn, spawned the production of *hadith* literature as a means of justifying opposing viewpoints, thus leading to standardization of *hadith* transmission and efforts to establish canonical collections in the Abbasid period. The primary use for these collections was legal, but *hadith*s were also used and arranged narratively in commemorative works that recorded the remarkably triumphant and disorienting achievements of the Prophet's time and the early Islamic period. As Khalidi states, 'It was under this "Science of *Hadith*" that historical writing first found shelter.'[3]

Among the early historical works that utilized *hadith*s as the building blocks of larger narratives were biographies of the Prophet, such as those of Ibn Ishaq (d. 151/761) and Ibn Hisham (d. 208/834), genealogical literature like al-Baladhuri's (d. 279/892) *Ansab al-ashraf*, biographical literature on the early Muslim community like the *tabaqat* of Ibn Saʿd (d. 230/845), the Annales or *Ta'rikh* of al-Tabari (d. 310/923), and *futuh* or conquest literature like al-Waqidi's (d. 207/823) *Maghazi* and al-Baladhuri's *Futuh al-buldan*.[4] In describing *futuh* literature, Khalidi observes that the alternating triumph and tragedy of the early Muslim conquests and civil wars provided great material for later generations to use when contemplating their own triumphs and tragedies, and sparked an interest in the edifying purpose of constructing narratives of those conquests. Although based on *hadith*s from the time of the earliest Muslim community, details of participants and problems in the conquests of the early Muslim state, *futuh* literature is nevertheless imbued with the heroic and the sentimental, serving as it does as a paradigm of the virtues of the Prophet, his Companions and the earliest Muslims.[5]

This is just as much true of al-Qadi al-Nuʿman's *Iftitah* (the title of which derives from the singular for *futuh*, *fath*). The *Iftitah* covers the spread of the Fatimid *daʿwa* and conquests of Abu ʿAbd Allah al-Shiʿi in North Africa until the establishment of the Fatimid state in 297/909.[6] As an example of Ismaili *futuh* or triumphal record of the Fatimid conquests, it presents the heroic exploits of Abu ʿAbd Allah, his policies, strategies and administration of conquered territory, as well as the flaws that led to his execution, very much in the mode of early *futuh* literature. In all this, Prophetic parallels are constantly, if implicitly, drawn by al-Nuʿman, e.g. Abu ʿAbd Allah's piety, knowledge and wisdom as leader of the *dar al-hijra*, his stunning political and military successes, as well as the setbacks and betrayals that ultimately cost him his life.[7] But, this is certainly not to say that al-Qadi al-Nuʿman equates him with the Prophet; rather that just as *futuh* of previous times commemorated the Prophet's career and achievements of his Companions, so al-Nuʿman's *Iftitah* commemorated the achievements of the Ismaili imam and his *awliya'* in his own time. And just as early *futuh* constructed a paradigm of Islamic triumph, so also did the *Iftitah* of Ismaili Shiʿi triumph.

Yet, and unlike Sunni *futuh* both of previous centuries and the same period, al-Nuʿman liberates the narrative of the *Iftitah* from the cumbersome apparatus and form of *hadith*-based history, such as the listing of the *isnad* or chain of transmission accompanying each record, and the juxtaposition of various records of the same event (although his sources, such as a lost biography of Abu 'Abd Allah, and the memoirs of Fatimid officials like Ibn al-Haytham and Ustadh Jawdhar, are acknowledged by inference). The reasons for this have already been discussed in Chapters 2 and 3; the effect is a seamless narrative that records in much detail the conquests leading up to the establishment of the Fatimid state. The value of the *Iftitah* has been demonstrated (in Chapter 1) as a source for the history of the Fatimid revolutionary period, and for numerous later Muslim historians as a source for communal histories (the *'Uyun al-akhbar* of the Ismaili *da'i* Idris 'Imad al-Din), regional histories (such as those of Ibn 'Idhari and al-Marrakushi), and the universal histories of Ibn al-Athir and al-Nuwayri.

In addition to being significantly different from Sunni *futuh* literature in terms of form, the *Iftitah* also differs significantly from other, and in particular Twelver Shi'i, forms of literature in terms of its content. Unlike the Fatimids who, as a result of the establishment of their state, needed to commission works like the *Iftitah* from al-Qadi al-Nu'man, the Twelver Shi'is had no comparable political triumph to commemorate and were discouraged from producing similar works by the 4th/10th century. On the contrary, having often been excluded from power and frequently oppressed, they were more inclined to develop a hagiographical rather than a historical literature to assert and commemorate their imams and their own community of followers. These include the *Nahj al-balagha* (a collection of reports by and from 'Ali b. Abi Talib) by al-Sharif al-Radi (d. 406/1015) and the *Kitab al-irshad* (a similar work on the twelve imams) by Shaykh al-Mufid (d. 413/1022). Although such works utilized many reliable *hadith* reports about historical events, legal philosophy and decisions, and other merits of the imams, they also include information on the miracles surrounding them and the supernatural abilities they exhibited (as was apparent from discussion of the *Kafi* and the *Risala* in the previous chapter). Ultimately, such works contributed to the construction of a mythical rather than a historical image of the imams, in keeping with the postponement of expectations and the messianism associated with the doctrine of occultation or *ghayba*.

Al-Nuʿman also produced works of *akhbar* literature in the larger Shiʿi tradition about shared Ismaili and Twelver imams, as well as particular Ismaili and Fatimid imams, such as the *Sharh al-akhbar* (which collected *hadith*s about all the imams to the Fatimid period), the *manaqib* and *fada'il* literature (which celebrated merits and virtues), and biographies of the Fatimid imams al-Mahdi, al-Qa'im, al-Mansur and al-Muʿizz, most of which are now lost, as noted in Chapter 2.[8] But in these works, too, al-Nuʿman does not list chains of transmission in the conventional Sunni manner of *hadith*-based history. More importantly, he aims at constructing a historical image of the imams, and thus includes information and contextualization beyond the immediate particulars of the imams' lives and achievements. The culmination of these efforts was the *Kitab al-majalis wa'l-musayarat*.

Composed like the *Daʿa'im* and the *Iftitah* in the time of al-Muʿizz, the *Majalis* deals with the life of this Fatimid imam-caliph, but in innovative ways different even from his earlier works.[9] The *Majalis*'s reports are based on al-Qadi al-Nuʿman's own personal experience and interactions, and these reports are recounted in a form usually associated with Sunni *adab* history – that is, sessions (*majalis*) between scholars that in the Sunni context involved the discussion of mainly secular topics, such as the merits of the knowledge and experience of the Ancients versus that of the Muslims, literature and theories of literary criticism, the debate between 'specialists' and 'generalists', and the debate on the respective merits of Arab and non-Arab cultures.[10] The literature that recorded these and other topics, each in the form of a report or *hadith*, without a chain of transmission, about the sessions in which they were discussed, include, for example, the *Nishwar al-muhadara* of al-Tanukhi (d. 384/994). Al-Tanukhi stated that his purpose was to edify the public on the basis of what he saw and heard from the intellectuals and scholars of his day, and in doing so the *Nishwar* illustrates 'the concept of history as lived experience, coupled with a heightened sense of the value of direct testimony and witness'.[11] Similarily, al-Nuʿman states in the introduction to his *Majalis* that his purpose is to impart some of the knowledge and wisdom of the imams as he had experienced it, and to relay what he had heard, seen and understood to future generations.[12]

The tradition of *majalis* among Ismailis, however, was one of religious instruction, as is clear from al-Nuʿman's description of Abu ʿAbd Allah's *majalis al-hikma* in the *dar al-hijra*. Considering that the imams' knowledge encompassed both the secular and the strictly religious, his referring to the *majalis* as such is not necessarily confusing. On the contrary, it allows him to exchange a linear narrative in the form of biography or *sira* recounting the life of al-Muʿizz for the record out of a vast number of anecdotes and accounts, broken down into 28 sections with no apparent order or classification, suitable for recitation and edification in public gatherings (which, in fact, was how it was used in later Fatimid history and Ismaili communities).[13] More important than al-Nuʿman's innovative adaptation of a genre already established in Sunni literature and a forum otherwise employed in the Ismaili context, is the image of al-Muʿizz that al-Nuʿman portrays in his *Majalis*. Contrary to Stern's characterization as 'mere hagiography',[14] the *Majalis*'s eyewitness and historical reports, so useful to both Ismaili and Sunni authors mentioned above, were intended to celebrate the example of an imam-caliph, or to establish the paradigm for the just rule of an imam.[15]

The presentation of al-Muʿizz in the *Majalis* incorporates many themes which, needless to say, are also found in other texts such as the *Daʿaʾim*. Many of the anecdotes that make up the work deal with his personal qualities as an imam, as well as his relations with the *daʿwa* and supporters from among his own Ismaili community. In reviewing the anecdotes about his personal qualities, one finds an emphasis especially on his knowledge, which is not surprising considering the importance of knowledge as a defining characteristic of *imama*. The range of the imam's knowledge and wisdom in the *Majalis* is not just religious, but extends to matters and examples not found in other discussions of his attributes and characteristics, and often to the mundane or prosaic, and even the scientific. What is more, the *Majalis* often portrays al-Muʿizz's knowledge in consonance with that of his predecessors.

In one account, for example, al-Nuʿman accompanies the imam al-Mansur and al-Muʿizz on an excursion. They stop in a valley where rainwater has been used to irrigate some farmland and a large dam built. Two men approach them and one complains that the other has obstructed the flow of water to his land, while the first argues that it was his right to do so. The imam and his son listen to the men, who each produce many proofs of the other's wrongdoing, to the confusion and dismay of the listeners. Eventually al-Mansur refers them to al-Muʿizz, who rules in favour of the one whose water supply had been obstructed.[16]

Al-Muʿizz's abilities are portrayed as so outstanding that his grandfather al-Qa'im had once exclaimed that were it not for his youth, he, al-Qa'im, would have designated him next in line.[17] Al-Nuʿman observes on another occasion that al-Muʿizz displayed much patience with some servants who had failed to prepare his bath after having been ordered to do so. As he waited while the servants finally prepared the bath, al-Muʿizz extolled the virtue of tolerance and forgiveness by recounting a *hadith* about Muhammad al-Baqir forgiving a servant girl who by accident fatally injured one of his sons.[18] Still, just as God had endowed the prophets with different capacities and abilities, so He also did with the imams. As Muʿizz observes on another occasion, even if some imams were more patient, compassionate or afflicted by hardship than others, yet each in his own way was appropriate to his age and each a proof of God on earth.[19]

For this reason, all that is good is reflected in the command of the imams,[20] and the imam can apprehend what others cannot apprehend, and although they would be satisfied without such responsibility, God has placed them in charge of the affairs of the world and the upholding of good and the forbidding of wrong.[21] In one account, the visit of messengers from the east occasions a lesson for al-Nuʿman on the convergence of the rulings of imams presiding in different eras, which to him is also one of the proofs of their *imama*.[22] That is why, in another account, al-Muʿizz argues that salvation and paradise will be obtained only by the followers of the imams, and why those who do not follow all the imams are held to be misled.[23]

Accounts such as these, while ultimately conceding an equality of virtue to all the imams, nevertheless distinguish certain abilities of al-Muʿizz from those of his Fatimid predecessors, al-Mansur, al-Qa'im and even al-Mahdi. This tendency is also revealed in accounts on the religious knowledge of the imams. The imams are all recognized for their superior knowledge of the Qur'an and its interpretation,[24] as well as for their ability to prove the ignorance and error of their enemies. But unlike previous Fatimids, al-Muʿizz's knowledge and discourse brings to mind imams such as ʿAli b. Abi Talib and Jaʿfar al-Sadiq, who were most famous for exposing the weak knowledge and position of some of their contemporaries.[25] Al-Muʿizz likewise takes on his contemporaries and demonstrates his superior knowledge with regard to the understanding and interpretation of the Qur'an, doctrines and a host of other topics.

In one account, for example, al-Muʿizz provides a lesson on the issue of *burhan* or proof. When the topic of *burhan* comes up in a *majlis*, al-Muʿizz asks al-Nuʿman what his understanding of the term is. Al-Nuʿman answers that it means an illustration (*bayan*) of something. Al-Muʿizz counters with a *hadith* from the Prophet which says that *bayan* can mean a form of magic, and then adds that such a meaning could not be applied to *burhan*, making the analogy incorrect. Al-Nuʿman is confused, for he has understood from the *hadith* of the Prophet that a *burhan*, like a *bayan*, is something which clarifies and establishes, and this is also how it appears in the Qur'an in numerous places. So al-Muʿizz sends al-Nuʿman off to research the matter.

Al-Nuʿman goes away and delves into works on language, consults the Qur'an and commentaries on the verses in which the term appears, and arrives always at the same conclusion, i.e. that the term means something that proves and clarifies. Finally, he consults the works of the imams for the *batini* or esoteric meaning of *burhan*, and then, with great unease, collects his findings and returns to the imam. As he enters the presence of the imam, it occurs to him that he had not researched the works of the philosophers for their understanding of the term. However, the imam launches into a discussion of the philosophers' definition and demonstrates how they also arrived at unsatisfying conclusions. Al-Nu'man is reassured. Nevertheless, some of those in attendance present a treatise which contains an explanation to a similar question put to two *da'is*, but this concurs with, and does not exceed, the findings of the philosophers. Then a *da'i* presents the imam with yet another (apparently extremist) philosophical treatise on *burhan*, which the imam glances at and throws down, exclaiming, 'What a catastrophe it is that such things are attributed to us by the *da'wa*!'

Finally, al-Mu'izz turns to al-Qadi al-Nu'man and asks him for his findings. Al-Nu'man hesitatingly submits his notebook to the imam, apologizing for its contents and noting that it contains only what he has found in works on the imams' sermons on the issue. He adds that more than what his research contains, only the imam himself could provide. Al-Mu'izz looks at the notebook, smiling and approving of the fact that al-Nu'man referred to the teachings of the imams above others, and comments that what he discovered resembled the meaning of the term. Al-Nu'man then rises and exclaims, 'May the imam himself continue!', at which point all those in the assembly rise also. Al-Mu'izz then interrogates al-Nu'man about God's creation of the universal intellect, and how it was said that when He created it, He intended to give, take, establish, reward and punish through it. This means, al-Mu'izz continues, that reason establishes what exists as *burhan* or proof (unlike what establishes *bayan* or the illustration of something), for proof does not exist without reason. Thus what is apprehended by right minds (like those of the imams) is what God intended to be established and what He rewards, and what is apprehended by weak minds (like those of others) needs to be rejected. Al-Mu'izz concedes that the philosophers originally presented a similar argument, but it was perverted by the people who thus made them produce ignorant opinions. After providing another example for the necessity of reason, he notes he is the first among the imams to establish this definition of *burhan*. Al-Nu'man then continues with praise for the imam's wisdom and knowledge, which he argues was apparent from his youth, which even the most learned could never surpass, and which encompassed knowledge of the *batin*, *fiqh*, what is permitted and forbidden, astrology, philosophy, and much else besides. (In this way, the imam resembled his forefather the Prophet, who despite his illiteracy was the most knowledgeable and wise man of his age.[26]) For example, the imam invents objects like the fountain pen,[27] demonstrates his knowledge of mathematics,[28] his ability to point out the weaknesses of grammarians,[29] to interpret poetry,[30] and so forth.

Of course, the knowledge of the imams and especially of al-Muʿizz enables them to know the *batin* and the *zahir*, the esoteric and the exoteric, of things.[31] They can foretell their deaths and the outcome of certain things through their dreams,[32] and in several of the accounts they elucidate points of *fiqh* and ritual such as prostration in front of the imams,[33] the prohibition against *mutʿa* (or temporary) marriage,[34] the necessity of *kitman* or secrecy,[35] the right of female relatives and slaves to inherit,[36] the status of orphans with guardians,[37] and the prohibition against mourning over the graves of the imams.[38] The imams, of course, inherit this knowledge from their predecessors,[39] through secret works[40] and training,[41] and the deathbed transmissions of their fathers.[42] While al-Muʿizz admits that the imams have knowledge of a kind which ordinary people do not possess, he emphatically denies that the imams have the knowledge of the 'unknown' that is exclusive to God.[43] In other accounts, al-Muʿizz upbraids certain *daʿis* for attributing knowledge of this 'unknown' domain to the imams.[44]

In addition to the imams' knowledge, another important issue or rather dynamic that the *Majalis* conveys is the often tense relationship between al-Muʿizz and his *daʿwa*, who sometimes propagate doctrines that he finds extremist, such as when, in the discussion of the meaning of *burhan*, a *daʿi* shows the imam something that contains a questionable interpretation derived from philosophy, as opposed to the teachings of the imam which al-Nuʿman had consulted, which then gets associated with the imams.[45] In yet other accounts al-Muʿizz complains about the deviation, corruption and insubordination of some *daʿis*,[46] and often finds he has to take action against those who seek to undermine his authority as imam. For example, al-Muʿizz recalls a visit made by one of the *daʿis* of the east, about whom reports had arrived indicating his corruption and deviation. So, al-Muʿizz continues, when the offending *daʿi* arrived he was made aware of the unacceptability of his ways. He repented in front of the imam and then asked permission to leave. But upon being advised that he intended to return to his old ways and to continue to corrupt the people, al-Muʿizz instructed the governor of Barqa to accompany him. When the two reached Tripoli, however, the *daʿi* insisted on preceding the governor. On the way, his party was attacked, and, when trying to escape his assailants, his mount threw him to the ground and he died. In this manner, says al-Muʿizz, God's hand protects the imams, and they rely on Him to execute what is right.[47]

Such accounts in the *Majalis* remind the reader that the extremism and antinomianism of some sections of the *daʿwa* from al-Mahdi's time lingered on in the time of al-Muʿizz, and were exacerbated by the distance between the Fatimid state and branches of the *daʿwa* outside Fatimid territory. They also portray al-Muʿizz's concern to disseminate correct doctrine, his rejection of extremism and his vigilance against the development of wayward beliefs among any and all Ismailis, including those in Sind, Iran and among the Qaramita, as previously noted, as well as his displeasure with unauthorized activities on the part of the *daʿwa* organization.[48] In all this al-Muʿizz, like al-Mahdi before him, hoped to suppress the tendency towards a more messianic understanding of his role, in favour of a historically living and ruling imam. Such accounts at the same time echo a well-established trope in Shiʿi literature generally, which routinely features an imam put upon by the well-intentioned but sometimes dangerous beliefs of his disciples.

Nonetheless, al-Muʿizz's relations with the *daʿwa* were on the whole positive. Al-Numʿan reports that he once heard the imam describe many of his *daʿis* as loyal, trustworthy and honest.[49] After all, the *daʿwa* organization was as crucial beyond their territories as within them, both in terms of doctrinal matters and revenue collection.[50] In one report, for example, a man approaches al-Nuʿman in a *majlis* and asks him who he should approach, when he returns home, to dispatch money to the imams. Al-Nuʿman informs him that each region has a *janah* (branch) of the *daʿwa*, and thus he will know who to approach. When al-Nuʿman informs al-Muʿizz of how he instructed this man, al-Muʿizz commends him for what he said, and adds that in every *jazira* (region), there are those who call people to the imams, for otherwise the imams would lose the allegiance of those who are far from them.[51]

As for al-Muʿizz's relations with other followers like the Kutama Berbers, they are generally painted in a positive light.[52] This is in large part because, as the *Majalis* reports indicate, Kutama support and military experience were crucial to the success of the conquest of Egypt. On one occasion, al-Muʿizz addresses a group of Kutama chiefs and promises them that he is confident that the east shall be conquered. He reminds them that the Kutama are from among the Berbers, who are after all the descendants of Goliath, and thus were driven out of the east when David defeated him.[53]

Of course, many of the reports in the *Majalis* convey aspects of the special relationship that al-Qadi al-Nuʿman himself had with al-Muʿizz.[54] Some also involve discussions about works that the imams commission from him, and thus have helped to complete the picture of his oeuvre.[55] Nevertheless, even al-Nuʿman experienced periodic anxiety over a possible loss of favour from his patrons. In one account al-Nuʿman reports that when al-Mansur was alive, he would always consult al-Muʿizz on everything he was ordered to do by al-Mansur. After al-Mansur's passing, al-Nuʿman did not hear from al-Muʿizz for a long time and began to worry that he would lose the guidance from al-Muʿizz on which he so depended. He therefore resolved to write to him to ask what he had done to displease his master, and why his master had forsaken him. Al-Muʿizz replied that al-Nuʿman had nothing to fear, that his favour with the imams had not diminished and that al-Nuʿman would continue to serve him as he had served his father.[56]

Al-Nuʿman's proximity to the imams also enabled him to

collect information about the evolving nature of their policies as rulers. For example, al-Nuʿman recalls that when he was once with al-Muʿizz, the imam brought up the topic of rebels and other troublemakers. At the time he had asked some people about what to do with such as these, and they had replied that he should do as al-Mansur had done with them (meaning Abu Yazid), that is, execute them and burn their possessions. Al-Muʿizz replied that whereas such policies were necessary in al-Mansur's time, there were times when the imam had to forgive, for forgiveness comes from God, who after all had given the imams the power of forgiveness. Moreover, if the imams always punished the crimes of the people, al-Muʿizz continued, they would only earn hatred and provoke rebellion in the people.[57] This account obviously speaks about the greater security and authority al-Muʿizz experienced during his reign, in contrast to the reigns of al-Qa'im and al-Mansur.

Al-Muʿizz's indulgence towards his subjects' shortcomings, however, did not extend to those of his administrators, as some accounts indicate. In one account, al-Muʿizz expresses concern about his tax collectors overburdening the people.[58] In another account the imam condemns those administrators and tax collectors who oppress the people, for just as God has warned against compulsion in religion, so the imams also are satisfied with what the people will give.[59] Other accounts describe al-Muʿizz's performance of such rituals of office as leading the Friday prayer,[60] and his personal interaction with the people. Once when he rode out to Mansuriyya, the people surrounded his mount, petitioning him about their needs. He, of course, made an effort to listen to them and delegated judges to hear their petitions, and was so crowded about that he was unable to move.[61] On another occasion when he went out for a stroll and was again beseeched by the needy, he stopped his guards from driving them away.[62]

In numerous accounts, al-Muʿizz is also concerned with the dissemination of the knowledge of the imams. On some occasions he commissions books (as we have seen with regard to al-Nuʿman), on others he receives or encourages questions from the people,[63] and personally conducts the *majalis al-hikma*. His concern for involvement with them, however, again does not blind him to the capabilities of the people. Al-Nuʿman recalls an instance when he was instructed to read to the people from the wisdom of the imams. The room in the palace in which he conducted his sessions became so crowded that many in the audience could not hear what he said. News of this reached the imam, as well as the fact that some of those in attendance aspired to hold positions in the *daʿwa* even though they understood little of what was being taught to them.[64] Later, al-Nuʿman was in the presence of the imam when the barber arrived to cut his hair. As was customary, al-Nuʿman prepared to leave like the others, but the imam detained him and then asked him whether the people were benefitting from his sessions. Eventually al-Nuʿman understood that the imam intended him to teach the people only what they were capable of learning, for otherwise their ignorance would be harmful to the imams.[65]

Other means by which al-Muʿizz sought to directly engage his subjects included the organization of spectacles. In one lengthy and rather extraordinary account (mentioned in the previous chapter), al-Muʿizz decides to commemorate the circumcision of his sons by ordering the governors of even the far reaches of his realm to announce to all the people that they also should participate by having their sons circumcised on the same day. This was to take place during Rabiʿ I 351/9 May–8 June 962[66] and those whose sons were circumcised were to receive money and robes from the imam. On the appointed day, the imam seated himself in the courtyard of the palace and ordered the setting up of pavilions to accommodate all those who were to participate in the ritual: the boys, as well as their parents and those servants whose masters desired them to be circumcised too. Those unable to attend were given seven years from that date to fulfil this duty.

The imam remained seated the whole day, reports al-Nuʿman, while all manner of people came and went. There were men to circumcise the boys in the pavilions and others to attend to the boys while they sat on chairs, and to collect the blood and skin that was shed. Incense burned and rose water was poured over the heads of the boys, and when some fainted they were revived.

Al-Nuʿman's account continues with a description of the gifts the people received on the occasion, such as the robes given out to the families, and the 100 to 150 dirhams that each boy received. The festivities went on for the remainder of the month, and at one time the imam pointedly observed to al-Nuʿman that unlike the worldly kings, the imams truly give of the wealth that God has granted them. Al-Nuʿman notes that about 5,000 to 10,000 boys in all were circumcised on that occasion.[67]

The image of the imam overseeing this ritual ceremony in the pavilions, amid the clamour of thousands of boys being circumcised, and their families attending and collecting the gifts, the palace staff and servants running back and forth with water and buckets, and so on, was clearly a spectacle no one had seen the like of before. But this would not be the only instance; the Fatimids became famous for their ceremonial and ritual. Paula Sanders points out that as Fatimid ceremonial developed it not only provided the imams with occasions on which to present themselves to the people and to exercise munificence, but also helped to bridge the gap between the Ismaili *khassa* or elite and the non-Ismaili *ʿamma* or general public, between the *mu'min* and the muslim.[68]

Apart from the details of the internal politics and policies of the early Fatimid state, the *Majalis* provides many accounts and reports that describe al-Muʿizz's relations with the Umayyads of Spain, the Byzantines, Abbasids and Ikhshidids, who all vied for control of the Mediterranean. As Dachraoui says, the information in the *Majalis* supplies, for the first time, a picture of Fatimid power at its peak in North Africa, and indicates how this power was perceived with anxiety by other states in the region.[69] One of the more noteworthy sections of the *Majalis* is a lengthy account of al-Muʿizz's attempt to undermine Umayyad power through a naval raid on the Iberian coast.[70] The account begins with a report that reaches al-Muʿizz concerning an Umayyad ship, coming from the east, colliding with a Fatimid vessel sailing from Sicily. The crew of the Umayyad vessel made off with the cargo of the Fatimid ship, including a letter from the Fatimid governor in Sicily, the Kalbid al-Hasan b. ʿAli, and left the Fatimid crew and passengers stranded on an island.

Al-Nuʿman reports that al-Muʿizz was much upset on hearing the news and resolved to send out a fleet from Sicily to the Iberian port of Almeria, where the Umayyads had a shipyard and their fleet was anchored. The Fatimid fleet, under al-Hasan b. ʿAli, succeeded in burning and destroying not only the Umayyad ships but also the port itself, with all its *matériel*, warehouses and shipyards. Al-Nuʿman adds that the Fatimid losses were negligible. Following these events, which took place in 345/955, the Umayyad ʿAbd al-Rahman III (also known as al-Nasir) reacted by seeking an alliance with the Byzantines in the eastern Mediterranean against the Fatimids, while the Byzantines, because of their concerns over Fatimid possessions such as Sicily, made an overture to the Fatimids against the Umayyads, offering a long-term truce. The three powers thus vied for control of the Mediterranean.

Al-Nuʿman then reports that al-Muʿizz called his council together to discuss his policy towards the Byzantines. When they advised a truce, al-Muʿizz reprimanded them for siding so quickly with the enemy. So instead of signing a truce with the Byzantines, he sent another fleet out from Mahdiyya to engage the Byzantines in battle off the coast of Sicily and inflicted defeat on them in their Sicilian lands.[71] In the meantime, the Umayyad caliph al-Nasir ʿAbd al-Rahman decided to take advantage of what he thought was an opportunity to launch an attack on the coast of North Africa, but was defeated again because al-Muʿizz had issued orders to his governors to prepare for such an attack. Having in this way defeated both powers from either end of the Mediterranean, al-Muʿizz reconsidered the situation and finally accepted the offer of a truce from the Byzantines, arguing that this time it was in the interests of the Muslims to do so.[72] With regard to the Umayyads, however, obviously there could be no compromise, for after all they claimed the caliphate. The rest of al-Nuʿman's account relates the various disputes between al-Muʿizz and ʿAbd al-Rahman, along with the imam's criticisms of the Umayyad, his genealogy and his treacherous alliances with the Byzantines, and condemnation of the rampant corruption and immorality in Umayyad domains.[73] His severest criticism, however, is reserved for al-Nasir's claim to the caliphal title.[74]

The caliphate was obviously also a major issue between al-Muʿizz and the Abbasids. It was the object of considerable anti-Fatimid polemic issued by the Sunni establishment under the Abbasids, and which the *Majalis* seeks to refute in several narratives.[75] Nevertheless, despite his emphatic denial of Abbasid claims to caliphal authority, most of al-Muʿizz's critique is directed against the Umayyads and, by extension, their vassals and supporters in the Maghrib. One such individual was the Midrarid governor of Sijilmasa, Ibn Wasul, who had attempted to ensure his autonomy from the Fatimids, again through that ultimate trump card of proclaiming himself caliph! Clearly this was more than al-Muʿizz could tolerate and, in any case, disciplining Ibn Wasul would provide the Fatimids with another opportunity for asserting their authority against the Umayyads, on this occasion in the contested arena of the far Maghrib. Al-Muʿizz dispatched an army under the general Jawhar al-Siqilli, and in the process Ibn Wasul was defeated and brought back a prisoner.[76] The expedition was to result in the famous incident in which, to show his master that his sway extended to the ends of the earth, Jawhar sent back a fish from the Atlantic when his army reached Fez. Although in many accounts Ibn Wasul is subjected to al-Muʿizz's anger and punished for his insubordination, al-Nuʿman on one occasion is moved to intercede for him with al-Muʿizz, so that he may attend Friday prayer,[77] to which al-Muʿizz reluctantly agrees. Al-Nuʿman's account of the treatment of Ibn Wasul was clearly intended to demonstrate to other vassals the virtue of remaining loyal to their Fatimid overlord.[78]

Perhaps because of these and many other accounts of al-Muʿizz's relations or disputes with the Umayyads (directly or indirectly through their allies in the Maghrib), Dachraoui suggests that there was a greater interest on the part of the Fatimids to extend their power in the western Mediterranean than other historians have conceded.[79] Nevertheless, despite all the space al-Nuʿman devotes to al-Muʿizz's problems with the Umayyads, in the end it is the Byzantines with whom al-Muʿizz seeks to make a deal, and with whom he intends to share the eastern Mediterranean. In one account, the imam receives a Byzantine ambassador bearing the yearly *jizya* (poll tax on non-Muslims) that they levied for the Fatimids in Calabria, and many gifts from the emperor.[80] The ambassador informs al-Muʿizz that the emperor wants to sign a treaty of friendship with the Fatimids. The imam first subjects the ambassador to a lecture on the rules of treaty making according to Islam, and then suggests to him that a treaty with the Byzantines would only be possible if it included the princes of the *bilad al-Sham* or Syrian territories, such as Sayf al-Dawla of the Hamdanid dynasty of Syria.[81] He then questions the ambassador about Byzantine attacks on the Syrian coast, off Tarsus, and how their forces were faring against the Hamdanids. Al-Nuʿman adds that those present at this interview looked at each other, puzzled as to why the imam was asking the Byzantine envoy about such details. When the envoy departed, however, al-Muʿizz explained to them that he did so in order to obtain the essential information he would need in time to use against the Byzantines. And this he clearly did, for when his general Jawhar conquered Egypt in 358/969, his *aman* or guarantee of safety to the Egyptians promised that the Fatimids would intervene to save Egypt and Syria from attacks by the Byzantines and their holding to ransom of Muslims in Syria.

In another account, al-Nuʿman provides the reasons for another attack that al-Muʿizz launched in 359/960 against the Byzantines.[82] This particular offensive was occasioned by Byzantine threats to the island of Crete, which had led the Cretans to appeal to their traditional protectors, the Ikhshidids of Egypt. This time, however, the Ikhshidids abdicated their responsibility, no doubt because of the increasing political and economic instability Egypt was facing. This gave al-Muʿizz the opportunity to champion the cause of Crete (and by extension *dar al-Islam*, the lands of Islam) in place of the Ikhshidids and their Abbasid overlords. Both these events demonstrate al-Muʿizz's long-term interest in the eastern Mediterranean and his careful political calculations for the conquest of Egypt. Notwithstanding his exchanges with the Umayyads of Spain, taking on the powerful

Byzantine hegemony in the eastern Mediterranean would, among other things, provide a greater demonstration of Fatimid claims to pan-Islamic rule, which naturally were greatly enhanced by the conquest of Egypt and its territorial extension in Syria.

All in all, the image the *Majalis* provides of al-Muʿizz's political career is impressive and consistent with the Islamic ideal of the just ruler: triumphant yet tolerant, knowledgeable and wise, able to provide the moral and political guidance that was exemplified by the Prophet and his family. The traditional and often mythic expressions of Twelver Shiʿi hagiography, preoccupied with the eschatological and soteriological function of an imam in occultation, are here countered by a very human and accessible portrait of a real historical figure. Al-Qadi al-Nuʿman's reports about the imam thus stands out from both the larger non-Ismaili Shiʿi literary tradition and the Sunni *adab* tradition in form and content. It is because of this that neither al-Nuʿman's *Majalis* nor his *Iftitah* fit neatly under the 'epistemic canopies' erected by Khalidi, and may account for him not casting the net of his conceptual framework wide enough to include the Ismaili Shiʿi tradition of historiography and the socio-political circumstances in which these works were created. The achievement of power by the Fatimids signified a shift in the larger Shiʿi context from hagiography to history, and a discourse that in certain respects resembled, even if it did not precisely imitate, the Sunni 'Arab Islamic' historiographical genres and traditions. In the next chapter, a number of additional similarities between the Sunni and Ismaili Shiʿi experience will be explored through an examination of the political and protocol literature of al-Qadi al-Nuʿman.

5

The *Zahiri* Order

Just as the Fatimids saw the necessity of a system of law and a historical narrative following the establishment of their state, so they also found the need for an appropriate protocol and political literature. These sorts of writings emerged in the Sunni tradition, especially after the rise of military states in the 4th/10th century and the increasing division of political and religious authority between military elites and the *'ulama'*, as noted in the Introduction. In the Fatimid context it emerges out of the complex relationship between a ruling Ismaili Shi'i minority and the larger non-Ismaili populace. In this chapter a theory of social order in the *Kitab al-himma fi adab atba' al-a'imma*, as well as a treatise on rulership in the *Kitab al-jihad* of the *Da'a'im al-Islam*, will be explored.

Al-Qadi al-Nu'man's *Kitab al-himma* provides something of a blueprint for the ideological basis that informed relations between the Fatimid imam-caliph and his subjects.[1] Unlike the Twelver Shi'is, for whom obedience to their occulted imam remained largely a matter of doctrinal belief, for Ismaili Shi'is obedience to a living imam acquired additionally a real and active sense or application. The forms that obedience took under the Fatimids were conditioned in some way by the status of the imam-caliphs and so included ceremonial. Research on Fatimid ceremonial, such as that undertaken by Canard and Sanders, has traced its development and described its elaborate and spectacular features and range.[2] Sanders' work especially has sought to move beyond the merely formal aspects to an assessment of Fatimid ceremonial as a ritual language. Nevertheless, such research has taken a largely descriptive approach and beyond that has been concerned with specific political uses of ceremony and court protocol. As for the political and fiscal aspects of obedience to the imam, again these have been dealt with in the context of studies of the administration in and policies of the Fatimid state, both medieval and modern.[3] The medieval sources and the studies based on them provide a wealth of detailed information on Fatimid policies and rule, without at the same time addressing the forms of social and political order envisaged or established by the Fatimids.

The classification and dating of the *Kitab al-himma* present a number of problems, more so even than al-Nuʿman's other *zahiri* works. As regards classification, the title of the work would seem to indicate an emphasis on the narrower field of protocol and etiquette. However, the *Kitab al-himma* is in fact concerned with placing obedience to the imam within a religio-political framework. Thus al-Qadi al-Nuʿman devotes several chapters to presenting the necessity of *imama* which, needless to say, cover the same ground and closely resemble the presentation of the same subject in the *Daʿaʾim*. At the same time, al-Nuʿman discusses the ramifications of the rule of an imam in terms of the political and fiscal obligations and responsibilities of different groups of the imam's subjects. And lastly, the work deals with issues of the protocol that governed behaviour in the presence of the imam, during processions, at banquets, special occasions, etc. The work thus lies somewhere between a credal statement in the manner of the Twelver Shiʿi Ibn Babawayh's *Risala*, and a manual of protocol after the *adab* and *rusum/marasim* (protocol) literature of the classical period.

As for dating, and unlike other works of al-Qadi al-Nuʿman, the introduction of the *Kitab al-himma* does not provide evidence of when and under whom it was composed. In works such as the *Daʿaʾim* and the *Majalis*, al-Nuʿman's introductions state that the work in question was commissioned by al-Muʿizz, for certain circumstances and in response to a need for enlightenment on a particular subject. The *Kitab al-himma*'s introduction, by contrast, begins with a discussion between al-Qadi al-Nuʿman and some unnamed benefactors (*mun'imin*), who present al-Nu'man with a short work which he assumes is about the *adab* for the servants and followers (*atba'*) of worldly kings (*muluk al-dunya*).[4]

Al-Nu'man admires it and expresses regret to one of the benefactors that it was not written for the more deserving, namely the imams. This benefactor then points out a letter in the text which reveals the identity of the author of the treatise, who is a follower of the imams. And so al-Nu'man decides to elaborate on the work, especially now that the imams had made themselves manifest, making it necessary for their followers to have a book that would tell them about what acts it was appropriate to perform out of respect and obedience.[5] Moreover, al-Nu'man adds, the imam's followers (*atba'*) had increased greatly and come to comprise all manner of classes and groups including, 'members of the imam's household, his retinue, the slaves of the court, the court servants, relations, members of the *da'wa* (*ahl al-diyanat min al-awliya'*), judges, scribes, pensioned officials, heads of *diwan*s, those in charge of *amanat*, tax collectors, messengers or postmen, military officers, the *ansar*, the slave classes, soldiers, craftsmen, merchants and peddlers, and the people (*ra'aya*)'.[6] For this reason, continues al-Nu'man, he has organized the material in chapters, most of which apply to all classes, but some of which specify only the obligations of certain groups. In addition, al-Nu'man states that he has kept his book short and its contents *zahiri* (or plain), so that it can be understood by all classes of people.[7]

To return to the rather enigmatic discussion between al-Nu'man and his 'benefactors' at the beginning of the *Kitab al-himma*'s introduction, it could indicate a number of things as regards dating. On the one hand, it could indicate that al-Qadi al-Nu'man was following the literary conventions of the *adab* genre (in which discussion of a topic would often begin with a hypothetical question posed by an unnamed interlocutor). Or it could mean that al-Nu'man composed the work early in his career in the Ismaili *da'wa*, before he had developed a close relationship with the imams (at which time he began identifying the imam who commissioned a particular work in its introduction). Thus his unnamed benefactors here could be members of the *da'wa* under whom he had received his early instruction, and the exercise of identifying the mysterious work on the *adab* of kings a type of test or examination of the kind given to initiates. Whatever the case, the *Kitab al-himma* outlines for the first time a distinctly Shiʿi and Ismaili vision of the body politic.

Perhaps its most significant aspect is the articulation of a social order which does not give a privileged position to the Ismailis at the expense of the majority non-Ismaili, mostly Sunni, community. As noted above, al-Nuʿman states that the purpose of his work is to instruct all the followers/subjects of the state in the proper forms of obedience to the imam. Some of these followers, of course, come from the elites of the Ismaili community, but many are clearly non-Ismaili employees of the Fatimid state or members of society who are nevertheless expected, on some level, to view their new rulers as imams. Al-Nuʿman argues that it is necessary for all the people (*jamiʿ al-ʿibad*) to believe that the rule of imams was intended by God. The proofs of this are in the Qur'an. The imams are the *ulu al-ʿamr* (4:59)[8] and the kinsmen (42:23) of the Prophet, whom God required the people to regard with loving kindness.[9]

Obedience to the imams, therefore, is not a matter of mere submission, as it is to the authority of a king, but rather is akin to obedience to the Prophet. All the people (*kaffat al-nas*) must believe this and strive to adhere to the imams more than they do to worldly kings and sultans, for, as the well-known *hadith* says, a look at them is an act of devotion, just as a glance at the Qur'an is an act of worship. So whoever hears a word from the imam must strive to understand it, and if he does not understand he must consult those who do, for the words of the imams are akin to the words of the Prophet, and in them there is wisdom and benefit.[10]

Moreover, al-Nuʿman continues, the imams are not only entitled to obedience, but also to the *amanat* (here to be understood under its definition as property deposited for safe keeping, in other words a tithe), which God has decreed must be returned to their rightful owners (4:58, 2:283, 8:27).[11] Not to return deposits to their owners constitutes a breach of trust. In this context, therefore, *amanat* are deposits owed to the imams, because they are a part of God's bounty towards humankind that the imams accept from the people on behalf of God. Thus not to give the imams the *amanat* is a breach of trust, which is a grave sin and error (8:27). This applies to non-followers as well. Even the poor and humble of rank give *amanat*, if only out of fear of damnation, and so it is even more imperative that the wealthy do not withhold the *amanat* due to the imams.[12]

This discussion on Fatimid legitimacy and on the right to *amanat* is directed at the general audience, which, as al-Nuʿman himself notes, includes non-followers. For this group, obedience to the imam entails belief in their rule as a divinely sanctioned state of affairs, and therefore binding on the community as in the Prophet's time, and the payment of *amanat* (which is to be understood in these terms as taxation). Situating the imam's rule within the *Sunna* of the Prophet is an attempt to not only distinguish the rule of the imams from the purely temporal authority of kings and sultans, but also to redefine obedience, changing it from a matter of coercion into a religious act ('to obey the imam is to obey God and His Prophet'), so that in paying *amanat* even the non-follower thereby acknowledges the imamate of the Fatimids.

As for the true followers, the members of the Ismaili community, they additionally take the pledge (*mithaq*) of allegiance to the imam. Al-Nuʿman continues his presentation with a discussion of the binding nature of the *mithaq*. He argues that there are those who say they believe in God and His Prophet, but do not believe in the binding nature of obedience to the imams. They are the faithless (*nakithun*), about whom God said, 'Those who pledge allegiance to you [the Prophet] pledge allegiance to God ... and he who breaks his oath, harms himself, whereas he who stays true, will receive a great reward' (48:10).[13] The *ʿahd* (covenant) of the imams is the same as the *ʿahd* of the Prophets and the *ʿahd* of God, and thus obedience to God and His Prophet must also include obedience to the imams. Those who have pledged to God, therefore, must ideally also take the oath (*mithaq*) to the imams, and abide by all that entails in terms of obedience and the giving of *amanat*. Pledging an oath to the imams and payment of *amanat* constitutes belief (*iman*), and defines those who are truly *mu'minin* or followers of the imam, as opposed to *muslimin* or ordinary Muslims. God has promised that their reward will be great (23:8–11).[14]

As for the obligations of those defining themselves as followers of the imam, they must also inform him truthfully about themselves, because God has promised salvation through the imams, and God loves those who repent and seek the intercession of the imams.[15] ʿAli b. Abi Talib said that the followers of the imams have to report their shortcomings to the imams so that they can appoint the right followers to the proper posts. Al-Nuʿman comments that it is only with the help of the imams that one can properly perform the duties to which one is assigned. Additionally, those who have taken the pledge must obey the imams without question, and this means that one should refrain from engaging in a *daʿwa* on behalf of the imam unless permitted by him to do so.[16] For, as the Imam Jaʿfar al-Sadiq said, it is best to be 'silent propagators', since the untrained will undermine the cause of the imams in front of those (unbelievers) who are more skilled in debate. It is wiser in such cases to refrain from engaging with those who seek to argue against the imams and to defer to those more knowledgeable. God has only given the knowledge of His secrets to a few, and for others they remain unknown (*ghayb*). This is the meaning of the *ghayb* (the hidden knowledge God-given for the imams only), and it is a test for the followers of the imams.

The followers of the imams should also have patience and be grateful to the imams through all the vicissitudes of fortune.[17] They are required to struggle for the sake of God alongside the imams, according to God's word, 'You are to believe in God and His Prophet, and to strive in God's path with your lives and possessions' (61:11).[18] And the followers are required to give part of their property in *khums*.[19] Even as the Muslims have confirmed that *zakat* is obligatory, so it is confirmed in the traditions of the imams that the *khums*, or fifth, has to be given to the imams, and the people have no share in it, nor can they question what is done with it. For the *khums* and *zakat* are the *amanat* due to the imams, and only when the *khums* is paid to the imams will the *mu'min* have discharged his duty.

The consequences of not fulfilling these obligations cannot be avoided. Al-Nuʿman points out that submission to the imams is obligatory for the *umma* as a whole. As for the followers, even when they do not understand the orders of the imams, or these appear to be unclear or unjust, they have to submit, for some of what the followers suffer is the penalty for sins they committed previously.[20] For example, a man once touched a woman in an indecent fashion at the Kaʿba and then fled. Later he was mistaken for a thief, and although he was in fact innocent of this crime his hand was cut off. He realized that God had in this manner punished him for the offence he had committed. Thus if one thinks one has been wrongly accused and punished for a crime, let him remember that God wills that some be punished in this world and postpones the punishment of others to the next.

If, on the other hand, there are followers who have been favoured by the imams (as, say, a reward for their loyalty), they should be grateful and continue to fear the imams.[21] They should not be proud of their proximity to the imams, nor try to please the imams seeking for worldly gain, nor fear material loss. For example, the imams have related that Jesus was once on a journey with his disciples in the desert, when they began to be afraid of thieves. Jesus asked one of them if he had anything valuable with him and the disciple showed him a piece of gold. Jesus told him to throw it away, and he did. Further on, Jesus stopped and asked them if they were afraid, and they responded that they no longer had any reason to be afraid. In other words, one should not allow the material rewards accrued through being a recipient of the imams' favour to come before loyalty to the imams themselves.

The *mu'minin* or followers of the imams should demonstrate their solidarity with each other. Al-Nuʿman argues that the followers should be friendly towards their brothers in faith and stand aloof from the enemies of the imams.[22] He adds that there are three classes of people: those who love the imams, those who are their enemies, and those who are weak-minded. Followers of the imams should be hostile to their enemies and appeal to the weak-minded by doing good deeds, for they are better than the outright enemies of the imams.

Identification and solidarity with the community, however, should never lead the followers to oppose or question the imams about the preference they might show for others, for they should consider their status as followers reward enough.[23] They should never do what is disagreeable to the imams,[24] and never become envious of those *mu'minin* to whom the imams show favour, nor slander innocent people in front of the imam, nor oppress other *mu'minin* by their outright hostility, or by usury, or ill will.[25] Humility is another trait which followers are to cultivate, for it is a form of worship.[26] If the imams' followers undergo hardship or wage war on behalf of the imams, they should not do it for the sake of their own glory, nor for the sake of material gain. And they should never complain that they do not receive preferential treatment, nor desire more money because of their proximity to the imam. If the judges and officials treat followers and non-followers and non-Muslims equally, they are only doing so on the orders of the imams, and the imams are just in whatever they do. And so, the followers are required to be humble and always thank and praise the imams in front of the people. Outstanding followers are those who are forbearing, calm, humble and forgiving; this is the way to behave in front of the imams and their officers.[27]

Lastly, it is forbidden to find fault with the imams.[28] Those who criticize the imams are ignorant, especially when they argue that the imams live surrounded by too much grandeur. These people would deny Solomon and David their kingdoms, exclaims al-Nuʿman, and forget that the imams have no love of pomp and luxury and maintain this state only to inspire awe in their enemies.

These sections or chapters outline general moral and behavioural guidelines for the neophyte and initiate of the Ismaili *daʿwa*, revealing some interesting things in the process. Clearly, while the distinction of the *mu'minin* from the *muslimin* carries certain spiritual rewards, it does not always bring privileges. Rather, it carries responsibilities, such as entitlement to office on the basis of ability rather than faith, the obligation to participate in jihad, and the payment of *khums* in addition to *zakat*. The followers, moreover, should not seek to be rewarded for supporting the imams, and they should accept punishment for wrongdoing from the imams without complaint. Most importantly, however, their status does not entitle them to preferential treatment or a more privileged status than non-Ismaili Muslims or the *ahl al-dhimma* (Jews and Christians). They are to submit to the imams and their officials, and never to question the word or decision or action of the imam.

Such instructions, besides asserting the imam's authority over all his subjects, also indicate the equal status of Ismailis and non-Ismailis before the authority of the state and its officials. This was a departure from the days of *dar al-hijra* under Abu ʿAbd Allah al-Shiʿi, with its exclusively Ismaili society. The move to consolidate the power and authority of the Fatimids obviously necessitated the identification of the interests of the state with those of non-Ismaili communities as well as their own constituency; hence the admonitions to the followers of the imam regarding expectations of preferential treatment, privilege and gain, and the injunction to obey the authority of the state's officials even when they appear to favour other groups at the expense of the Ismailis.

As for other groups, al-Qadi al-Nuʿman devotes three sections or chapters to *adab* for the relatives of the imam, the officers of state and the *daʿwa* organization. As far as the relatives of the imam are concerned, al-Nuʿman reminds them that they are not entitled to exemptions simply because of their kinship with the imams.[29] This is the meaning of God's words, 'Warn those of near kinship' (26:214), and the meaning of the *hadith* that has come from Jaʿfar al-Sadiq in which he said that those who do not acknowledge the imam of their time die the death of the *jahiliyya*, that is, of ignorance. The Prophet, in his time, had warned the Banu ʿAbd al-Mutallib that on the Day of Judgement their relationship to him would not be a substitute for having done good works, and ʿAli b. Abi Talib, in his time, had suffered the betrayal of Talha and Zubayr when they laid claim to a greater share of booty than others based on their ties to the family of the Prophet. The relatives of the imams are neither exempt from good works, nor are they exempt from complete obedience and loyalty to the imam. Furthermore, relatives of the imams have no right to claim a greater share of dues or booty. In fact, they are as liable to punishment for neglecting to do good works, or for disbelief, or rebelling against the imams.

On officials of the state, al-Qadi al-Nuʿman states that what pertains to those officials appointed to oversee the collection of the imam's revenue, or the *amanat*, pertains generally to all the people.[30] They should be as accountable to God and the imams for their own behaviour as others are accountable to them. By way of analogy, al-Nuʿman points out that a doctor who is himself sick cannot be expected to treat others, and so the imams' officials must themselves practise what they preach. In fact they must behave in an exemplary manner, and take care to discharge their duties and responsiblities as best they can.

This applies even more to the *daʿwa*, continues al-Nuʿman, for they are the representatives of the imam and the faith.[31] Just as the lesson for the officials applies to the *muslimin* in general, the lesson of this chapter applies to all the *mu'minin*, says al-Nuʿman. He cites again Jaʿfar al-Sadiq on the need to be 'silent propagators', for it is this that will attract the people to the imam, rather than brashly publicizing his cause. And when the *daʿis* do publicize the cause of the imam, they should do so wisely and with discretion, for otherwise they will fail, as many indeed have done. The *daʿi* must assess his audience and approach them in a manner in accordance with their abilities, and he must know his own shortcomings and defer to those who have higher authority.

Al-Qadi al-Nuʿman concludes by noting the importance to the imam of the last two groups (the officials/tax collectors and the *daʿwa*), and as representatives of the state the need for their behaviour to be exemplary in front of the people. At the same time, he argues that it is especially important that these two groups submit to the authority of the imams in all matters. As regards the officers and tax collectors, this is a self-evident requirement. As regards the *daʿwa*, on the other hand, it places emphasis on good works and instructional service to the people, rather than the continuation of the overtly political or antinomian activities that occurred in the time of al-Mahdi. The advice on methods of instruction or pedagogy in the chapter on the *daʿwa* also emphasizes the necessity for strict adherence to the hierarchy within the *daʿwa*, and to the official curriculum prescribed by the imam.

As argued above, this kind of advice and instruction in the *Kitab al-himma* constitutes another evidence of a transition. Prior to the establishment of the Fatimid state, the Ismaili community had defined itself as autonomous and distinct from others through mechanisms such as a *dar al-hijra*. This autonomy was abandoned with the foundation of the state and as the boundaries, physical as well as religio-political, separating the Ismailis from others became obscured. At the same time, the state's attempt to assert its authority and to expand its constituency to include non-Ismailis necessarily undermined the former exclusivist atmosphere within the community. The new state order necessarily imposed a political hierarchy consisting of the Ismaili Shiʿi imam and his officials at the top, and the various communal and occupational groups below.

And insofar as there was opposition to this new order, it is implied in some of the *Kitab al-himma*'s examples and digressions, such as those dealing with the protection of the interests of the *ahl al-dhimma* and non-Ismaili communities, the necessity of accepting the authority of officials of the state, as well as the pomp and ceremony of the court. Nevertheless, the vision of the state that the *Kitab al-himma* articulates is that of an imamate approximating, in theory at least, to the theocratic rule of the Prophet, and thus differing from mere kingship or *mulk*. The comparisons made with the relations between the Prophet and the early community, the requirement of *amanat/khums* and jihad, all confirm the just and necessary rule of the imams, and thus the religious and obligatory nature of obedience to them. Moreover, the obligations incumbent on all those who now came under the jurisdiction of the ruling imam entailed a universal acceptance of the legitimacy of the Fatimid imam-caliphs, and therefore a redefinition of the community on a broader basis.

It is also in this light that the *Kitab al-himma*'s instructions on court protocol and ceremonial are to be understood. Six chapters are devoted to the topics of dress, submitting requests, order for processions, audiences, salutations and address, and attending repasts in the company of the imams, all of which discuss protocol in terms of its religious symbolism and significance. As regards how one should appear before the imams, for example, al-Nuʿman argues that one's appearance before them must be governed by the rules that apply to entering a sacred area or place of worship and to the performance of religious obligations such as prayer.[32] That is, God said, 'O sons of Adam, adorn yourselves and enter the mosques' (7:31), and, as the Prophet said, he whom God has blessed must show it. So those who wish to attend the *majalis* (audiences) with the imams and to appear before them must clean their hair and coif it, they must wear the best that they have, and beautify themselves, for it is the right of the imams to see the blessings that God has conferred on their followers in their audiences and celebrations and processions, and this constitutes a proper show of respect, for one is in holy presence when one is with them.

Similarly, continues al-Qadi al-Nuʿman, glorifying the imams when addressing and speaking to them is like glorifying God.[33] This is done by prostration in front of the imam. Just as their heirs kiss the ground in greeting them, so too should the followers of the imams. Contrary to what the riffraff within the population say, prostration before the imams is not the same as prostration in prayer, although by doing it one shows respect for God. The followers must greet the imams by saying, 'Blessings of God be upon you, O Commander of the Faithful', and then kiss the ground before them, unless the imam speaks first.

Also, when standing in front of the imams, al-Nuʿman argues that one should assume the posture of prayer,[34] since gazing on them is an act of worship, and when speaking to them one should not raise one's voice above theirs, just as was the practice when speaking to the Prophet in his time,[35] and when the imam speaks to anyone, all should listen, since his every word is full of wisdom.[36] Moreover, out of reverence for them, one should not laugh, nor move one's eyes about, nor dispute or argue, nor prolong a discourse in the imam's presence,[37] and whatever transpires in a meeting with the imam must be kept secret.[38] And requests to the imams must be made efficiently and to the point. One should never insist on a request for worldly advantage, and if a request is made for some spiritual benefit, it should be made without show. As for those who accompany the imam in procession, they should always maintain the prescribed distance between themselves and the imam and never move from their designated positions. If they are called, they should approach quickly and they should never turn their backs on the imam as they withdraw or return to their designated places.[39]

Al-Qadi al-Nuʿman provides numerous other guidelines and details, with examples to illustrate many points of protocol. As it is not the aim to catalogue them here, and since their symbolism and development have already been explored in other works on Fatimid ceremonial, suffice it to note, first of all, that al-Nuʿman's discussion of court protocol and ceremonial is fundamentally concerned with its rationale rather than its detail. Fatimid ceremonial in any case was fully elaborated later, as has been pointed out by Sanders.

Even though couched in terms of the rituals of worship, al-Nuʿman's advice on protocol in the *Kitab al-himma* clearly borrows from and appropriates what was regarded as the secular protocol of the worldly king's court.[40] Hence the frequent comparisons with the protocol of the *muluk al-dunya* (worldly kings). Many features of protocol in the *Kitab al-himma*, such as the aesthetic and symbolism of prostration, lowered eyes, respectful silence, standing as opposed to sitting, withdrawal, and so forth, are in fact characteristic of the ritual of royalty integral to life in the courts of medieval Islam and elsewhere.

If the symbolism of ceremonial and protocol outlined in the *Kitab al-himma*, as well as its vision of and explanation for the relationship between the imam and his followers, reflects the process of transformation from revolution to state, this is also expressed in another text, an *ʿahd* or treatise on rulership in the *kitab al-jihad* of the first volume of the *Daʿaʾim*.[41] In his introduction to the *ʿahd*, al-Qadi al-Nuʿman claims that it was composed by ʿAli b. Abi Talib, or the Prophet himself, and is addressed to a governor, providing him with instructions on how to rule wisely and justly. The *ʿahd* appears abruptly, and seemingly out of context in a presentation of the prescriptions for jihad (which include, for example, discussions on conducting oneself during warfare, the treatment of prisoners, and the like). Because of this, it has been subject to an analysis of its provenance and content by Wadad al-Qadi.[42] The inclusion of the *ʿahd* in the *Daʿaʾim* demonstrates its continuing significance to the Fatimid state and its requirements in the time of al-Muʿizz.[43] At that time, the Fatimid state was expanding into Egypt, and thus the imam did not have the same degree of control over all territories within the Fatimid state. Documents such as the *ʿahd* were therefore a blueprint for governance in those areas where governors had necessarily to be given increased powers of supervision and greater authority. This was particularly the case with Egypt, which for four years was governed by the Fatimid general Jawhar al-Siqilli while al-Muʿizz tied up loose ends in Ifriqiya and made the necessary preparations for the transfer of the court to his new capital of Cairo.

Briefly put, the *ʿahd* exhorts its addressee, a king/governor (*malik*), to exercise a policy of ethical governance by paying heed to his subjects and ruling wisely, mercifully and justly. This requires him to remember that his power is only of this world, and so he should fear God and obey Him in all that he does, abstaining from the greed and arrogance that in the end brought about the demise of his predecessors. It also requires his awareness of the different classes of people, and the need to deal differently with each while keeping in mind that his power, security and well-being depend upon showing mercy towards the people, paying the soldiery and avoiding courtiers and confidants who seek rather to please him than to enlighten and inform him truthfully of the state of affairs in his kingdom.

The preamble of the *ʿahd* contains some biographical information that indicates 'the addressee's humble origin, the change in his fortune so that he became a ruler', the necessity of keeping within his limits … 'of not amassing fortunes for his children, of not giving too much to the people, of not feeling so proud and strong in his position as to go against his duties to God (and therefore his imam) for he cannot run away from his power',[44] and so on. This address would certainly be meaningful to Jawhar, who while ruling Egypt in 358–362/969–973 had virtual control of this province, which at the time also included the territorial extension into Syria and the Hijaz. Jawhar al-Siqilli was also of humble origin and possessed a great deal of power in his time, ruling Egypt before al-Muʿizz's arrival.[45] When al-Muʿizz finally arrived in 363/973, Jawhar lost control over the bureaucracy, but remained in control of the army, conducting campaigns to subdue the Qaramita who were threatening to invade Egypt from Syria.[46] He was replaced as governor by the former Jewish vizier of the previous Ikhshidid regime, Ibn Killis, and ʿUsluj b. Hasan who had accompanied al-Muʿizz to Cairo, and who were subsequently put in charge of state finances.[47] In 366/976, the first year of al-Muʿizz's successor al-ʿAziz's reign, Jawhar conducted another campaign against the Qaramita, but was ignominiously defeated. On his return, al-ʿAziz, apparently in anger, dismissed him from his position (it seems he was succeeded in it by his son Hasan), and he then retired to follow a quiet life in Cairo until his death in 381/992.[48]

In appreciating the degree to which Jawhar's actions as Fatimid governor of Egypt might have been informed by the advice of the *ʿahd*, more needs to be said about its descriptions and prescriptions. For example, the state and society described in the *ʿahd* consisted of five classes of people (the army, the administrators, landholders and farmers, merchants and artisans, and the poor and needy); a judiciary; a complex administration (including 'overseers' or spies/informants); an economy based largely on agriculture (made possible through inundation and irrigation), and from which the state extracted a large percentage of revenue in *kharaj* or land tax; a merchant and artisan class, among whom are those that had been known to hoard their wealth; the poor and needy who had been repeatedly subject to plague and famine; and external threats that required considered military intervention.[49]

Thus the addressee of the treatise is advised to rely on the support of the people (appearing before them as an upholder of good works, restraint and humility) and seek their contentment above that of his retainers. At the same time, the ruler should avoid sycophantic viziers and confidants, especially those of previous regimes, and reward the soldiery amply in order to retain their support and protection and prevent them from resorting to brigandage. In the event of disagreement among the judges he is to consult the imam, and he should choose administrators that are reliable and trustworthy, and appoint overseers to supervise them and acquire intelligence about them. Also, he should refrain from collecting the land tax in times of hardship, as long-term healthy cultivation of the land is more important than raising revenue in the short term (that is, in case of blockages in the irrigation system, over-inundation of land, or plague and disease, he should lighten the people's burden by relieving them from paying taxes for a year).[50] He should appoint his followers to the secretariats in order to safeguard secrets, confidential paperwork and mail (and place informers among them as well), and punish hoarders and avaricious members of the merchant class. Lastly, he should pay heed to the needs of the poor (and let the overseers inform the ruler of their needs as well), remain accessible to the people, and avoid unnecessary warfare and shedding of blood.

Egypt at the time of Jawhar's conquest was in a chaotic state and in dire need of just this sort of ruler. For a time after its conquest by the Muslims in 1st/7th century, Egypt was a flourishing province, first under the Rashidun, then the Umayyads, followed by the Abbasid caliphs. However, during the Abbasid period, many of the governors appointed by the central power in Baghdad were able to use the wealth of Egypt as leverage in order to acquire a great measure of autonomy, and this was the case with the Ikhshidid dynasty that governed Egypt in the 4th/10th century. Before the appointment of the first Ikhshidid in 323/935, there had been a political vacuum in Egypt for about 30 years (from 292/905), which the Fatimids had tried to exploit by attempting a conquest both in the time of al-Mahdi and al-Qa'im (which failed because of the efforts of an Abbasid general, Mu'nis al-Khadim, who, luckily for the Abbasids, was quick to respond). By 355/966 the Ikhshidid regime was in tatters, as much due to political instability (and the proxy rule of one of their Nubian slaves, Kafur) as to constant attacks from the east by the Qaramita in Syria, from the south by Nubians and from the Fatimids to the west. In addition, and because of the chaos and instability of the regime, care and maintenance of vital aspects of agriculture such as irrigation lapsed, resulting in increasing hardship and then famine. According to Ibn Khallikan, the notables of Egypt wrote to al-Muʿizz and actually asked him to take over the state because conditions had deteriorated so much. Shortly after Kafur's death, the Fatimids took Egypt.[51]

The social order envisaged by the *Kitab al-himma*, placing as it did the interests of the state and its officials before those of its communal constituencies, and the latitudinarianism of al-Nuʿman's other works and also of al-Muʿizz's policy, is reflected in the very tolerant terms of Jawhar's *aman* proclaimed as he entered Egypt. In addition to guaranteeing the safety of the Egyptians and promising to protect Egypt from the infidels (Byzantines), Jawhar also promised to restore the pilgrimage and create secure conditions for travel (which had been threatened by the Qaramita's actions in Syria and the Hijaz), to abolish illegal taxation and extortionist fiscal practice, enhance the value of the currency, build new mosques and renovate old ones, ensure regular payment of religious officials and uphold religious rites common to all Muslims.[52]

Jawhar's policies as governor of Egypt before al-Muʿizz's arrival would also seem to reflect the advice of the *ʿahd*. For example, its exhortations to undertake good works, to rely on expertise and information from the knowledgeable and pious, and seek the approval of the people are reflected in his promises to undertake the repair and building of mosques, the distribution of alms, supervision of the vizier and judiciary, and the appointment of North Africans to the various *diwan*s of the administration. His reliance on viziers and confidants of the previous Ikhshidid regime echoes some of the *ʿahd*'s cautionary advice. As for the military, lack of pay was precisely the reason behind the disturbances and unruly behaviour of the Kafuriyya and Ikhshidiyya in Egypt, which he solved through a temporary increase in land tax. Jawhar's expeditions into Syria were aimed at consolidating the borders of the new Fatimid empire, and this is reflected in the *ʿahd*'s advice to the ruler, which is in essence to proceed with caution when undertaking military activities. Regarding the fiscal advice offered to the 'ruler' in the *ʿahd*, as noted, before the Fatimid conquest Egypt experienced famine as well as periods of drought (brought on by low water levels during the yearly inundation of the Nile). According to one report the level of the Nile had dropped from 16 or 17 degrees to 12, which resulted in tremendous inflation and ruin, and a plague that took some 600,000 souls.[53] The *ʿahd*'s advice to lower agricultural taxes, or repeal them for a period of a year in times of hardship, would later be echoed in the fiscal practice of the Fatimids, which put possession of all land in the hands of the imam, with the result that it was possible to lower land tax overall, at least for a while.[54]

In the end, and more important than establishing the provenance of the *ʿahd* or whether or not Jawhar based his policies in Egypt on it, is the fact of its inclusion in the *Daʿaʾim*, making it an Ismaili Shiʿi example of the 'Mirror for Princes' genre. The secular language of the *ʿahd*, its ambiguous tone, the complex society it describes, as well as its equally complex instructions for just governance, certainly reflect the reality of Fatimid rule in al-Muʿizz's time (rather than that of al-Mahdi), and further indicate how Fatimid achievement of power had generated a need for political manuals, as well as the protocol outlined in the *Kitab al-himma*. While the *Kitab al-himma*'s vision of the social order asserts the ultimate centralizing authority of the imam, the *ʿahd* provides a manual or blueprint for the just rule of his governors, in a state where it was their merit, piety, ethics and sound judgement that furthered the prosperity and well-being of the state and all its subjects, rather than their conformity to a particular creed or ideological construct of the rulers. In this, as in his legal and historical works, al-Qadi al-Nuʿman was able to once again provide a *zahiri* discourse that reflected the transition from Shiʿi revolution to statehood.

Conclusion

Between *Zahir* and *Batin*

In focusing on the *zahiri* works of al-Qadi al-Nuʿman, this study does not intend to discount the importance of his *batini* or esoteric works, or the importance of *batini* discourse in Ismaili Shiʿism in general. In fact, the esoteric and spiritual aspect of Ismailism continued to engage the *daʿwa* throughout the Fatimid period, and the instructional sessions known as the *majalis al-hikma* became a regular forum for the dissemination of esoteric wisdom within the Ismaili community. Indeed, the Qadi himself composed an esoteric interpretation of his *Daʿaʾim al-Islam* under the title of *Taʾwil al-Daʿaʾim*, which was intended to present to his Ismaili audiences the *batini* hermeneutics of the ritual prescriptions of Islam.

The establishment of institutions such as *majalis al-hikma*, and centres of education and propagation such as al-Azhar and later the Dar al-ʿIlm, as well as the prominent role of the Ismaili *daʿwa* in these institutions and abroad, is well documented. After al-Nuʿman's death in 363/974, certain Ismaili *daʿis*, such as Hamid al-Din al-Kirmani (d. after 411/1020), al-Muʾayyad fi'l-Din al-Shirazi (d. 470/1078) and Nasir-i Khusraw (d. after 462/1070), made major contributions to Ismaili theology, philosophy and esoteric thought, reflecting a continuing commitment of the Fatimids to the specifically Ismaili doctrinal bases of their legitimacy and authority.[1]

At the same time, the process of transformation from *daʿwa* to *dawla* required the Fatimids to develop a *zahiri* discourse of their doctrines. We have seen the imam's role was articulated in the *Da'a'im* in terms that could be historically and doctrinally defended to all communities, including the Sunni majority. Unlike the eschatological expectations of the imam which found expression in the *da'wa* during the pre-Fatimid period of *satr* or concealment, the *Da'a'im* focused on the ruling Fatimid imam as the guarantor of law and a just society in this world. The historical evidence of 'Alid succession constituted the foundation of his right to rule. In the *Kitab al-himma*, the imam's role was broadened to include the Dar al-Islam or the *umma* as a whole, rather than the select community of the faithful. And in the *Kitab al-majalis*, al-Nu'man reconstructs an image of ideal Islamic rule through the presentation of *akhbar* about the Fatimid imams.

In many ways, then, the attempts, especially by al-Mu'izz, to achieve a rapprochement with the Sunni world which the Fatimids found themselves ruling, obliged them to depart from the *dar al-hijra* model of the revolutionary period to seek common ground with Sunni tradition. This was possible insofar as these were undertaken by al-Qadi al-Nu'man, who was particularly able in his works to negotiate the transition from a minoritarian position, previously based on a predominantly esoteric doctrine, to a more universal or majoritarian and discursive universe that maintained both the *zahir* and the *batin* as necessary and complementary aspects of Ismaili Shi'ism, and by extension of the Islamic faith as a whole.

Nevertheless, the suppression of eschatological tendencies in the Fatimid *da'wa*, and all that it entailed in terms of doctrine and understanding of the *imama*, did not altogether disappear. Such tendencies resurfaced from time to time, notably during the reign of al-Hakim bi-Amr Allah (d. 411/1021) who had to deal with the extremism of the nascent Druze community. The Fatimid *da'wa* was further shaken by a series of schisms generated by succession crises and political instability, such as that which followed the death of al-Mustansir bi'llah in 487/1094 and resulted in the division between the Musta'li and Nizari branches of Ismailism. Even in the twilight of the Fatimid state, succession crises resulted in important schisms, such as the emergence of the Tayyibis following the death of the caliph al-Amir in 524/1130.

The Fatimids responded to these challenges by giving renewed attention to the doctrinal basis of their legitimacy as ruling imams and an increasing reliance on the *daʿwa* to prepare the necessary responses and formulations. Thus, in the time of al-Hakim, the *daʿi* Hamid al-Din al-Kirmani was given the responsibility of addressing the Druze dissidents, which he did in a number of works defending the legitimacy of the imamate and the principle of maintaining equilibrium between *zahir* and *batin*.[2] The same principles were vigorously championed by al-Mu'ayyad fi'l-Din al-Shirazi, the chief *daʿi* of al-Mustansir, in the *majalis* he held at the Dar al-ʿIlm in Cairo. Even as late as the time of al-Amir and the Tayyibi–Hafizi schism, the efforts undertaken by the Fatimids to shore up their legitimacy reveal, if nothing else, the undeniable importance of a specifically Ismaili theology to Fatimid rule.[3]

In sum, the primary contribution of al-Qadi al-Nuʿman was to negotiate a path between the legitimate needs and traditions of both the Ismaili Shiʿi and Sunni communities, a political arrangement that enabled the Fatimids to enjoy a relatively peaceful and prosperous era until the time of al-Mustansir. Al-Nuʿman's contribution in this regard is clearly attested to in the evidence we have not only of the prevalence of his works in the curriculum of *daʿwa* institutions and the courts of Fatimid Egypt, but also in the distinguished positions he occupied in the judicial and religious administration of the Fatimid state for almost 50 years, as well as the continuing prominence of his descendants in the judiciary for several generations.[4]

After al-Qadi al-Nuʿman his works continued to be propagated in the *majalis* within Fatimid territories, and the application of his *Daʿa'im* in the Ismaili courts of the land, but there were no further legal developments of significance in Ismaili jurisprudence, and historiography appears to have become the preserve of non-Ismaili officials of state and outside observers. In the later period of dynastic schisms, military intervention and political decline, Fatimid protocol and ceremonial became progressively shorn of their ideological content. Nevertheless, following the demise of the Fatimid state, al-Nuʿman's intellectual legacy was preserved among the Ismaili communities of Syria and Yemen, and among the Tayyibi Ismailis in particular his *Daʿaʾim al-Islam* continues to be followed to this day as the most authoritative source of Ismaili law.

Notes

Introduction: The Fatimids and the Ismaili Shiʿi Century

1. Muhammad b. Jarir al-Tabari (d. 310/923), *Ta'rikh al-Tabari*, ed. M. Abu'l-Fadl Ibrahim (Cairo, n.d.), vol. 10, pp. 41–42. Important decisions or policies were often presented as presaged by dream prophecies in biographies and descriptions of royal and religious figures. On dreams and dream portents in Islamic tradition, see T. Fahd, 'The Dream in Medieval Islamic Society', in G. von Grunebaum and R. Caillois, eds., *The Dream and Human Societies* (Berkeley, CA, 1966), pp. 351–363, and T. al-Hibri, *Reinterpreting Islamic Historiography* (Cambridge, 1999).
2. A similar dream is recounted by Abu'l-Hasan ʿAli b. al-Husayn b. ʿAli al-Masʿudi (d. 345/956) in his *Muruj al-dhahab wa-maʿadin al-jawhar*, ed. Y.A. Daghir (Beirut, 1965), vol. 4, pp. 181–182. In it, al-Muʿtadid saw an old man sitting on the banks of the Tigris river, whose waters rose and receded seemingly in response to gestures the old man made with his hands. Told that he was ʿAli b. Abi Talib, the caliph approached the old man and was informed that the throne would soon be his, and was told to treat his (ʿAli's) descendents well when he came to power.
3. In contrast to some of his predecessors, al-Muʿtadid (r. 279–289/892–902) was in fact especially concerned to acquire Shiʿi support. Because of their competing claims to leadership of the community, Abbasid reactions to Shiʿi groups ranged from appeasement to open hostility. The second Abbasid caliph, al-Mansur (r. 136–158/754–775), sought the *bayʿa* or oath of allegiance from the ʿAlid imam or leader of his time, Jaʿfar al-Sadiq (d. 148/765), which the latter declined to offer; and his grandson al-Ma'mun (r. 198–218/813–833) temporarily proclaimed another ʿAlid imam,

'Ali al-Rida (d. 203/818), his successor as caliph. Al-Ma'mun also attempted to forge a compromise with Shi'ism through enforcement of the doctrine of Mu'tazilism, which earned him the enmity of the Sunni *'ulama'* during the episode known as the *mihna* or inquisition. Consequently, his nephew and al-Mu'tadid's grandfather, al-Mutawakkil (232–247/847–861), revoked his predecessor's policies in the hope of gaining their favour. But the appeasement of the Sunni *'ulama'* did not enable the Abbasids to offset the influence of provincial governors and the military, nor obviously did it help with the Shi'i opposition, and so al-Mu'tadid again reversed official policy and tried to court Shi'i groups that were acquiring popularity in Abbasid territories. On Abbasid–Shi'i relations, see B. Lewis, ''Abbasids', *EI2*; H. Kennedy, *The Prophet and the Age of the Caliphates: The Islamic Near East from the Sixth to the Eleventh Century* (London, 1986); M.A. Shaban, *Islamic History AD 600–750 (AH 132): A New Interpretation* (Cambridge, 1976), vol. 2; and M. Cooperson, *Classical Arabic Biography: The Heirs of the Prophet in the Age of al-Ma'mun* (Cambridge, 2000).

4. Mu'awiya emerged as the main opponent of 'Ali's caliphate and, following the latter's assassination in 40/661, founded the Umayyad dynasty. In addition to supporters of the Umayyads, the Abbasids faced the opposition of groups espousing the merits of Companions of the Prophet such as the caliphs Abu Bakr and 'Uthman b. 'Affan, who were by this time viewed by many of the Shi'a as usurpers, with the rightful succession belonging to 'Ali b. Abi Talib. On the activities and disruptive role of such groups in Abbasid society see A. Mez, *The Renaissance of Islam*, tr. S. Khuda Bukhsh and D.S. Margoliouth (London, 1937), pp. 63–71.
5. Al-Tabari, *Ta'rikh*, vol. 10, pp. 54–63.
6. In contrast to the Shi'is, who espoused the leadership of the Prophet's cousin and son-in-law 'Ali and his descendants, the legitimacy of the Abbasid caliphs rested on their descent from the Prophet's uncle, Ibn 'Abbas.
7. The Buyids (or Buwayhids) controlled the Abbasid state until the mid-5th/11th century, retaining the Abbasid caliphs as figureheads.
8. The Idrisid dynasty held power from 172 to 375/789 to 985.
9. The Hamdanids gained a foothold in the time of al-Mu'tadid and ruled from 293 to 394/906 to 1004, the 'Uqaylids from 380 to 564/990 to 1169, the Mazyadids from 350 to 545/961 to 1150, and the Qaramita (or Qarmatis) held sway in their territories from 273

to 470/886 to 1078.

10. See, for example, J. Berkey's survey, *The Formation of Islam* (Cambridge, 2003), pp. 130–140, where many of these arguments resurface.
11. The general approach in Western scholarship has been to focus on establishing a Muslim orthodoxy, while historical and regional studies have imposed geographical boundaries on the Islamic world, marginalizing the presence of Shiʿism within regional classifications. Anthropological research has focused on the uniquely local and so has often missed links and continuities, thus divorcing the particularly Shiʿi in certain cases from the generally Islamic.
12. The link between empire and monotheism in the period of Late Antiquity is the subject, for example, of Garth Fowden's *Empire to Commonwealth: Consequences of Monotheism in Late Antiquity* (Princeton, NJ, 1993).
13. See Aziz Al-Azmeh, *Muslim Kingship: Power and the Sacred in Muslim, Christian, and Pagan Polities* (London, 1997), pp. 83–115.
14. Fowden, following R.W. Bulliet in *Conversion to Islam in the Medieval Period* (Cambridge, MA, 1979), connects the emergence of Shiʿism to conversion, arguing that conversion to Islam resulted in the 'multiplication of heresy' such as Shiʿism. A competition between Sunni and Shiʿi Islam ensued, resulting in the 'fragmentation of the Islamic world empire' and its replacement with an 'Islamic commonwealth', or a world where political unity was abandoned in favour of a shared cultural framework. See his *Empire to Commonwealth*, pp. 163–165.
15. On non-ideological causes for the fragmentation of the Abbasid empire, such as the role of court elites and the military, economic problems and centre–periphery relations, see Kennedy, *The Prophet and the Age of the Caliphates*, and Shaban, *Islamic History*, vol. 2.
16. On the origins of Shiʿism, see W. Madelung, *The Succession to Muhammad: A Study of the Early Caliphate* (Cambridge, 1997), and S.H.M. Jafri, *Origins and Early Development of Shiʿa Islam* (Beirut, 1979).
17. See Madelung's *Succession to Muhammad* on these issues and events. Asma Afsaruddin, in her *Excellence and Precedence: Medieval Islamic Discourse on Legitimate Leadership* (Leiden, 2002), challenges Madelung's contention that the Shiʿi call for succession in the Prophet's family had precedents in pre-Islamic Arab political culture, arguing that demands for ʿAli b. Abi Talib's

succession 'were inspired by motives not fully known to us' (p. 1), and that kinship to the Prophet became primary in Shiʿi tradition only after the 3rd/9th century, in response to the occultation of the last of the Ithnaʿashari imams and the acceptance of the merits of successors to the Prophet like Abu Bakr.

18. The rebellion of the Prophet's wife ʿA'isha, and the Companions Talha and al-Zubayr in 35/656, was launched ostensibly to bring to justice those they accused of involvement in the assassination of the previous caliph, ʿUthman.
19. The first civil war lasted from 37/657 to 40/661 and was also ostensibly to do with ʿUthman's murder. In this case, justice was demanded by ʿUthman's relative, the founder of the Umayyad dynasty, Muʿawiya b. Abi Sufyan. The Umayyad dynasty lasted from 40/661 to 132/750.
20. Kharijism emerged as an opposition movement within ʿAli b. Abi Talib's camp, as a result of his agreeing to Muʿawiya's demand for arbitration to resolve the civil war. See G. Levi Della Vida, 'Kharidjites', *EI2*.
21. The most dramatic instance of the persecution of ʿAlid descendants was the martyrdom of Husayn, the son of ʿAli b. Abi Talib, at the hands of Muʿawiya's son, Yazid, at Karbala in 61/680. The event is commemorated by the Shiʿa on 10 Muharram, which is known as ʿAshura.
22. Al-Mukhtar launched his revolt on behalf of another of ʿAli b. Abi Talib's sons, Muhammad b. al-Hanafiyya, in 66/685. In 122/740, a major Shiʿi revolt was launched by Zayd b. ʿAli, the son of ʿAli Zayn al-ʿAbidin, who was the only surviving son of Husayn after Karbala.
23. Distinctions between these three main branches of Shiʿism are addressed in Chapter 3. For an overview of Shiʿi divisions generally, see H. Halm, *Shiism*, tr. J. Watson (Edinburgh, 1991).
24. On the Abbasid revolution, see M. Shaban, *The Abbasid Revolution* (Cambridge, 1970); M. Sharon, *Black Banners from the East: The Establishment of the ʿAbbasid State* (Jerusalem and Leiden, 1983); and R. Stephen Humphreys, 'Modern Historians and the Abbasid Revolution', in his *Islamic History: A Framework for Inquiry* (Princeton, NJ, 1991), pp. 104–127.
25. The identification of the Abbasid caliphate with Sunni currents became more explicit after the *mihna*, during which the Abbasids had supported the rational theology of Muʿtazilism against the literal interpretations of Traditionists (*muhaddithun*) like Ibn

Hanbal. This bid to exercise their religious authority as caliphs failed and the influence of these Traditionists led the Abbasids to abandon support for philosophers, the Muʿtazilis and the Shiʿa, whose doctrines had certain affinities with each other. See M. Hinds, 'Mihna', *EI2*; Cooperson, *Classical Arabic Biography*; and M. Qasim Zaman, *Religion and Politics under the Early ʿAbbasids: The Emergence of the Proto-Sunni Elite* (Leiden, 1997), for three interpretations of the *mihna*'s consequences.

26. The term 'imam' broadly speaking means a leader or authority. In the Sunni context, the title is given to anyone who has religious authority, such as the leader of the Friday or communal prayer, or the founder of a legal school. The Shiʿi meaning of 'imam' is supreme spiritual and political authority, and so it is reserved for the descendents of specific lines of the Prophet's family that each branch of Shiʿism recognizes as the only legitimate successors to leadership of the Muslim community. The Fatimids, thus, were spiritual heads of the Ismaili Shiʿi community (including those outside Fatimid territories) and political heads of all those within their empire.
27. L. Massignon, 'Mutannabi, devant le siècle Ismaélien de L'Islam', in *Al Mutannabî: Recueil publié à l'occasion de son millenaire* (Beirut, 1936), p. 1.
28. Sunni literature on Shiʿi groups is generally polemical, since Shiʿi causes challenged the increasingly autonomous and powerful role of the Sunni *ʿulama'* under the Abbasids. On Sunni political thought see A.K.S. Lambton, *State and Government in Medieval Islam* (Oxford, 1981). The Ismaili Shiʿa and the Fatimids were particularly attacked in tracts sponsored by the Abbasids, such as that of the ʿAlid Muhammad b. ʿAli, known as Akhu Muhsin (ca. 370/980), who elaborated on earlier anti-Ismaili works and attributed Christian gnostic origins to the Fatimids, and also in works such as al-Ghazali's *Fada'ih al-batiniyya* ('The Scandals of the Esotericists'), written for the Abbasid caliph al-Mustazhir (d. 512/1118) and thus also known as *al-Mustazhiri*. Later works attached to Ismaili groups abusive labels such as *hashishiyya*, which metamorphosed in European languages into 'assassins'. Despite their clearly polemical nature, such literature has nevertheless engaged many modern scholars, and much ink has been spilt examining these claims. See, for example, M.G.S. Hodgson, *The Order of Assassins: The Struggle of the Early Nizari Ismaʿilis against the Islamic World* (The Hague, 1955); H. Hamdani, *On the*

Genealogy of Fatimid Caliphs (Cairo, 1958); B. Lewis, *The Origins of Ismaʿilism* (Cambridge, 1940) and *The Assassins* (London, 1967); and F. Daftary, *The Assassin Legends: Myths of the Ismaʿilis* (London, 1994).

29. Michael Brett, *The Rise of the Fatimids: The World of the Mediterranean and the Middle East in the Fourth Century Hijra/Tenth Century CE* (Leiden, 2001).
30. See R. Mottahedeh, *Loyalty and Leadership in an Early Islamic Society* (Princeton, NJ, 1980), pp. 20–25.
31. In a similar vein, see also A. Hamdani, 'Did the Turkicization of Asia Minor lead to the Arabization of North Africa?', *The Maghreb Review*, 24 (1999), pp. 34–41. Here it is argued that the entry of the Seljuks into the Middle East prompted a new wave of Arab expansion into North Africa and the Near East, and as a result its Arabization.
32. To that end, Paul E. Walker's recent *Exploring an Islamic Empire: Fatimid History and its Sources* (London, 2002) reviews the source material for the study of Fatimid history in particular, and provides a valuable bibliography of primary and secondary sources on the Fatimids. See also F. Daftary's *Ismaili Literature: A Bibliography of Sources and Studies* (London, 2004).
33. See F. Daftary, *The Ismaʿilis: Their History and Doctrines* (Cambridge, 1990), pp. 91–93 for a discussion of problems in early Fatimid and Ismaili historiography and the issue of sources.
34. This was due in particular to the efforts of Ismaili scholars such as Zahid ʿAli, Husayn al-Hamdani and Asaf A.A. Fyzee, as well as the Russian orientalist Wladimir Ivanow, who encouraged the study of the Ismaili literature found in Iran, Central Asia and the Indian subcontinent. See F. Daftary, 'The Bibliography of the Publications of the Late W. Ivanow', *Islamic Culture*, 45 (1971), pp. 55–67, and 56 (1982), pp. 239–240.
35. See Daftary, *The Ismaʿilis*, pp. 1–31, and his *Ismaili Literature*, Chapters 1 and 2; and Walker, *Exploring an Islamic Empire*, pp. 228–235.
36. For a complete list see Daftary, *The Ismaʿilis*, pp. 726–734, and *Ismaili Literature*, Chapter 3; Poonawala's *Biobibliography*; and Walker, *Exploring an Islamic Empire*, pp. 228–235.
37. In addition, M. Talbi's *L'Émirat Aghlabide* (Paris, 1966), although about the Aghlabid period which preceded the Fatimid state, deals extensively with Fatimid revolutionary activity leading up to the establishment of their state in the Maghrib.

38. Hence the research of French orientalists such as Sylvestre de Sacy (d. 1838), *Exposé de la religion des Druzes* (Paris, 1838); E.M. Quatremère (d. 1857), 'Notice historique sur les Ismaëliens', *Fundgruben des Orients*, 4 (1814), pp. 339–376; and C. Defrémery (d. 1883), 'Nouvelles recherches sur les Ismaéliens ou Bathiniens de Syrie', *JA*, 5 (1854), pp. 373–421, and 5 (1855), pp. 5–76. All these works focused on the Druze and Nizari Ismaili communities of Syria, increasingly an area of French political interest.
39. Ivanow produced his own arguments on the origins of Ismaili Shiʿism and the Fatimids in his *Ismaili Tradition Concerning the Rise of the Fatimids* (London, 1942), as well as smaller studies on aspects of the same, on Nizari Ismailism, and his important *Ismaili Literature: A Bibliographical Survey* (Tehran, 1963).
40. For example, Massignon, 'Ésquisse d'une bibliographie Qarmate', in T.W. Arnold and R.A. Nicholson, eds., *A Volume of Oriental Studies Presented to Edward G. Browne* (Cambridge, 1922), pp. 329–338.
41. Claude Cahen, 'Quelques chroniques anciennes relatives aux derniers Fatimides', *BIFAO*, 37 (1937–1938), pp. 1–27.
42. See the articles in his *Miscellania Orientalia* (London, 1973).
43. See, for example, his *Cyclical Time and Ismaili Gnosis*, tr. R. Manheim and J. Morris (London, 1983).
44. Among other works on the same, see A. Hamdani, 'A Critique of Casanova's Dating of the *Rasa'il*', in Daftary, ed. *Mediaeval Ismaʿili History and Thought*, pp. 145–152, and Paul E. Walker, *Early Philosophical Shiism: The Ismaili Neoplatonism of Abu Yaʿqub al-Sijistani* (Cambridge, 1993).
45. W. Madelung, 'Fatimiden und Bahrainqarmaten', *Der Islam*, 34 (1959), pp. 34–88, English trans., 'The Fatimids and the Qarmatis of Bahrayn', in F. Daftary, ed., *Mediaeval Ismaʿili History and Thought*, pp. 21–73; and 'Das Imamat in der frühen ismailitischen Lehre', *Der Islam*, 37 (1961), pp. 43–135; S.M. Stern, 'Ismaʿilis and Qarmatians', in *L'Élaboration de l'Islam* (Paris, 1961), pp. 99–108; 'The Epistle of the Fatimid Caliph al-Amir (al-Hidaya al-Amiriyya) – its Date and Purpose', *JRAS* (1950), pp. 20–31, and 'Heterodox Ismaʿilism at the time of al-Muʿizz', *BSOAS*, 17 (1955), pp. 10–33; as well as other articles in his *Studies in Early Ismaʿilism* (Jerusalem and Leiden, 1983).
46. F. Daftary, *A Short History of the Ismailis: Traditions of a Muslim Community* (Edinburgh, 1998), translated into French, German, Portuguese, Russian, Arabic, Persian, Urdu and Gujarati.

47. See also S. Goitein, 'From the Mediterranean to India', *Speculum*, 29 (1954), pp. 181–197, and Abbas Hamdani, *The Sira of al-Mu'ayyad fi'l-din al-Shirazi* (Ph.D. thesis, University of London, 1950), pp. 1–6, on economic history. On minorities see, for example, Marlis Saleh, *Government Relations with the Coptic Community in Egypt during the Fatimid Period* (Ph.D. thesis, University of Chicago, 1995); Mark Cohen, *Jewish Self-Government in Egypt* (Princeton, NJ, 1980); Walter J. Fischel, *Jews in the Economic and Political Life of Mediaeval Islam* (New York, 1969); and Jacob Mann, *The Jews in Egypt and Palestine under the Fatimid Caliphate* (London, 1920–1922).
48. Also on art, see J.M. Bloom, 'The Origins of Fatimid Art', *Muqarnas*, 3 (1985), pp. 30–38; I.A. Bierman, *Writing Signs: The Fatimid Public Text* (Berkeley, CA, 1998); and Thomas Leisten, 'Dynastic Tombs, or Private Mausolea: Observations on the Concept of Funerary Structures of the Fatimid and 'Abbasid Caliphs', in M. Barrucand, ed., *L'Égypte Fatimide son art et son histoire* (Paris, 1999), pp. 465–479. See also, S. Hossein Nasr, ed., *Isma'ili Contributions to Islamic Culture* (Tehran, 1977), for other aspects of Ismaili cultural influence.
49. Similarily, A. Hamdani, 'Evolution of the Organisational Structure of the Fatimi Da'wah: The Yemeni and Persian Contribution', *Arabian Studies*, 3 (1976), pp. 85–114; and Paul E. Walker, 'The Isma'ili Da'wa in the Reign of the Fatimid Caliph al-Hakim', *Journal of the American Research Center in Egypt*, 30 (1993), pp. 161–182.
50. A case in point is *The Advent of the Fatimids: A Contemporary Shi'i Witness*, ed. and tr. W. Madelung and Paul E. Walker (London, 2000), which is an edition and translation of a recently discovered memoir by Ibn al-Haytham, the *Kitab al-munazarat*, dating from the early Fatimid period in North Africa.
51. Regarding the early Ismaili *da'wa* and its split in the late 3rd/9th century into the Fatimid and Qarmati branches, scholars have offered a variety of possible explanations. Stern, for example, argued in his 'Isma'ilis and Qarmatians' that there was no link between the original Ismaili movement and the later Fatimid and Qarmati movements. Madelung in his 'Fatimiden und Bahrainqarmaten', on the other hand, maintains that the movements were in fact originally one and the same, but a split occurred because of a rearticulation of Fatimid doctrine from belief in the return of Muhammad b. Isma'il, to a belief in his descendants as

imams. The Qarmatis rejected this claim and went their own way. In contrast to both these opinions, there are the arguments of Husayn al-Hamdani in his *On the Genealogy of Fatimid Caliphs* and Abbas Hamdani (with F. de Blois) in 'A Re-Examination of al-Mahdi's Letter to the Yemenites on the Genealogy of the Fatimid Caliphs', *JRAS* (1983), pp. 173–207. Both scholars maintain that the movement was continuous and all along the cause of the Fatimid imams, but because of the need for secrecy, the identity of the imams became obscured, giving rise to confusion and ultimately the disagreements that resulted in the Fatimid/Qarmati split.

52. This is reflected in another major debate in Ismaili and Fatimid studies, namely the identity of the Brethren of Purity or Ikhwan al-Safa', who composed important philosophical epistles or *Rasa'il* that were widely circulated in the 3rd/9th century. Because they did not identify themselves or leave clear textual evidence as to their identity, scholars have once again offered a variety of explanations for their identity and the significance of their work. Most recently, A. Hamdani's research has argued that references to the *Rasa'il* in Ismaili texts indicate that the Ikhwan al-Safa' were probably an Ismaili group, and their epistles might therefore constitute evidence of the wide appeal of the early Ismaili movement. See his 'Brethren of Purity, a Secret Society for the Establishment of the Fatimid Caliphate', in *L'Égypte Fatimide*, pp. 73–82.
53. The few facts of al-Nu'man's life have been discussed most recently in Poonawala's *Biobibliography*, pp. 48–68, and his 'Al-Qadi al-Nu'man and Isma'ili Jurisprudence', in Daftary, ed., *Mediaeval Isma'ili History*, pp. 117–144. See also the introduction to Poonawala's recent revision of Fyzee's English translation of the *Da'a'im* entitled *The Pillars of Islam*, vol. 1, *Acts of Devotion and Religious Observances* (New Delhi, 2002), pp. xxv–xxxiii.
54. Ed. S.T. Lokhandwala (Simla, 1972).
55. Ed. M. Kamil Husayn (Cairo, 1948).

Chapter 1: From Revolution to State

1. The detailed accounts of the Fatimid revolution have been dealt with most recently in H. Halm's *The Empire of the Mahdi* and Dachraoui's *Le Califat Fatimide au Magreb.*
2. The only means of succession to the Shi'i imamate was through *nass* or explicit designation, a practice that had been established during the time of Muhammad al-Baqir (d. ca. 114/732), the father

of Ja'far al-Sadiq. Once given it was considered irreversable, since the imam was deemed infallible and possessed of supernatural knowledge. For this reason, Twelver Shi'ism has argued that Ja'far al-Sadiq, knowing that his son Isma'il would not survive him, could not possibly have designated him as his successor. This argument enabled the Twelver Shi'i community to justify the eventual succession of Isma'il's half-brother, Musa al-Kazim.

3. H. Modarressi Tabataba'i, in his *Crisis and Consolidation in the Formative Period of Shi'ite Islam* (Princeton, NJ, 1993), provides a detailed account of the succession crisis during Ja'far al-Sadiq's time.
4. See H. Halm, *Shi'ism*. Regarding claims that a given imam had not died, as will be further explained below, this was a strategy commonly used by his followers adhering to a particular inclination or doctrine that other branches of the family had abandoned or disavowed.
5. Among the most controversial members of the imam's circle was Muhammad b. Abi Zaynab known as Abu'l-Khattab (d. 145/762), whom Ja'far al-Sadiq allegedly repudiated because of teachings he publicly attributed to al-Sadiq with which the imam was uncomfortable. These teachings included belief in the divine light of the imams, a ranking of prophets, imams and others according to a cosmic hierarchy and cyclical hierohistory, and the use of numerological exegesis, all of which subsequently did become, to varying degrees, part of both Twelver and Ismaili Shi'i doctrines. See Daftary, *The Isma'ilis*, pp. 86–97.
6. Twelver Shi'i heresiographers of the period such as al-Qummi in his *Kitab al-maqalat wa'l-firaq*, ed. M. Mashkur (Tehran, 1963), p. 81, and al-Nawbakhti in his *Kitab firaq al-Shi'a*, ed. H. Ritter (Istanbul, 1931), pp. 58–59, for example, linked the early Ismailis with Abu'l-Khattab and his followers.
7. W. Madelung, 'Fatimiden und Bahrainqarmaten'. On the concept of the *mahdi* in Shi'ism generally, see Madelung, 'al-Mahdi', *EI2*.
8. Al-Nawbakhti, *Kitab firaq al-Shi'a*, pp. 61–64, and al-Qummi, *Kitab al-maqalat wa'l-firaq*, pp. 83–86.
9. On the Qarmati movement, in addition to Madelung and Stern, see M. de Goeje, *Mémoire sur les Carmathes du Bahraïn et les Fatimides* (2nd ed., Leiden, 1886), the first major study on the Qaramita, and problematic; W. Ivanow, 'Ismailis and Qarmatians', *JBBRAS*, New series, 16 (1940), pp. 43–85; and T. Wali, *al-Qaramita* (Beirut, 1981).

10. The succession to the imamate of the descendants of Muhammad b. Isma'il was official Fatimid doctrine, even if there was confusion over the actual genealogy of the imams of the *satr* period, as discussed in H. al-Hamdani's *On the Genealogy of Fatimid Caliphs*. This study deals with a letter sent to the Yemeni *da'wa* by 'Abd Allah al-Mahdi. In it al-Mahdi asserts his legitimacy as imam in his own time by arguing his descent going back to Muhammad b. Isma'il. See Hamdani and de Blois, 'A Re-Examination of al-Mahdi's Letter', which further clarifies and explains al-Mahdi's attempt to establish his lineage.
11. For details, see F. Daftary, 'A Major Schism in the Early Isma'ili Movement', *SI*, 77 (1993), pp. 123–139.
12. In addition to the above-mentioned letter from al-Mahdi to the Yemeni *da'wa*, there were later communications such as a letter from the fourth Fatimid caliph al-Mu'izz (d. 365/975) to the Qaramita, written after they attacked the Fatimid armies that had conquered Egypt. See al-Maqrizi, *Itti'az al-hunafa' bi akhbar al-a'imma al-Fatimiyyin al-khulafa'*, ed. J. al-Shayyal and M. Hilmi M. Ahmad (Cairo, 1967–1973), vol. 1, pp. 189–202; and Madelung, 'Das imamat', p. 101.
13. See Halm, *The Empire of the Mahdi*, pp. 79–88, on the career there of the *da'i* Zikrawayh b. Mihrawayh (or Zikroye b. Mihroye) and his sons.
14. On the careers of Mansur al-Yaman and 'Ali b. al-Fadl, see al-Nu'man, *Risalat iftitah al-da'wa wa-ibtida' al-dawla*, ed. F. Dachraoui (Tunis, 1975), pp. 2–26; H. al-Hamdani, *al-Sulayhiyyun wa'l-haraka al-Fatimiyya fi'l-Yaman* (Cairo, 1955), pp. 27–48; and Halm, *The Empire of the Mahdi*, pp. 31–38.
15. Daftary, *The Isma'ilis*, pp. 134–135.
16. Idris 'Imad al-Din, *Ta'rikh al-khulafa' al-Fatimiyyin bi'l-Maghrib*, ed. M. Ya'lawi (Beirut, 1985), pp. 83–89; and S. Jiwa, 'The Initial Destination of the Fatimid Caliphate: The Yemen or the Maghrib?', *BSMESB*, 13 (1986), pp. 15–26.
17. Muhammad al-Yamani, *Sirat al-hajib Ja'far*, ed. W. Ivanow, *Bulletin of the Faculty of Arts, University of Egypt*, 4, Part 2 (1936), p. 121. The *Sirat Ja'far* is the autobiography of 'Abd Allah al-Mahdi's chamberlain, recorded soon after his death (or before 386/996), and thus an important intimate source on the early period of Fatimid history.
18. *Iftitah*, pp. 26–30, 34–38, 40. This episode was apparently far from a coincidence. According to al-Nu'man, the *da'wa* hierarchy

was well aware of the presence of the Kutama in Mecca and their previous exposure to Shiʿism, because of two earlier *daʿis* who had travelled to North Africa in the time of Jaʿfar al-Sadiq: one by the name of Abu Sufyan, who had settled in the Lesser Kabylia and converted local towns such as Marmajanna, Nafta and al-Urbus (Laribus) to Shiʿism, and another known as al-Hulwani who was also active among the Kutama. See also W. Madelung, 'Some Notes on Non-Ismaʿili Shiism in the Maghrib', *SI*, 44 (1977), pp. 86–97; Talbi, *L'Émirat*, pp. 566–579; and Halm, *The Empire of the Mahdi*, pp. 38–42.

19. Of these states, the Aghlabid (184–296/800–909) was perhaps the most important. Ifriqiya had been the traditional seat of Arab administration for the whole of North Africa from the time of the Umayyads, and thus the Aghlabids inherited the role of provincial governors for the empire of their time, the Abbasid caliphate. As for the Idrisids (172–348/788–959), the Rustamids (144–296/761–908) and the Midrarids (140–366/757–977), they ruled small city-states, controlling important trans-Saharan trade routes. They depended heavily on alliances with the surrounding Berber tribal confederations, and their independence from external control found ideological expression in their espousal of Maliki Sunnism (in the case of the Idrisids, despite their Shiʿi dynastic origins), or Kharijism (as in the case of the Rustamids and Midrarids). On Berber tribes and their history in the medieval period, see the *Kitab al-ʿibar wa-diwan al-mubtada' wa'l-khabar fi ayyam al-ʿArab wa'l-ʿAjam wa'l-Barbar* of Ibn Khaldun (Beirut, 1956–1960), French trans. *Histoire des Berbères et des dynasties musulmanes de l'Afrique septentrionale*, tr. W. MacGuckin de Slane (Paris, 1968–1969). See also A. Laroui's *History of the Maghrib*, tr. R. Manheim (Princeton, NJ, 1977), pp. 105–156, for an analysis of Berber relations with local states in North Africa during the medieval period.
20. Or alternatively, Ifkan: see Ibn Hawqal's *Kitab surat al-ard*, ed. J.H. Kramers (Leiden, 1938), pp. 88–89, where mention is made of the fortress.
21. By 282/895, within two years of his arrival, only the cities remained unconverted, according to al-Nuʿman in *Iftitah*, pp. 88–89 and 116–117.
22. According to Halm, *The Empire of the Mahdi*, p. 104, Abu ʿAbd Allah's *dar al-hijra* was modelled on the Ismaili sanctuaries of Iraq. More extensive knowledge of the *daʿwa* organization dates from later periods. See for example, W. Ivanow, 'The Organization of the

Fatimid Propaganda', *Journal of the Bombay Branch of the Royal Asiatic Society*, 15 (1939), pp. 1–35; S. Stern, 'Cairo as the Centre of the Isma'ili Movement', *Studies*, pp. 234–253; and A. Hamdani's 'Evolution of the Organisational Structure of the Fatimi Da'wah', *Arabian Studies*, 3 (1976), pp. 85–114. See also Stern's 'Fatimid Propaganda among Jews according to the Testimony of Yefet b. 'Ali the Karaite', in his *Studies*, pp. 84–95, 'Isma'ili Propaganda and Fatimid Rule in Sind', *Islamic Culture*, 23 (1949), pp. 298–307, repr. in his *Studies*, and 'The Early Isma'ili Missionaries in North-West Persia and in Khurasan and Transoxiana', *BSOAS*, 23 (1960), pp. 56–90, repr. in his *Studies*, on other instances and evidence of *da'wa* activity.

23. For an overview of the Arab Muslim conquest of North Africa and the spread of Islam there, see J. Abun-Nasr, *A History of the Maghrib* (London, 1971), as well as Laroui's *History of the Maghrib*.
24. 'Alid politics, the spiritual flavour of Shi'ism as practised by the Ismaili *da'wa*, as well as Abu 'Abd Allah's *mashriqi* or Middle Eastern origin, added to the *da'wa*'s prestige. From the periphery of North Africa, all things originating in the Mashriq appeared superior. In fact the term *mashriq* became identified with Ismaili Shi'ism at this time, according to I.K. Poonawala, 'A Reconsideration of al-Qadi al-Nu'man's *Madhhab*', *BSOAS*, 37 (1974), pp. 572–579. As he explains, 'The Arabic word for conversion to Shi'i Isma'ili faith is *tasharraqa* [to become Eastern] meaning "to become an Isma'ili". With the lapse of time the terms '*al-mashriqi*' and '*al-mashariqa*' were replaced by al-Shi'i and al-Shi'a; the verbal form remained in use, however.'
25. The *Iftitah* was a source for the later Ismaili history, the '*Uyun al-akhbar* of the Yemeni *da'i* Idris 'Imad al-Din (d. 872/1468) as well as Sunni regional and universal histories such as Ibn al-Athir (d. 630/1233), *al-Kamil fi'l-ta'rikh*, ed. C.J. Tornberg (Leiden, 1851–1876; repr., Beirut, 1965–1967); Ibn 'Idhari (d. 712/1312), *Bayan al-mughrib fi akhbar al-Andalus wa'l-Maghrib*, vol. 1, ed. G.S. Colin and É. Lévi-Provençal (Leiden, 1948); and Shihab al-Din Ahmad al-Nuwayri (d. 733/1322), *Nihayat al-arab fi funun al-adab*, vol. 28, ed. M. Amin and M. Hilmi M. Ahmad (Cairo, 1992). For a complete English translation of the *Iftitah*, see Hamid Haji, *Founding the Fatimid State: The Rise of an Early Islamic Empire* (London, 2006).
26. *Iftitah*, pp. 99–109.
27. Occasionally, these *mashayikh* abused their power according to al-Nu'man, provoking opposition from the ousted tribal leadership,

and contributing to sporadic instability within the nascent community. See *Iftitah*, pp. 124–126.

28. *Ibid.*, pp. 109–110.
29. *Ibid.*, pp. 119–120. Halm suggests that the practice of excommunication was observed in Berber communities from before the coming of Islam. See his *The Empire of the Mahdi*, p. 105.
30. *Iftitah*, pp. 121–124. Al-Nu'man remarks that Abu 'Abd Allah, with all his piety, tended to be solemn and serious. But he adds that this was in keeping with the example of the Prophet (p. 129). On the Prophetic paradigm and Abu 'Abd Allah's attempt to emulate it, see J.E. Lindsay, 'Prophetic Parallels in Abu 'Abd Allah al-Shi'i's Mission among the Kutama Berbers, 893–910', *IJMES*, 24 (1992), pp. 39–56.
31. Initiates were required to take a pledge, or *mithaq*, which consisted of a confessional statement and pledge of allegiance to the imam, and a vow to conceal (*kitman*) their true beliefs and identity from enemies or non-Ismailis. The pledge remains a rite of passage and a mark of membership in the Tayyibi Ismaili, or Bohra, community to this day, and as such reflects the need Shi'is generally and historically felt for *taqiyya* or dissimulation, as a minority within Islam.
32. *Iftitah*, pp. 49–52.
33. *Ibid.*, pp. 128–129.
34. *Ibid.*, pp. 131–132. Apparently when training women and others, the Ismaili *da'wa* tailored its message by using vocabulary and references that would suit its audiences. Thus the tenets of Ismaili doctrine were explained to women by reference to items of jewellery and to the home (whereas craftsmen, for example, would be addressed with reference to the tools of their trade). See also Ibn al-Haytham's *Kitab al-munazarat* in W. Madelung and Paul E. Walker, eds., *The Advent of the Fatimids*, Arabic, p. 122, trans., pp. 169–170.
35. The *Kitab al-'alim wa'l-ghulam*, ed. and tr. J.W. Morris as *The Master and the Disciple: An Early Islamic Spiritual Dialogue* (London, 2001).
36. The *Kitab al-munazarat* of Abu 'Abd Allah Ja'far b. Ahmad b. Muhammad b. al-Aswad b. al-Haytham (b. ca. 273/886 and d. after 334/945) was discovered by Paul E. Walker in a much later manuscript entitled the *Kitab al-azhar* by Hasan b. Nuh al-Bharuchi (d. 939/1532). It covers the crucial period between the taking of Raqqada and Qayrawan by Abu 'Abd Allah and the installation of

al-Mahdi as caliph, or the events of the year 297/909. At the height of his career Ibn al-Haytham was sent by al-Mahdi to al-Andalus to support the efforts of Ibn Hafsun, a Christian rebel against the Umayyads, who declared his loyalty to the Fatimids. Subsequently, and although Ibn al-Haytham continued to serve the Fatimids as *daʿi* until the time of al-Mansur, he seems to have fallen out of favour. The editors contend that the *Kitab al-munazarat* was written in about 334/945 and it was perhaps designed to bring the author to the attention of al-Mansur and improve his situation. The contents of the memoir also seem to indicate that Ibn al-Haytham was seeking to defend the reputation of Abu ʿAbd Allah al-Shiʿi and his brother Abu'l-ʿAbbas, both of whom were killed in 299/911 on al-Mahdi's orders for plotting a coup against him.

37. Among the Ancients that Ibn al-Haytham studied were Plato, Aristotle on logic, the Epistles of St Paul, works in his family's library, as well as Hippocrates, Empedocles, Galen and Dioscurides. He mentions their names especially in a lengthy conversation with Abu'l-ʿAbbas, who was the more learned of the two brothers. Madelung and Walker, *The Advent of the Fatimids*, English intro., pp. 50–52, Arabic, pp. 87–92, trans., pp. 137–141.
38. W. Madelung, 'The Sources of Ismaʿili Law', *JNES*, 35 (1976), pp. 29–40.
39. Madelung and Walker, *The Advent of the Fatimids*, English intro., pp. 24–26, Arabic, pp. 59–64, trans., pp. 111–116.
40. As Walker has observed, Ibn al-Haytham's recourse to a variety of teachers, including Hanafis and Jews, indicates that the local Shiʿis lacked their own educational institutions and thus could not receive the kind of training that other more well-established Shiʿi communities in the east had enjoyed. It is not surprising, therefore, that Ibn al-Haytham, like others, identifies himself as a Shiʿi from a Zaydi family, who studied Hanafi law and Muʿtazili theology, which were subjects common to the less specifically Shiʿi Zaydi curriculum (Madelung and Walker, *The Advent of the Fatimids*, Arabic, pp. 59–60, trans., pp. 111–112). It was not until Ibn al-Haytham studied with Muhammad al-Kufi, the Sicilian émigré, that he developed a more intense interest in Shiʿism and a desire for a more specific identification (Madelung and Walker, *The Advent of the Fatimids*, English intro., pp. 24–26, Arabic, pp. 60–61, trans., pp. 112–114).
41. On the conversion of Shiʿis, Hanafis and others in Qayrawan during the early days of the Fatimid state, see the author's 'Dialectic of

Power: Sunni–Shiʿi Debates in Tenth-Century North Africa', *SI*, 90 (2000), pp. 5–21.

42. See E. Wagner, 'Munazara', *EI2*.
43. Madelung and Walker, *The Advent of the Fatimids*, Arabic, pp. 6–40, trans., pp. 67–95. According to Ibn al-Haytham, Abu ʿAbd Allah was so eager to debate with him that others were kept waiting. When another *daʿi* sought to relieve Abu ʿAbd Allah, he commented that he had spent 18 years debating with the likes of him but that 'This one has what we want', and so continued to instruct Ibn al-Haytham personally. When compared with Abu ʿAbd Allah's less erudite Kutama disciples, it is not difficult to understand why Ibn al-Haytham appeared so impressive and why Abu ʿAbd Allah was so eager to draw him in.
44. Polytheism or *shirk* is defined as the associating of others with God, and as such proscribed in Islam.
45. For example, 'We found most of them were not true to their covenant' (7:102), and 'Those who pledge allegiance to you [Muhammad] pledge allegiance to God, thus whoever breaks the covenant violates his own soul' (48:10). The first verse refers to people who turned against previous prophets, while the second refers to those who pledged allegiance to Muhammad at the time of the treaty of Hudaybiyya in 6/628, when he negotiated a truce with the still non-Muslim Meccans. Some of his party would have preferred that he conquer Mecca instead, and knowing this, Muhammad asked the Muslims to take a pledge to support him whatever course he decided to take.
46. The first caliph Abu Bakr (10–12/632–634) denied Fatima a share in an oasis near Medina, which had been given to her by her father. Also at the time of the Prophet's death, Abu Bakr and ʿUmar tried to compel ʿAli to accept Abu Bakr's succession, and so Fatima threatened to remove the veil from her hair (thus indicating their violation of her) as she defended her husband in their home. For a thorough account of these and other incidents in the lives of ʿAli and Fatima, see Madelung, *The Succession to Muhammad*.
47. Ibn al-Haytham refers here to the *falta* (or unexpected show of allegiance) engineered by ʿUmar and Abu Bakr at the time of the Prophet's death. Sunni tradition accepts Abu Bakr's succession despite evidence of the hasty maneouvering on his and ʿUmar's part. Zaydi Shiʿis also accept the succession of Abu Bakr and ʿUmar, arguing that since ʿAli b. Abi Talib himself in the end accepted it, they could not legitimately reject the caliphate of these

other Companions.

48. Madelung and Walker, *The Advent of the Fatimids*, Arabic, p. 9, trans., p. 70.
49. The reference here is to the wars of apostasy or *ridda*. See Kennedy, *The Prophet and the Age of the Caliphate.*
50. The allusions here are to events, *hadith*s and Qur'anic verses, which are further explained in Chapter 3 of the present book.
51. Madelung and Walker, *The Advent of the Fatimids*, Arabic, pp. 41–54, trans., pp. 95–10. Shortly after, Ibn al-Haytham asks Abu 'Abd Allah to disclose to him the name of the true imam and although Abu 'Abd Allah tries to put him off, he insists. Curiously, Abu 'Abd Allah states that the imam's name is Muhammad b. Isma'il, and not as one might suspect, 'Abd Allah al-Mahdi himself (Arabic, pp. 55–56, trans., p. 107). The wording of the text, however, seems to indicate that this is meant allegorically, and subsequently Ibn al-Haytham refers to al-Mahdi as the imam and commander of the faithful or *amir al-mu'minin*, the title employed for caliphs (for example, Arabic, pp. 84, 119, 127, trans., pp. 135, 167, 174).
52. Ja'far b. Mansur al-Yaman was the son of Ibn Hawshab, or Mansur al-Yaman, who as previously noted, first spread the Ismaili *da'wa* in the Yemen with 'Ali b. al-Fadl. When 'Ali b. al-Fadl fell away from the official *da'wa*, Mansur al-Yaman remained loyal, as did his son Ja'far after him. His dates of birth and death are uncertain; we know that he was born and lived the early part of his life in Yemen, and later migrated to North Africa during the reign of the second Fatimid Imam-caliph al-Qa'im (d. 334/946) and died during the reign of al-Mu'izz (d. 365/975). See Morris, *The Master and the Disciple*, pp. 22–27.
53. *Iftitah*, pp. 53–54.
54. *Ibid.*, pp. 79–84 and al-Nuwayri, *Nihaya*, vol. 28, pp. 81–84.
55. Talbi, *L'Émirat*, pp. 633–641. Ibrahim II died during the Sicilian campaign in 289/902 and was succeeded by his son 'Abd Allah II. His reign was cut short by his uncle Ziyadat-Allah III, who had him and all other potential claimants killed in 290/903.
56. Al-Jawdhari, *Sirat al-Ustadh Jawdhar*, ed. M.K. Husayn and M. 'Abd al-Hadi al-Sha'ira (Cairo, 1954), pp. 116–122; *Iftitah*, pp. 163–164; Halm, *The Empire of the Mahdi*, pp. 91–95, 128–129.
57. *Iftitah*, pp. 172–173.
58. Abu'l-'Abbas then returned to back to Tripoli, where al-Mahdi had left his mother when he fled to Sijilmasa. Ibn 'Idhari, *Bayan*, vol. 1, p. 139.

59. The town of Baghaya was the strongest fortress to the west of Qayrawan, and so when it was taken by Abu ʿAbd Allah the Aghlabids were far more vulnerable. See Halm, *The Empire of the Mahdi*, pp. 112–113.
60. Attempts to rally people behind the Aghlabids included presenting the sum of 50 dinars to anyone willing to wage war against Abu ʿAbd Allah and followers. See *Iftitah*, pp. 198–200, and also Halm, *The Empire of the Mahdi*, pp. 114–115.
61. *Iftitah*, pp. 207–227.
62. *Ibid.*, pp. 227–232.
63. Al-Yasaʿ b. Midrar had already been informed in a letter from Ziyadat-Allah III of al-Mahdi's identity and his relations with Abu ʿAbd Allah and the *daʿwa*, but he had apparently seen no reason to act on the information purely for Ziyadat-Allah's sake, and thus had left al-Mahdi, his son and his entourage alone until Sijilmasa was approached by Abu ʿAbd Allah and the Kutama army (Halm, *The Empire of the Mahdi*, pp. 132–133).
64. In Rabiʿ II 297/January 910, or about five months after al-Mahdi's rescue from Sijilmasa in Dhu'l-Hijja 296/August 909.
65. On Ziyadat-Allah III's reign see M. Talbi, *L'Émirat*, pp. 623–699. Ismaili sources, including the *Iftitah* (pp. 151–156), also attribute Aghlabid defeat to their last ruler's frivolity, decadence and depravity. For all these reasons, according to al-Nuʿman, he was reviled by the people (pp. 197–198).
66. Ibn ʿIdhari, *Bayan*, vol. 1, pp. 141–142. See also *Iftitah*, pp. 173–178. Islamic law does not allow for the taxing of Muslims except in a few cases, such as, for example, *zakat* (poor due), and thus rulers would often have to meet deficits by imposing temporary or arbitrary taxes.
67. *Iftitah*, pp. 215–218.
68. *Iftitah*, pp. 185–191.
69. ʿIzz al-Din Abu'l-Hasan ʿAli, known as Ibn al-Athir, a historian at the time of the Crusades, and partial to the Zangid regime ruling in Syria, which was famous, among other things, for its attempts at Sunnification and antipathy towards Shiʿism. See his *al-Kamil*, vol. 8, pp. 45–50.
70. *Ibid.*, p. 46.
71. *Ibid.*, pp. 48–49. The figures given here for the duration of the three dynasties whose rule was terminated by the Fatimids are incorrect. The Midrarids actually ruled for 160 years, and the Rustamids for 130 years.

72. Ibn ʿIdhari, *Bayan*, vol. 1, p. 158. Abu'l-ʿAbbas Ahmad b. Muhammad b. ʿIdhari al-Marrakushi lived under the Maliki Sunni Marinid dynasty of Morocco and served as an administrator in their capital, Fez. His history concerns itself primarily with North Africa and Spain, and exhibits the Maliki bias predominant in the region.
73. *Iftitah*, pp. 253–257, 270–275, 279–280, 294–299.
74. *Ibid.*, pp. 253–257. An amendment was attached to the declaration sent to Sicily, a province inherited from the Aghlabids, which detailed capitulations specific to the island. Abu ʿAbd Allah's declaration at the time of al-Mahdi's release also describes how al-Yasaʿ b. Midrar's refusal to cooperate and release al-Mahdi and his cowardly retreat from Sijilmasa had all aided the victory of the 'friends' of God in support of the cause of the Commander of the Faithful (*amir al-mu'minin*) and 'son' of the Prophet (*ibn Rasul-Allah*) (pp. 281–286).
75. *Ibid.*, pp. 293–300.
76. *Ibid.*, pp. 302–303. They were also given some of the concubines of the Aghlabid harem, instructed to comport themselves appropriately as governors by improving their dress and to adorn their steeds so as to appear distinguished.
77. See Halm, *The Empire of the Mahdi*, pp. 149–154, in particular p. 151.
78. *Iftitah*, pp. 303–304, 315; Ibn ʿIdhari, *Bayan*, vol. 1, pp. 151, 159.
79. Ibn ʿIdhari, *Bayan*, vol. 1, p. 167.
80. Halm, *The Empire of the Mahdi*, pp. 153–154.
81. Ibn ʿIdhari, *Bayan*, vol. 1, p. 162. Abolishing the *diwan al-insha'* was probably due to availability within the *daʿwa* of trusted members to undertake some of the scribal and chancery responsibilities it had previously handled.
82. *Iftitah*, pp. 303–304.
83. Ibn ʿIdhari, *Bayan*, vol. 1, p. 159.
84. See B. Roy and P. Poinssot, *Inscriptions Arabes de Kairouan* (Paris, 1950–1958). In discussing the Grand Mosque, they note that the oldest inscriptions are Aghlabid (all three are from the early 3rd/9th century, pp. 10–16), and subsequent inscriptions date from the Zirid period or 5th/11th century (pp. 18–21, 25–30). This of course indicates that either the Fatimids did not in fact excise Aghlabid names from monuments, or that their own names were excised after the defection of the Zirids to the Abbasid camp.
85. See, for example, H. Monès, 'Le Malékisme et l'échec des Fatimides en Ifriqiya', in *Études d'orientalisme dediées à la mémoire de Lévi-*

Provençal (Paris, 1962), vol. 1, pp. 197–220.

86. These sources include histories such as Ibn ʿIdhari's *Bayan* as well as *tabaqat* works, or biographical dictionaries, of the Sunni and especially Maliki *ʿulama'* of North Africa during the Fatimid period. The latter include the *tabaqat* of Abu'l-ʿArab Muhammad b. Ahmad al-Tamimi (d. 333/945) and Muhammad b. al-Harith al-Khushani (d. 371/981), combined and edited as *Classes des savants de l'Ifriqiya* by Muhammad b. Cheneb (Beirut, n.d.), and the 5th/11th century *Riyad al-nufus* of Abu Bakr ʿAbd Allah b. Muhammad al-Maliki, ed. B. al-Bakkush (Beirut, 1981–1983).
87. Madelung, 'Some Notes on Non-Ismaʿili Shiism in the Maghrib'.
88. *Iftitah*, pp. 26–30.
89. Halm, *The Empire of the Mahdi*, pp. 243–245.
90. *Bayan*, vol. 1, pp. 154–155.
91. The case of Ibn al-Birdhawn took on almost mythical proportions in later *tabaqat* works like Abu Bakr al-Maliki's *Riyad al-nufus*, which describes Ibn al-Birdhawn heroically facing down the triumvirate of al-Mahdi, Abu ʿAbd Allah and Abu'l-ʿAbbas, who ask him to testify that al-Mahdi is the messenger of God. Ibn al-Birdhawn refuses and is put to death cruelly. W. Madelung, 'The Religious Policy of the Fatimids toward Their Sunni Subjects in the Maghrib', in *L'Égypte Fatimide*, pp. 99–101.
92. For example, a brawl broke out near Qayrawan between a Kutama Berber and a merchant in 298/911, and a similar but more serious incident occurred in Qayrawan in 299/912. See *Iftitah*, pp. 320–322.
93. Halm, *The Empire of the Mahdi*, pp. 159–168.
94. See for example, Qadi ʿAbd al-Jabbar (b. Ahmad al-Hamadhani, d. 415/1025), *Tathbit dala'il al-nubuwwa*, ed. A. ʿUthman (Beirut, 1966), vol. 2, pp. 380–391.
95. The *Iftitah* borrows heavily from a lost autobiography or *sira* of Abu ʿAbd Allah for information on his career and conquests.
96. *Iftitah*, pp. 317- 318.
97. The Kutama found allies in some members of the former Aghlabid dynasty who joined them in a revolt soon after the execution of Abu ʿAbd Allah and Abu'l-ʿAbbas. See Madelung and Walker, *The Advent of the Fatimids*, trans., p. 172, n. 186.
98. Halm, *The Empire of the Mahdi*, p. 172; *Iftitah*, p. 234; and Ibn ʿIdhari, *Bayan*, vol. 1, pp. 166–167.
99. *Iftitah*, pp. 319–320.
100. On Mahdiyya see, for example, M. Talbi, 'al-Mahdiyya', *EI2*, and

A. Lézine, *Mahdiya: Recherches d'archéologie islamique* (Paris, 1965).

101. As Madelung notes in his 'The Religious Policy of the Fatimids', pp. 101–104, both al-Mahdi and al-Qa'im basically followed the precedence set by Abu 'Abd Allah al-Shi'i that only Shi'is were appointed to religious offices. But al-Mansur, after successfully putting down the rebellion of Abu Yazid, realized that greater flexibility was needed in order to avert such a rebellion in the future. So he appointed a Maliki *qadi* over Qayrawan to replace the Ismaili judge whom the rebels had killed, and 'in practice ... jurisdiction was henceforth split in the Fatimid realm. The towns where Maliki Sunnism prevailed had Maliki judges ... while Ismaili communities were subject to Ismaili jurisdiction.'

Chapter 2: From *Batin* to *Zahir*

1. Again, on the evolution of Shi'i thought concerning the imams see Daftary, *The Isma'ilis*, pp. 32–90; and W. Madelung, 'al-Mahdi', *EI2*.
2. Daftary notes: 'The *ta'wil*, literally meaning to lead back to the origin or to educe the *batin* from the *zahir*, may be distinguished from *tafsir*, to explain and comment upon the apparent meaning of the sacred texts, and from *tanzil*, which refers to the revelation of the religious scriptures through angelic intermediaries. The *ta'wil* practised by the early Isma'ilis was often of a cabalistic form, relying on the mystical properties and symbolism of letters and numbers. Although similar processes of interpretation and of spiritual exegesis had existed in the earlier Judeo-Christian traditions and among the Gnostics, the immediate origins of the Isma'ili *ta'wil* are Islamic and may be traced especially to the Shi'i circles of the 2nd/8th century' (Daftary, *The Isma'ilis*, p. 138).
3. *Ibid.*, pp. 91–143, and especially pp. 136–141. The cyclical view of history was probably inspired by the ancient Greeks and their observations of planetary revolution. These cosmological cycles were, in turn, applied by Muslim thinkers to human history, and in the Ismaili context the cyclical view of history supported the inevitability of political change or revolutions, culminating in the *qiyama* or Day of Resurrection. For an analytical overview of this subject, see Henry Corbin, *Temps cyclique et gnose Ismaélienne* (Paris, 1982), tr. R. Manheim and J. Morris as *Cyclical Time and Ismaili Gnosis* (London, 1983).

4. Apparently the awaited imam was expected to be more youthful than the 35-year-old al-Mahdi (Halm, *The Empire of the Mahdi*, pp. 146, 159–161), and this was maybe why a youth like that of the Banu Mawatnit featured in the episode of the false *mahdi*, which occurred in 299/912, two years into al-Mahdi's reign. Moreover, according to his detractors, 'Abd Allah al-Mahdi displayed worldly tendencies: he was pleased to arrive in Qayrawan because its residents resembled the more civilized population of the Mashriq (*Iftitah*, p. 292), and he ordered the Kutama to dress in a way appropriate to their new status as governors (*Ibid.*, pp. 302–303).
5. Abu'l-Qasim was declared al-Mahdi's successor and given the title al-Qa'im, significantly in the spring of 299/912, a year after the execution of Abu 'Abd Allah al-Shi'i (and the disturbances that occurred in the wake of his death), and at the time of the episode of the rival *mahdi* (*Iftitah*, p. 234).
6. To the Sunni community, messianic titles were familiar from Abbasid practice. Unlike the Umayyads, who retained their given names on assuming power, the Abbasids routinely adopted messianic or religious titles as symbolic of the general religious authority they claimed for the caliphate.
7. See H. al-Hamdani, *On the Genealogy of Fatimid Caliphs* and Hamdani and de Blois, 'A Re-examination of al-Mahdi's Letter'. Given that the exact genealogy of the Fatimids was less an issue for non-Ismailis, it is not surprising that there was no general proclamation to the Sunni community on this matter.
8. Problematic doctrinal dissidents included those who demanded that al-Mahdi perform miracles and who indulged in occasional outbursts of antinomian activity. According to Sunni sources, al-Mahdi apparently had 200 *da'is* from Qayrawan, Baja and Tunis put to death in 309/921 for openly drinking wine and eating pork during Ramadan (Ibn 'Idhari, *Bayan*, vol. 1, pp. 185–186). Even if these are gross exaggerations, al-Nu'man notes the Fatimids did punish errant *da'is* from time to time (*Iftitah*, pp. 328–329; *Kitab al-majalis wa'l-musayarat*, pp. 457–460; *Da'a'im al-Islam*, vol. 1, pp. 68–69).
9. See again Hamdani, 'Dialectic of Power'.
10. *Iftitah*, pp. 269–270.
11. Madelung and Walker, *The Advent of the Fatimids*, Arabic, pp. 69–70, trans., pp. 122–123.
12. Ibn al-Haytham lists some of those debated by Abu 'Abd Allah: Ibn 'Abdun, Sa'id b. al-Haddad (the prominent Maliki *faqih*), Musa al-

Qattan, Himas (b. Marwan, the Maliki judge of Qayrawan, who had caused Ibn al-Haytham trouble over his inheritance) and al-Sudayni (or al-Sadini, the Hanafi judge of Qayrawan before Himas b. Marwan) (Madelung and Walker, *The Advent of the Fatimids*, Arabic, p. 65, trans., pp. 117–118). He also states that Abu ʿAbd Allah ordered him to debate with the local Sunnis himself, and describes one such occasion when he debated with prominent Hanafis on the question of female inheritance which Shiʿis, unlike Sunnis, allow in full in the absence of a spouse or male siblings (*Ibid.*, Arabic, pp. 67–68, trans., pp. 120–121).

13. Abu ʿUthman Saʿid b. Haddad (d. 302/915) was a student of Ibn Sahnun, son of the author of the important Maliki legal compendium, the *Mudawwana*, and the teacher of many of the Malikis of Qayrawan. He was also a specialist in disputation and thus no doubt led the attack against the Ismaili *daʿwa* on behalf of the Malikis on most occasions. On Ibn Haddad, see al-Khushani, *Tabaqat* in *Classes des savants*, ed. M. Ben Cheneb (Paris, 1915), pp. 148, 198–212, and al-Maliki, *Kitab Riyad*, ed. Bashir al-Bakkush (Beirut, 1981–1983), vol. 2, pp. 57–115.
14. A reference to Qur'an 33:6: 'The Prophet is dearer to the believers than themselves', which the Prophet received before he declared ʿAli *mawla*.
15. Madelung and Walker, *The Advent of the Fatimids*, Arabic, p. 70, trans., p. 123. Ibn al-Haytham also mentions other debates (on the imamate, what constituted the *Sunna*, fasting and chastity) that took place between Ibn al-Haddad and Abu'l-ʿAbbas (*Ibid.*, Arabic, p. 114, trans., p. 161).
16. In Ibn al-Haytham's account the debates took place with Abu ʿAbd Allah, whereas in both al-Nuʿman's *Iftitah* and al-Khushani's *Tabaqat*, the debates took place with Abu'l-ʿAbbas. Al-Khushani's transcript is probably based on the account of Saʿid b. al-Haddad which Ibn al-Haytham mentioned refuting. Another version of these debates occurs in al-Maliki's *Kitab Riyad* (Beirut, 1981–1983), vol. 2, pp. 75–96, where they take place between the Malikis and both Abu ʿAbd Allah and Abu'l-ʿAbbas. See also M. Yaʿlawi's *al-Adab bi-Ifriqiya fi'l-ʿahd al-Fatimi* (Beirut, 1986), pp. 40–60; Halm, *The Empire of the Mahdi*, pp. 240–242; and Monès, 'Le Malékisme et l'échec des Fatimides en Ifriqiya'.
17. Al-Khushani, *Tabaqat* in *Classes des savants*, p. 198.
18. 'O you who believe, kill not game while in the state of pilgrimage. If you do so intentionally, the compensation is an offering brought

to the Ka'ba, of a domestic animal equivalent to the one killed, or as adjuged by two just men from among you' (5:95).

19. According to Muslim tradition, when Abu Bakr and 'Umar could not break the resistance of the enemy at the Battle of Khaybar, the Prophet called on 'Ali, 'a man who loves God and His Prophet, and whom God and His Prophet love'. 'Ali carried the day by killing the enemy's shaykh, and wielding a fortress door as a shield and using it as a bridge for the Muslims.
20. Maliki *fiqh* does not incorporate the tradition of 'Ali b. Abi Talib, and early on the school tended to spread in an anti-'Alid milieu such as Basra. See J. Schacht, 'Malik b. Anas', *EI2*.
21. Al-Khushani, *Tabaqat* in *Classes des savants*, pp. 199–202.
22. *Ibid*., pp. 202–203.
23. *Ibid*., pp. 203–207.
24. *Ibid*., pp. 208–210.
25. See Talbi, *L'Émirat*, pp. 540–543.
26. *Ibid*., p. 540. 'Abd Allah II appointed as supreme judge or *qadi al-qudat* al-Sudayni or al-Sadani, one of those who Ibn al-Haytham claimed to have debated with Abu 'Abd Allah, and who was a known Hanafi and Mu'tazili.
27. Al-Khushani, *Tabaqat* in *Classes des savants*, pp. 215–218, 223–224, 230. 'Abd al-Malik's conversion enabled him to derive an income from drawing up contracts, for which permission was required by the Fatimid authorities.
28. *Ibid*., p. 223. See also I.K. Poonawala, 'A Reconsideration of al-Qadi al-Nu'man's *Madhhab*', *BSOAS*, 37 (1974), pp. 572–579.
29. Al-Khushani, *Tabaqat* in *Classes des savants*, p. 225.
30. *Ibid*., pp. 225–226. A section on those who were tried/punished contains the entries of ten *'ulama'* who were put on trial by Fatimid judges and administrators. Eight of these men were Malikis and were tried generally for disobeying legal and ritual guidelines set by the Fatimids (on issues such as marriage contracts, the *adhan*, taxation, and so on), and for otherwise displeasing the government or antagonizing Shi'is, as in the case of Ibn al-Birdhawn. One Shafi'i was tried for reasons unrecorded, and one Shi'i, Abu 'Ali b. Abi Minhal, for the illegal confiscation of goods. As for the judges of Qayrawan, al-Khushani records the names of six, beginning with al-Marwadhi, who eventually was put to death for fraudulent practices. A Qamudi, by the name of Muhammad b. al-Mahfud, succeeded him in this office until 306/919. Then Ishaq b. Abi Minhal was appointed. The Ismaili governor of Qayrawan,

Abu Sa'id Musa b. Ahmad al-Dayf, was soon after removed, and succeeded by Muhammad b. 'Imran al-Nafti, who had previously been *qadi* of Tripoli. The latter died after one year in office and was replaced by Ishaq b. Abi Minhal who served in this position into the reign of al-Qa'im. He died in office and was succeeded by Ahmad b. Bahr, the last *qadi* recorded by al-Khushani, who had also previously been *qadi* of Tripoli. The former Aghlabid capital of Raqqada had during this time been given to the Kutami Aflah b. Harun, and Mahdiyya's judge was Zurara b. Ahmad, whom al-Khushani characterized as a fanatical Shi'i (*Ibid.*, pp. 227–233).

31. See, for example, the *Kitab al-jami'* of Abu Muhammad b. Abi Zayd al-Qayrawani (d. 386/996), ed. A.M. Turki (Beirut, 1990); R. Brunschvig, 'Fiqh Fatimide et histoire de l'Ifriqiya', in his *Études Islamologiques* (Paris, 1976), vol. 1, pp. 63–70; and H.R. Idris, *La Berbérie orientale sous les Zirides, Xe-XIIe siècles* (Paris, 1962). These studies deal with the impact of Ismaili and Sunni *fiqh* on each other later during Fatimid rule in North Africa.
32. Poonawala, 'Al-Qadi al-Nu'man and Isma'ili Jurisprudence', p. 120.
33. Ahmad b. Muhammad b. Khallikan (d. 681/1282), *Wafayat al-a'yan*, ed. I. Abbas (Beirut, 1972), vol. 5, pp. 415–423.
34. Taqi al-Din Ahmad b. 'Ali al-Maqrizi (d. 845/1499), *Kitab al-mawa'iz wa'l-i'tibar bi-dhikr al-khitat wa'l-athar (al-Khitat)* (Bulaq, 1270/1853), vol. 1, pp. 390–391, and vol. 2, pp. 341–342.
35. Early biographical notices on al-Nu'man include: R.J.H. Gottheil, 'A Distinguished Family of Fatimide Cadis (al-Nu'man) in the Tenth Century', *JAOS*, 27 (1906), pp. 217–296; A.A.A. Fyzee, 'Qadi an-Nu'man, the Fatimid Jurist and Author', *JRAS* (1934), pp. 1–32; and M.K. Husayn, *Fi adab Misr al-Fatimiyya* (Cairo, 1955), pp. 42–54. Standard biographical sources are discussed by Poonawala in his two articles, 'Al-Qadi al-Nu'man's Works and the Sources', *BSOAS*, 36 (1973), pp. 109–115, and 'A Reconsideration of al-Qadi al-Nu'man's *Madhhab*', *BSOAS*, 37 (1974), pp. 572–579. Despite the frequency with which al-Nu'man is included in such sources, very little biographical information exists on him. Ibn Khallikan's *Wafayat*, for example, offers little other information on the career or writings of al-Nu'man, derived mainly from the now lost works of Ibn Zulaq (d. 386/996) and al-Musabbihi (d. 420/1029); an excerpt from the latter's *Akhbar Misr*, ed. A.F. Sayyid and Th. Banquis (Cairo, 1978), contains information on the lives and careers of his sons and grandsons.

36. Ibn Khallikan, *Wafayat*, vol. 5, p. 415.
37. Poonawala observes: 'With the decline of the Buyids in Baghdad and their ensuing fall, Fatimid Cairo proved to be a refuge for Shiʿis; and many Imamis [Twelver Shiʿis] were attracted to this new centre. The existence of a large number of Imamis in the Fatimid capital is attested to by the proclamation of the Imami faith as the official creed of the Fatimid empire by Abu ʿAli Ahmad (nicknamed Kutayfat) b. Afdal, the grandson of Badr al-Jamali, in the year 524/1129–1130, and the appointment of an Imami *qadi* along with three others. It is not improbable, therefore, that such a group of Imamis might have been instrumental in introducing al-Qadi al-Nuʿman's works to the Imami circles and also in giving him an Imami character' (Poonawala, '*Madhhab*', p. 573). Subsequently (or by the 11th/17th century), al-Nuʿman was appropriated by most Twelver Shiʿi scholars and biographers.
38. Idris ʿImad al-Din states that al-Nuʿman was eventually given membership of the *daʿwa* in its highest ranks. *ʿUyun al-akhbar*, ed. M. Ghalib (Beirut, 1978), vol. 6, p. 39. Fyzee, in his article 'Qadi an-Nuʿman', deduces from this that 'the *ʿUyun* does not mention exact rank, but he is generally supposed to have attained the rank of *hujjat* in the hierarchy of the Ismaʿili *Daʿwat*' (p. 12).
39. Idris ʿImad al-Din, *ʿUyun*, vol. 6, p. 50.
40. Poonawala notes: 'al-Nuʿman states … that he embarked on the collection of a vast number of legal *hadith*s transmitted from the family of the Prophet by scrutinising various sources accessible to him. … Out of this material he compiled the *Idah*. … It was a voluminous composition comprised of some 3000 folios (*waraqa*)' ('Al-Qadi al-Nuʿman and Ismaʿili Jurisprudence', p. 121).
41. W. Madelung, 'Some Notes on Non-Ismaʿili Shiism', *SI*, 44 (1977), pp. 87–97. The founder of this school was one Ibn Warsand, who apparently flourished in the 3rd/8th century.
42. Madelung, 'The Sources of Ismaʿili Law'. Madelung argues, 'Ismaʿili law thus appears in the *K. al-idah*, both materially and theoretically, as a compromise between Imami and Zaydi law. Materially it is based on sources accepted as authoritative in Imami *fiqh* as well as those accepted as authoritative in Zaydi *fiqh*. Theoretically, al-Nuʿman recognises, in agreement with the Zaydis, the authority of the *ahl al-bayt*. … But he makes a concession to the Imami position in granting the imams superior authority to that of the other ʿAlids' (p. 32). See also T. Nagel, *Frühe Ismailiya und Fatimiden im Lichte der Risalat Iftitah ad-Daʿwa* (Bonn, 1972), which attributes

Hasanid Shiʿi and Muʿtazili influence to the works of al-Nuʿman.

43. *Fihrist al-kutub wa'l-rasa'il*, ed. A.N. Munzavi (Tehran, 1966). Its author, Ismaʿil b. ʿAbd al-Rasul al-Majduʿ, was given the name *al-majduʿ* (mutilated) as punishment for his son Hibat-Allah's attempt to gain leadership of the Tayyibi-Ismaili community in India, by claiming that he was in contact with the imam. Al-Majduʿ's *Fihrist* remains an important bibliography of works in the possession of the Ismaili community in India and includes information on literature of the pre-Fatimid, Fatimid and post-Fatimid periods.
44. Fyzee, 'Qadi an-Nuʿman', pp. 2–3. See also, the *Fihrist* of al-Majduʿ, and Gottheil's 'A Distinguished Family of Fatimide Cadis'. Ibn Nadim's *Fihrist al-kutub* is one of the earliest bibliographies available of the literature of the classical period in Islam and it was written in Baghdad. Ibn Hajar al-ʿAsqalani's *Rafʿ* is a biographical dictionary that includes entries for a variety of scholars.
45. There are sometimes discrepancies in the classification systems employed by these bibliographers. Poonawala disagrees with Fyzee on his classification of, for example, the *Kitab al-majalis wa'l-musayarat* as *waʿz* or sermons. See Poonawala's 'Al-Qadi al-Nuʿman's Works and the Sources'.
46. Idris ʿImad al-Din,ʿ*Uyun*, vol. 6, p. 42.
47. Poonawala, 'Al-Qadi al-Nuʿman and Ismaʿili Jurisprudence', pp. 121–122.
48. Poonawala, *Biobibliography*, p. 52.
49. *Ibid.*, pp. 62 and 53 respectively. The *Mukhtara* has been edited by Poonawala (Montreal, 1970), and the *Muntakhaba* exists only in manuscript form.
50. Ed. M.W. Mirza (Damascus, 1957); Poonawala, 'Al-Qadi al-Nuʿman', p. 122.
51. Poonawala, 'Works and the Sources'. Ivanow, in his *A Creed of the Fatimids* (Bombay, 1936), p. 7, mentions another work by al-Nuʿman that was composed during al-Mansur's reign, the *Tathbit al-imama li-mawlana ʿAli b. Abi Talib*, which is cited in the *Daʿa'im al-Islam*. A similarly titled work is in the possession of the Hamdani family, although it is attributed to al-Mansur himself.
52. Poonawala, *Biobibliography*, p. 60.
53. *Kitab al-majalis*, p. 108.
54. This distinction between Ismaili and Twelver Shiʿi treatment of the issue of *imama* will be discussed further in the following chapter. For a look at the categories and contents of Twelver Shiʿi legal works, see H. Modarressi Tabataba'i, *An Introduction to Shiʿi Law*

(London, 1984), pp. 13–22.

55. Thus, the first book of the *Da'a'im al-Islam*, al-Nu'man's most important legal work, begins with a section on faith or *iman*, in which is incorporated the concept of *walaya*, or the necessity of devotion and obedience to the imam, and the second book reiterates the significance of *walaya* and *imama* in relation to *wasaya*, or inheritance and wills. See A.A.A. Fyzee, *The Ismaili Law of Wills* (London, 1933) for discussion of the relationship of *imama* to *wasaya*.
56. Poonawala, *Biobibliography*, pp. 52–55. With the exception of *Kitab al-iqtisar* and the *Da'a'im*, the rest of the abridgements here listed are available only in manuscript form or are lost. A discussion of the *Da'a'im* as an abridgement of the *Kitab al-idah* is provided in Madelung, 'The Sources of Isma'ili Law'.
57. Now lost (Poonawala, *Biobibliography*, p. 58).
58. This work has been recently published (Tehran, 1412/1991–1992). Poonawala also says that one part of the total 16 was also printed by al-Jami'ah al-Sayfiyah in Surat, India (Poonawala, *Biobibliography*, p. 60).
59. *Ibid.*, p. 58.
60. Usually known as Ibn al-Qasim, al-'Utaqi (d. 191/806) was a disciple of Malik, and considered responsible for spreading the *madhhab* in Egypt and then North Africa. He was part author of and a primary source for material on Malik in the *Mudawwana* of Ibn Sahnun, the most important Maliki figure in North Africa. See J. Schacht, 'Ibn al-Kasim', *EI2*.
61. Ibn Qutayba (d. 276/889) served the Abbasids and was known mostly for his literary works, although he also wrote several important religious works which upheld the Traditionist or Hanbali views that came into favour after the Abbasid *mihna*. See G. LeComte, 'Ibn Kutayba', *EI2*.
62. Ibn Surayj al-Baghdadi was a well-known Shafi'i scholar of the 3rd/9th century. He was apparently quite prolific, although none of his works seem to have been preserved. Many of them were in fact ripostes, but there does not seem to be any indication that he addressed the Ismailis. He died in 306/918 in Baghdad. See J. Schacht, 'Ibn Suraydj', *EI2*.
63. Poonawala, *Biobibliography*, pp. 62–63.
64. Begun in the time of al-Mansur, according to the *Majalis*, p. 125.
65. Poonawala, *Biobibliography*, p. 63.
66. This work has been edited by 'Arif Tamir (Beirut, 1960).

67. Poonawala, *Biobibliography*, p. 64.
68. *Ibid.* Both volumes were edited by Muhammad A'zami, and one volume by 'Adil al-'Awwa. There is some doubt as to whether in fact al-Nu'man was the author of this work.
69. This work is mentioned by Idris 'Imad al-Din, *'Uyun*, vol. 6, p. 174.
70. Poonawala, *Biobibliography*, p. 65. Poonawala notes that although the author of this work is thought to be al-Mu'izz himself, 'It is very likely that Nu'man undertook its compilation at the behest of al-Mu'izz though later it came to be ascribed to the Imam.'
71. Ed. M. Kamil Husayn (Cairo, 1948). There is also an unreliable and abridged translation by Jawad Muscati and A.M. Moulvi as *Selections from Qazi Noaman's Code of Conduct for the Followers of Imam* (Karachi, 1950).
72. This work provides a discussion of *tawhid* (unity/oneness of God), based on the teachings of al-Mu'izz (Poonawala, *Biobibliography*, p. 66).
73. *Ibid.*

Chapter 3: The *Zahiri* Framework

1. On the development of Sunni law see J. Schact, *The Origins of Muhammadan Jurisprudence* (Oxford, 1950), and N. Calder, *Studies in Early Muslim Jurisprudence* (Oxford, 1993). By the 4th/10th century the main Sunni schools either emphasized a modified use of independent judgement or *ijtihad* (as it came to be called), as did the Hanafi school, or a reliance on Prophetic *hadiths*, sometimes to the exclusion of *ijtihad*, as in the Maliki, Zahiri and Hanbali schools. The Shafi'i school was originally not a school; al-Shafi'i (d. 204/820) rather saw himself as establishing a method for deriving law. He is credited with establishing the *usul al-fiqh*, or sources of law, which he set down for the first time in his *Risala*. On al-Shafi'i see in addition E. Chaumont, 'al-Shafi'i', *EI2*.
2. On the development of Twelver Shi'ism in the aftermath of Ja'far al-Sadiq's death, and then the occultation of Muhammad al-Mahdi, see again Modarressi Tabataba'i, *Crisis and Consolidation*.
3. The effect of Fatimid success on Shi'i communities in the Mashriq is indicated by reports that some Shi'is left Baghdad for the Maghrib when al-Mahdi assumed power, in order to lend their solidarity and encourage him to conquer the east; see Halm, *The Empire of the Mahdi*, p. 182, and also F. Daftary, 'A Major Schism in the Early

Isma'ili Movement', *SI*, 77 (1993), pp. 123–139.

4. Production of authoritative doctrinal and legal works in Twelver Shi'ism continued throughout the medieval period, and then especially from the Safawid period onwards (beginning ca. 1501) when Twelver Shi'ism became dominant in Iran. See S.H. Nasr, 'Ithna 'Ashariyya', *EI2*.
5. Al-Kulayni underwent training in Qumm and eventually moved to and taught in Baghdad. While there he compiled what later came to be considered Twelver Shi'ism's most authoritative collection of *hadiths*, the *Kitab al-kafi*, a multi-volume work intended to be a comprehensive reference work. Arranged according to subject matter, the *Kafi*'s 'books' or volumes include the *Usul* (which deals with theological issues, including the *imama*), *Furu'* (which deals with *fiqh*) and *Kitab al-rawda* (which covers a miscellany of subjects), each containing only those *hadith*s considered to be established in the Shi'i tradition. See W. Madelung, 'al-Kulayni', *EI2*, and Modarressi Tabataba'i, *Crisis and Consolidation*. The other author of the 'four books' was Shaykh al-Ta'ifa Muhammad b. al-Hasan al-Tusi (d. 460/1067), whose *Istibsar* and *Tahdhib al-ahkam* are considered two of the four authoritative early Twelver Shi'i books. Sayyid Sharif al-Radi (d. 406/1015) collected the sayings and sermons of 'Ali b. Abi Talib in the equally important *Nahj al-balagha*.
6. Ibn Babawayh, also a prominent and prolific Twelver Shi'i Traditionist, composed *Man la yahduru-hu'l-faqih*. He came from a well-known family of theologians and taught in Baghdad. In his time the Abbasid state had been taken over by the Buyids. Ibn Babawayh often entered into the scholarly controversies that took place at their court. See A.A.A. Fyzee, 'Ibn Babawayh', *EI2*.
7. *Al-Usul min al-kafi* (Tehran, 1388 Sh./1968), vol. 1.
8. *Risalat al-i'tiqadat*, tr. A.A.A. Fyzee as *A Shi'ite Creed* (Bombay, 1942).
9. W. Madelung, 'The Religious Policy of the Fatimids', in *L'Égypte Fatimide*, p. 101.
10. A few minor incidents attended al-Qa'im's succession in 322/934. There was much public display of mourning over the death of al-Mahdi, and some *da'is* had assumed that he would have no successor (*Majalis*, p. 497). In another incident, some Berbers rallied around a false *mahdi* in Tripoli (*Iftitah*, p. 332).
11. Halm, *The Empire of the Mahdi*, p. 278.
12. *Ibid.*, pp. 298–325. The account of Abu Yazid's revolt is based prima-

rily on a report from Ahmad al-Marwadhi, son of the first Ismaili *qadi* of Qayrawan, who accompanied al-Mansur on his campaign. His account is also preserved, for example, by Ibn Hammad (d. 617/1220) in his *Akhbar muluk Bani 'Ubayd wa-siratihim*, ed. J. al-Badawi (Algiers, 1977).

13. Ibn Hammad, *Akhbar muluk bani 'Ubayd*, p. 47.
14. Madelung, 'The Religious Policy of the Fatimids', in *L'Égypte Fatimide*, p. 103.
15. Al-Jawdhari, *Sirat al-Ustadh Jawdhar*, ed. M.K. Husayn and M. 'Abd al-Hadi al-Sha'ira (Cairo, 1954), p. 113.
16. Al-Nu'man, *Majalis*, pp. 223, 426.
17. *Ibid.*, pp. 515–518.
18. Ibn 'Idhari, *Bayan*, vol. 1, p. 223.
19. The conquest of Egypt had been attempted three times before al-Mu'izz: twice during al-Mahdi's reign and then again during al-Qa'im's reign. On al-Qa'im's campaigns see, for example, Ibn 'Idhari, *Bayan*, vol. 1, pp. 170–173, 181–182, 209; al-Maqrizi, *Itti'az*, vol. 1, pp. 68–69, 71–72, 74; and Halm, *The Empire of the Mahdi*, pp. 196–213, 284–285. When the Fatimid general Jawhar al-Siqilli finally succeeded in conquering Egypt, he issued a guarantee of safety whose tone was very different from that issued by Abu 'Abd Allah on his conquest of Raqqada and Qayrawan. Jawhar's guarantee does not criticize the immorality of the Egyptian regime or the illegitimacy of their Abbasid overlords. Rather he argues that Fatimid presence in Egypt protected the Egyptians from threats posed by the Byzantines (who had been raiding the Syrian extension of Egyptian territory) and the Qaramita who had threatened the pilgrimage route when they seized the stone of the Ka'ba (in 317/930); see al-Maqrizi, *Itti'az*, vol. 1, pp. 103–106. During the four years between the conquest (358/969) and al-Mu'izz's arrival (in 362/973), moreover, it appears that Jawhar simply added Ismaili officials to the Egyptian administration, rather than dismissing the Sunnis already in post. See again al-Maqrizi, *Itti'az*, vol. 1, pp. 102–133, on Jawhar's initial appointments; A.F. Sayyid, *al-Dawla al-Fatimiyya fi Misr* (Cairo, 1992); and M.J. Surur, *Misr fi 'asr al-dawla al-Fatimiyya* (Cairo, 1960). On Jawhar al-Siqilli's life and career see H. 'Ali, *Ta'rikh Jawhar al-Siqilli* (Cairo, 1963).
20. The Fatimids would rule Egypt (and from there North Africa, Yemen, Syria and the Hijaz) from 358 to 567/969 to 1171.
21. Al-Nu'man, *Majalis*, for example, pp. 182–183, 216–217, 241–244, 338–342, 371–378, 391–392, 431–433, 437–439, 439–444.

22. Al-Maqrizi, *Itti'az*, vol. 1, pp. 189–202.
23. According to al-Mu'izz, Maymun was one of a number of pseudonyms devised and used by the Fatimid imams in the period of *satr* to conceal their identity from their enemies (*Majalis*, pp. 375–378). See Hamdani and de Blois, 'A Re-examination of al-Mahdi's Letter', and S. Stern, 'Heterodox Isma'ilism at the Time of al-Mu'izz', *BSOAS*, 17 (1955), pp. 10–33.
24. Al-Nu'man, *Majalis*, pp. 374–375, 439–444. On the Fatimid *da'wa* in Sind, see A. Hamdani, *The Beginnings of the Isma'ili Da'wa in Northern India* (Cairo, 1956), and S. Stern, 'Isma'ili Propaganda and Fatimid Rule in Sind', *Islamic Culture*, 23 (1949), pp. 298–307.
25. In al-Nu'man's *Asas al-ta'wil*, ed. 'A. Tamir (Beirut, 1960), and more particularly in his *al-Risala al-mudhhiba* (in *Khams rasa'il Isma'iliyya*, ed. 'A. Tamir, Beirut, 1956, pp. 27–87); and Ja'far b. Mansur al-Yaman's *Ta'wil al-zakat*, as quoted in Madelung, 'Das Imamat'.
26. For example, al-Nu'man, *Majalis*, p. 393. Al-Mu'izz apparently himself composed works defending his imamate in the context of expectations for the return of Muhammad b. Isma'il. Excerpts from these are found in later Ismaili works (see Daftary, *The Isma'ilis*, p. 178).
27. Abu Ya'qub Ishaq b. Ahmad al-Sijistani was executed for heresy by the governor of Sistan sometime after 361/971. On his contribution to Ismaili thought and especially Neoplatonic approaches in Ismaili philosophy, see Walker, *Early Philosophical Shiism: The Isma'ili Neoplatonism of Abu Ya'qub al-Sijistani*.
28. Ed. 'A. Tamir (Beirut, 1966).
29. See Daftary, *The Isma'ilis*, pp. 193, 197, 213–215, 215–218, for an overview and references on these *da'is*.
30. Wadad al-Qadi, 'An Early Fatimid Political Document', *SI*, 48 (1978), pp. 71–108.
31. Al-Qadi al-Nu'man, *Kitab al-walaya* (from *Da'a'im al-Islam*), tr. A.A.A. Fyzee as *The Book of Faith* (Bombay, 1974), pp. xii–xiii.
32. *'Uyun*, vol. 6, pp. 42–43.
33. W. al-Qadi, in her 'An Early Fatimid Political Document', dates the *Da'a'im* to around 347/958, whereas Poonawala dates the work to 349/960 in 'al-Qadi al-Nu'man and Isma'ili jurisprudence', pp. 126–127.
34. *Da'a'im al-Islam*, English trans. ed. I.K. Poonawala (New Delhi, 2002), vol. 1, p. 2.
35. *Ibid.*

36. Shiʿi law in general favours *hadith*s transmitted on the authority of the imams and rejects those from the Companions or others from the early Muslim community.
37. *Daʿaʾim*, vol. 1, pp. 5–17.
38. As a result of his widespread reputation, Jaʿfar al-Sadiq was frequented even by Sunnis of repute and founders of Sunni legal schools, such as Malik b. Anas and Abu Hanifa, while Twelver Shiʿism refers to its legal school as the Jaʿfari *madhhab*. See J. Schacht, 'Djaʿfar al-Sadiq', *EI2*, and Modarressi Tabatabaʾi, *Crisis and Consolidation*.
39. The Murjiʾa emerged, centred in Kufa and Basra, during the late Umayyad period and became prominent during the lifetime of Jaʿfar al-Sadiq. They argued that some benefit of doubt had to be given to those who professed faith but appeared not to hold to its obligations. As applied to politics, this doctrine rationalized unjust rule in the hope of avoiding the kind of civil wars that had plagued the Muslims, especially during the Umayyad period. See, for example, I. Goldziher, *Introduction to Islamic Theology and Law*, tr. A. and R. Hamori (Princeton, NJ, 1981).
40. *Daʿaʾim al-Islam*, ed. A.A.A. Fyzee (Cairo, 1951–1961), vol. 1, pp. 3–4.
41. This is a reference to those who migrated with the Prophet from Mecca to Medina in 622 (the first year of the *hijra* or emigration and beginning of the Islamic calendar), when he fled from persecution by the Meccan tribe of Quraysh for Medina, where the first Islamic state was established.
42. The duties of the heart include: avowal of faith, knowledge, complying with God's covenant, contentment, submission to the unity of God, and belief in Muhammad's prophecy and the prophets and revelations sent before him. Without this, one's profession of faith is unacceptable to God, for He said '[There are] those who said "we believe" with their mouths, but did not believe with their hearts' (5:41), and He said, 'Only with remembrance of God will the heart have rest' (13:28). The duties incumbent upon other parts of the body, in turn, involve making manifest the faith that resides in the heart. So, for example, the tongue expresses the faith of the heart, the ears permit the believer to hear the prescriptions of the faith, the eyes permit the believer to gaze on the lawful, the hands and feet to perform ablutions and prayers and to testify against the claims of the mouth on the Day of Judgement, etc. Similar *hadith*s are found in al-Kulayni, *al-Usul min al-kafi*, vol. 1, pp. 169–171,

also on the authority of Ja'far al-Sadiq.

43. *Da'a'im*, vol. 1, pp. 8–11.
44. *Ibid.*, pp. 12–13. The discussion of *iman* versus *islam* occurs in the book of *iman* and *kufr* in the second volume of the *Usul al-kafi*. The distinction also exists in the Sunni tradition: see 'Iman', *EI2*.
45. Again, a reference to the wars of the *ridda* or apostasy waged against certain Arab tribes who reverted to paganism in the first decade after the Prophet's death.
46. Knowledge here is *ma'rifa*, not the usual *'ilm*; *ma'rifa* tends to signify spiritual knowledge or gnosis.
47. According to a *hadith* from 'Ali b. Abi Talib and Ja'far al-Sadiq, whereas *kufr* or unbelief had to be condemned and fought against, those who do not acknowledge the imam of the age are merely misguided (*Da'a'im*, vol. 1, p. 11).
48. *Ibid.*, pp. 20–28.
49. On the Sunni understanding or interpretation of this verse, see for example al-Tabari's *Jami' al-bayan*, ed. M.M. Shakir (Cairo, 1950), vol. 8, pp. 495–504.
50. Abu Dharr al-Ghiffari (d. 31/651–652) was an outspoken supporter of 'Ali b. Abi Talib during the succession crisis after the Prophet's death. He is therefore considered one of the pillars of the early Shi'i cause and a reliable source for Shi'i *hadiths*.
51. *Da'a'im*, vol. 1, pp. 24–28. The *hadith* on the authority of 'Ali defines the imams as the *ahl al-dhikr* (people of remembrance) of 16:43, and the *hadith* on the authority of Abu Dharr al-Ghiffari likens the imams to Noah's ark. Both these are standard in Shi'i compilations. See E. Kohlberg, 'Some Shi'i Views of the Anti-Diluvian World', *SI*, 52 (1980), pp. 41–66; repr. in *Belief and Law in Imami Shi'ism* (Aldershot, 1991), article XVI.
52. According to Islamic tradition, Abraham was the first monotheist and thus the progenitor of not only the Judeo-Christian prophets through his son Isaac, but also of the Muslim prophet Muhammad, through his son Ishmael or Isma'il. His importance to the genealogy of monotheism is reflected in Islam's annual commemoration of his supreme test (his attempted sacrifice of his son Isaac in the Judeo-Christian tradition and of Isma'il in the Islamic tradition) as proof of his love for God.
53. *Da'a'im*, vol. 1, pp. 28–38.
54. This particular reference to the majority is directed at the Hanbalis.
55. Ja'far al-Sadiq notes references to David's family in 34:13, Pharaoh's

family in 40:28, the houses of Moses and Aaron in 2:248, as well as the family of Yasin (*Al* Yasin, instead of *il*-Yasin in 37:130).

56. Also 14:37, in which Abraham says, 'I have settled some of my children, Lord, in a valley near Your sacred house, so that they may constantly worship; so put in the hearts of men some kindness for them [his descendants].' Ja'far al-Sadiq adds that this refers to the Prophet, 'Ali, Fatima, Hasan and Husayn, as they were the only ones from among the 'progeny' of Abraham who did not worship idols (*Da'a'im*, vol. 1, p. 33).
57. The community is of Abraham's descendants, about whom it is said (3:104): 'Let there be a community from among you who call to the good and command what is permissible, and forbid what is wrong. They are the ones who will be successful.'
58. *Da'a'im*, vol. 1, pp. 35–38.
59. *Ibid.*, pp. 15–16. Also, see al-Tabari, *Jami' al-bayan*, vol. 9, pp. 516–531, for a Sunni commentary on 5:3, and vol. 10, pp. 467–472, for a commentary on 5:67. Reflecting Sunni tradition, al-Tabari does not associate these two verses with the designation of 'Ali, but rather with a final restatement of faith at the time of the Farewell Pilgrimage.
60. See *Kafi*, vol. 1, p. 287, for a variant. Here 'Ali gives a beggar 1,000 dinars that had been sent to the Prophet by the Negus of Ethiopia.
61. *Da'a'im*, vol. 1, pp. 15–16. The clan of 'Abd al-Muttalib, the Prophet's grandfather, was led after his death by a number of his sons in succession. Shortly after the Prophet's birth, his own father 'Abd Allah died and his grandfather assumed guardianship over him. When both the Prophet's mother and grandfather later also died, he became the ward of his uncle Abu Talib (the father of 'Ali) who was now the leader of the clan. When Abu Talib died, the next in line for leadership of the clan was Abu Lahab who, unlike his brothers or other uncles of the Prophet, disliked his nephew (and therefore refused to assume guardianship over him), and conspired with his enemies to persecute the Prophet. Abu Lahab's breach of tribal traditions of conduct and his animosity towards the Prophet earned him the dubious honour of being the only enemy of Islam to earn divine condemnation by name, in *Surat al-Lahab* or *Surat al-masad* (Qur'an, sura 111): 'The power of Abu Lahab will perish, and this for all his wealth and profit, for he will be plunged in hell-fire, and his wife the "wood-carrier" will be choked by a halter of flaming palm-fibre (*masad*).'
62. *Da'a'im*, vol. 1, pp. 17–18. In addition, the verses 9:19–21, 11:17 and

7:142 also convey 'Ali's preferred status over other Companions, his designation as successor and his relationship to the Prophet being as Aaron's was to Moses (pp. 18–20).

63. *Da'a'im*, vol. 1, pp. 38–45. See Azim Nanji, 'An Isma'ili Theory of *Walayah* in the *Da'a'im al-Islam* of Qadi al-Nu'man', in Donald Little, ed., *Essays On Islamic Civilization Presented to Niyazi Berkes* (Leiden, 1976), pp. 260–273, and the introduction to *Urjuza al-mukhtara*, ed. I.K. Poonawala (Montreal, 1970).
64. Mu'tazilism is a rationalist theological school that held that the Qur'an was created and not eternal with God. The political ramifications of this position meant that if the Qur'an was created then it was open to interpretation by the leader or imam according to the circumstances of his era. The doctrine of the created Qur'an became official under the Abbasid caliph al-Ma'mun (d. 218/833) and was later suppressed under Caliph al-Mutawwakil (d. 247/861). On the Murji'a, see note 39 above.
65. The Kharijis (from the Arabic *khawarij* or 'those who go out') held that in agreeing to arbitration at the Battle of Siffin in 37/657, 'Ali b. Abi Talib had betrayed himself as rightful imam (since 'judgement is God's', they argued), and had thus lapsed into unbelief.
66. See, for example, Ibn Qutayba's *al-Imama wa'l-siyasa* ('Leadership and Politics'), ed. K. Mansour (Beirut, 1997). Ibn Qutayba presents a generally Sunni position on the issue of Abu Bakr's succession to the Prophet and the succession after him of the remaining caliphs, as well as the Umayyads and the Abbasids up to the time of Harun al-Rashid (d. 170/786). However, in the section dealing with Abu Bakr's election he includes a *hadith* from Ibn 'Abbas where he goes to pledge allegiance to 'Ali after the Prophet's death, in light of Ghadir Khumm. But 'Ali asks him first if the Companions would accept this. So Ibn 'Abbas goes to Abu Bakr and asks him whether or not he had been deputized by the Prophet in any way, and he says no. Then Ibn 'Abbas asks the same of 'Umar and receives the same reply (p. 8). The incorporation of this *hadith* in Ibn Qutayba's narrative is indicative of the Sunni acknowledgement that 'Ali's rights had been usurped, even if by such worthwhile individuals as Abu Bakr and 'Umar.
67. 'Amr b. al-'As (d. 43/663) was a late convert and a military commander who most famously conquered Egypt in 19/640. 'Usama b. Zayd was the son of the Prophet's adopted son Zayd, who led a military expedition to Syria in the time of Abu Bakr.
68. *Da'a'im*, vol. 1, pp. 40–42.

69. *Ibid.*, pp. 43–45.
70. *Ibid.*: 'On the stations of the imams' (pp. 45–55); 'On the counsel of the imams' (pp. 55–67); 'On loving kindness for the imams' (pp. 67–78).
71. *Ibid.*, p. 47.
72. *Ibid.*, p. 49. Al-Mughira b. Sa'id was also known for attempting to introduce pre-Islamic Manichaean gnostic ideas into Shi'i thought, such as an anthropomorphic description of God and belief in the mystical properties of letters. On his influence and the tendency that he initiated, see Daftary, *The Isma'ilis*, pp. 72–73.
73. *Da'a'im*, vol. 1, pp. 49–50. On Abu'l-Khattab and his followers, see again Daftary, *The Isma'ilis*, pp. 89, 96–100.
74. *Da'a'im*, vol. 1, pp. 51–53.
75. *Ibid.*, pp. 54–55.
76. *Ibid.*, p. 56.
77. *Ibid.*, pp. 57–58. See also p. 59 for a *hadith* from Ja'far al-Sadiq in which he supports al-Mufaddal's rejection of some followers in Kufa who did not perform the obligatory acts or *fara'id*. Al-Mufaddal b. 'Umar al-Ju'fi was one of the more radical members of Ja'far al-Sadiq's circle early on, who nevertheless modified his views after the imam's death. And although he ultimately supported the cause of Musa al-Kazim, he did not condemn the followers of Isma'il.
78. *Da'a'im*, vol. 1, pp. 56–67.
79. *Ibid.*, p. 59.
80. *Ibid.*
81. *Ibid.*, p. 60.
82. *Ibid.*, pp. 60–61.
83. *Ibid.*, pp. 62–67.
84. *Ibid.*, pp. 64–65.
85. *Ibid.*, p. 62.
86. *Ibid.*, pp. 67–78.
87. *Ibid.*, pp. 68–69, 71. 'Abd Allah b. 'Abbas (d. ca. 60s/680s) was also the progenitor of the future Abbasid caliphs. In Sunni tradition, Ibn 'Abbas's position is given a different interpretation. See al-Tabari, *Jami' al-bayan*, vol. 25, pp. 23–25. Here several transmissions of a *hadith* from Ibn 'Abbas are provided, in which he identifies *qurba* (kinsmen) as all of the Prophet's relations among the Quraysh. Al-Nu'man acknowledges this when he argues elsewhere that Ibn 'Abbas changed his position when he became excluded from the succession himself.
88. Hasan al-Basri (d. 110/728) was an early and famous ascetic, who

was also inclined to Mu'tazili thought. He is known mostly as an exemplar in the Sufi tradition. See 'Hasan al-Basri', *EI2*, and al-Tabari's *Jami' al-bayan*, vol. 25, p. 26, for Hasan al-Basri's interpretation of *qurba*, which he also rejects.

89. *Da'a'im*, vol. 1, p. 72.
90. And also in verses 39:9, 29:49 and 58:11; *Da'a'im*, vol. 1, p. 79.
91. For example, the well-known *hadith* of the Prophet, 'Many a learned man is not a jurist, and many a jurist conveys knowledge to one more learned', and one from 'Ali in which he states, 'Let not the ignorant be ashamed to learn, or the learned be too arrogant to confess their ignorance' (*Ibid.*, pp. 80–81).
92. *Ibid.*, p. 80.
93. *Ibid.*, p. 81. Referring to another *hadith* saying that the learned should not engage in the world, al-Nu'man comments that the Prophet meant they should not seek power. He adds further that this refers to the leaders of the rebels and wrongdoers, not to the imams.
94. *Ibid.*, p. 84.
95. *Ibid.*, pp. 85–86.
96. *Ibid.*, pp. 86–87.
97. *Ibid.*, p. 87.
98. *Ibid.*, pp. 88–89.
99. *Ibid.*, p. 91.
100. *Ibid.*, pp. 92–95.
101. This recalls the debates of the early Fatimid period, and the occasional agreement between Hanafis and Ismailis in them.
102. *Da'a'aim*, vol. 1, pp. 95–98.
103. *Ibid.*, p. 98.
104. In fact Prophetic *hadith*s began to be important much earlier, in the time of the Umayyads. T. Khalidi, in his *Arabic Historical Thought in the Classical Period* (Cambridge, 1994), argues that *hadith*s came to play a role in justifying or opposing Umayyad rule in the time of 'Abd al-Malik (d. 86/705) and the second civil war, and began to be recorded and systematized at that time for the purpose of wider dissemination (pp. 17–28). Regarding al-Shafi'i's role in establishing Sunni *usul al-fiqh*, see W.B. Hallaq, 'Was al-Shafi'i the Master Architect of Islamic Jurisprudence?', *IJMES*, 25 (1993), pp. 587–605; and his *Islamic Legal Theories: An Introduction to Sunni usul al-fiqh* (Cambridge, 1997). Hallaq plays down al-Shafi'i's role in the development of Sunni *usul*, arguing that the *Risala* does not clearly establish the acceptable sources of law.

105. Having presumably established the importance of Prophetic *hadith*s, al-Shafiʿi's *Risala* was surprisingly not followed by any other systematic treatment of *usul* from the Sunnis until the 5th/11th century. Al-Nuʿman's *Ikhtilaf* thus stands out as a significant contribution to the development of Islamic legal theory, and might well have prompted subsequent Sunni formulations.
106. Al-Nuʿman, *Ikhtilaf*, ed. Lokhandwala, pp. 91–92.
107. As opposed to the *furuʿ* section of the *Kafi*, which are the volumes that actually deal with *ʿibadat* and *muʿamalat*, that correspond to the *Daʿaʾim*'s two *ajzaʾ*.
108. Al-Kulayni, *Kafi*, vol. 1, pp. 2–9.
109. *Ibid.*, p. 8.
110. *Ibid.*, p. 180. Muhammad al-Baqir said: '[The knowledge of God] is belief in God and His Messenger, and ʿAli and the rightly guided imams.'
111. *Ibid.*, p. 187. Also, Muhammad al-Baqir adds that 'Love of us is *iman*, and hatred of us is *kufr*' (p. 188). Similarly Jaʿfar al-Sadiq says in the *Daʿaʾim*, 'He was asked about the saying of the Prophet: "He who dies without knowing the imam of his time, dies the death of 'ignorance' (*jahiliyan*)"' (vol. 1, p. 25).
112. *Ibid.*, pp. 178–179.
113. *Ibid.*, pp. 192–193.
114. *Ibid.*, p. 194.
115. E. Kohlberg, 'Imam and Community in the Pre-Ghayba Period', in S. Arjomand, ed., *Authority and Political Culture in Shiʿism* (Albany, NY, 1988), pp. 25–53; repr. in his *Belief and Law in Imami Shiʿism* (Aldershot, 1991), article XVI.
116. Al-Kulayni, *Kafi*, vol. 1, pp. 223–227. ʿAli inherited knowledge of 120,000 prophets before him, and the imams have knowledge of all versions of scripture.
117. *Ibid.*, pp. 227–228.
118. *Ibid.*, pp. 230–231.
119. *Ibid.*, pp. 238–240.
120. *Ibid.*, pp. 242–253.
121. *Ibid.*, pp. 256–258.
122. *Ibid.*, pp. 258–260.
123. *Ibid.*, pp. 223–227, 230–238.
124. *Ibid.*, pp. 292–297.
125. This was the occasion for the revelation of verse 57:25, 'For We have sent messengers before with the Book and the Balance that men may stand forth in justice'.

126. al-Kulayni, *Kafi*, vol. 1, p. 294.
127. *Ibid.*, pp. 296–297.
128. *Ibid.*, pp. 214–216, 232–233, on other talismans believed to be in the possession of the rightful imams, and pp. 235–242, on the *mushaf* of Fatima.
129. Fyzee, *A Shiʿite Creed*, pp. 92–93.
130. *Ibid.*, p. 95.
131. *Ibid.*
132. *Ibid.*, pp. 96–98.
133. *Ibid.*, pp. 113–116.
134. *Ibid.*, pp. 107–108.

Chapter 4: *Zahiri* Paradigms

1. Khalidi neglects Shiʿi literature, however, and only once addresses Ismaili Shiʿism in his discussion of different approaches to historical time in Islamic thought. After considering the influence of Neoplatonic ideas on the philosophy of history in the works of Ibn Rushd, Ibn Sina and al-Farabi, he nevertheless dismisses the formulation of the contemporary Ismaili philosopher Abu Yaʿqub al-Sijistani, commenting that the 'Ismaʿili vision of time and prophecy bears little resemblance to any Arabic Islamic conception of time' (Tarif Khalidi, *Arabic Historical Thought in the Classical Period*, Cambridge, 1994, p. 162).
2. *Ibid.*, p. xi.
3. *Ibid.*, p. 83.
4. *Ibid.*, pp. 17–81.
5. *Ibid.*, pp. 62–63.
6. Written around 346/957 in the time of the Imam-caliph al-Muʿizz, like the *Daʿaʾim*, the *Iftitah* came at the end of a process of refinement preceded by other historical works, and during a period in Fatimid rule of consolidation and preparation for the conquest of Egypt.
7. See J. Lindsay, 'Prophetic Parallels in Abu ʿAbdallah al-Shiʿi's Mission among the Kutama Berbers'.
8. They include the *Maʿalim al-Mahdi*, *Dhat al-mihan* (dealing with the rebellion of Abu Yazid as well as the biographies al-Qa'im and al-Mansur), the *Dhat al-minan* (on al-Muʿizz), the *Kitab al-manaqib wa'l-mathalib* (on the virtues of the Banu Hashim and the vices of the Umayyads).
9. Stern concluded that the *Majalis* was completed no later than

351/962 ('Heterodox Isma'ilism in the time of al-Mu'izz'). However, the editors of the text argue that it was written between 358 and 360/968 and 971, based on an account in it which mentions the forthcoming marriages of al-Nu'man's sons, which, given their births in 329/941 and 340/951–952, could not have occurred before 358/968 (*Kitab al-majalis wa'l-musayarat*, ed. H. Faqi, I. Shabbuh and M. Ya'lawi, Tunis, 1978; 2nd ed. Beirut, 1997, pp. 18–19).

10. Khalidi, *Arab Historical Thought*, p. 97. About *adab*, Khalidi says, 'One could argue that the classical Greek "Paideia" is a more accurate rendering of the term since *adab*, like Paideia, refers to a process of moral and intellectual education designed to produce an *adib*, a gentleman-scholar' (*Ibid*., p. 83).
11. *Ibid*., p. 114.
12. *Majalis*, p. 43.
13. Al-Maqrizi, *al-Khitat*, vol. 1, pp. 390–391, M.K. Husayn, *Fi adab Misr al-Fatimiyya*, pp. 23–41, and S. Stern, 'Cairo as the Centre of the Isma'ili movement', in *Colloque international sur l'histoire du Caire* (Cairo, 1972), pp. 437–450.
14. Stern, 'Heterodox Isma'ilism at the Time of al-Mu'izz'.
15. The historical value of the *Majalis* also led to excerpts from it being presented early on in Ivanow's *Creed of the Fatimids*, and along with the *Iftitah* it is the major source for Dachraoui's *Le Califat Fatimide au Maghreb* and Halm's *The Empire of the Mahdi*.
16. *Majalis*, pp. 60–65.
17. *Ibid*., pp. 94–95. See also pp. 501, 542, and 555.
18. *Ibid*., pp. 210–211.
19. *Ibid*., pp. 283–284. For other accounts that deal with al-Mu'izz's abilities see also pp. 69, 126, 133, 248–249 and 286.
20. *Ibid*., p. 240.
21. *Ibid*., pp. 251–252.
22. *Ibid*., pp. 266–267.
23. *Ibid*., pp. 382–383. See also pp. 433, 463, 466, 514, and 521–523.
24. *Ibid*., for example, p. 132.
25. *Ibid*., for example, pp. 64, 93, 121–123.
26. *Ibid*., pp. 142–148.
27. *Ibid*., pp. 319–320.
28. *Ibid*., for example, p. 295.
29. *Ibid*., pp. 309–310.
30. *Ibid*., pp. 85–86.
31. *Ibid*., pp. 54, 56, 209, 213, 258–289, 313, 343, 362–363, 515. In one session al-Nu'man recalls al-Mu'izz complaining about the follow-

ers of his predecessors, al-Mahdi, al-Qa'im and al-Mansur, who did not record anything of their wisdom and knowledge, except for the outward meaning of their orders, and their management of the affairs of the world during their respective reigns (pp. 156–157). And yet the merit of the imams is their wisdom and knowledge of the *zahir* and *batin* (pp. 327–329), and that is why al-Nu'man desires to record this imam's every word (p. 224).

32. See, for example, *ibid.*, pp. 129, 133, 239, 253, 311–312, 364, 385, 508, 556. In one dream, al-Mansur is approached by a man with a piece of paper inscribed with several circles. As al-Mansur looks on, a spot of black ink expands to cover almost the entire page. The man tells al-Mansur to put his finger on the page, and wherever he does, the ink recedes. In this manner, al-Mansur realized he would defeat Abu Yazid (pp. 113–114). Some of the imams' dreams also feature exceptional historical figures. For example, with regard to a new palace that he seeks to build, al-Mu'izz has a dream in which he consults with the classical astronomer Ptolemy on the most auspicious date to begin the project (pp. 326–327).
33. *Ibid.*, pp. 57–59.
34. *Ibid.*, p. 65.
35. *Ibid.*, p. 83.
36. *Ibid.*, pp. 97 and 393–394 respectively.
37. *Ibid.*, p. 107.
38. *Ibid.*, p. 535.
39. Al-Mansur gives al-Mu'izz a large book in the hand of al-Mahdi and instructs him to copy it, and recalls how he had been made to do the same in the time of al-Qa'im. Then al-Qa'im appears to him in a dream and instructs him in its meaning (pp. 130–131).
40. Al-Mahdi gives al-Mansur a large book which deals with medicine for the soul or *'ilm al-batin* (pp. 502–503). In one account, al-Mu'izz discusses the Prophet's bequest of the sword Dhu'l-fiqar to 'Ali, and likens it to the knowledge that he transmitted to his descendants (pp. 208–209).
41. Al-Mansur trains al-Mu'izz in disputation and debate (p. 117).
42. Al-Mu'izz recalls when al-Mansur instructed him on what to do as he lay on his deathbed (pp. 93, 96 and 241). It is because the imams inherit knowledge from God through each other that they know what will happen in future generations (pp. 271–272).
43. See, for example, *ibid.*, pp. 83–85.
44. *Ibid.*, pp. 84–85.
45. When the imam had continued to demonstrate the use of reason

in establishing truth, al-Nuʿman marvels at the profundity of his explanation and then contemptuously notes that the *daʿis* present could not even comprehend the *zahir* of what the imam was saying (*Ibid.*, p. 147).

46. On one occasion al-Nuʿman recalls the imam mentioning a certain *daʿi* who had allowed the forbidden and instructed people to sin in order to prove that God was forgiving. Al-Muʿizz exclaims that such apostates defame the imams and ascribe repugnant things to them, and the imams wash their hands of such deviants and curse them (*Ibid.*, p. 105). See also pp. 198–199, 216, 237, 406–408, 419–420, 452, 478–481, 496–499, 515–516, 524, 548–550.
47. *Ibid.*, pp. 198–199.
48. See especially Stern, 'Heterodox Ismaʿilism'. For the use of the *Majalis* for information on *daʿwa* organization and hierarchy, see A. Hamdani's 'Evolution of the Organisational Structure of the Fatimi Daʿwah', and Ivanow's 'The Organization of Fatimid Propaganda'.
49. By way of illustration, al-Nuʿman mentions one *daʿi* who had been entrusted with purchasing items for the imams. One of the things he was ordered to buy was musk, which he would test on his own clothing. Because its scent lingered, he took from his own money the cost of the fragrance he had used and added it to the items he was sending to the imams (*Majalis*, pp. 91, 157).
50. In one session on the virtues of some of the members of the *daʿwa*, al-Muʿizz recalls receiving a book on the activities of the *daʿwa* in the east, and this leads him to praise some of its members, and to remember their trustworthiness in collecting dues for the imams from their respective *jaziras* (*Ibid.*, pp. 405–407). This account, however, continues with the imam's complaints about other *daʿis* who deviated by permitting the forbidden and mixing philosophy with religion. These are possibly oblique references to al-Muʿizz's problems with the writings of *daʿis* like Abu Yaʿqub al-Sijistani. (See Daftary, *The Ismaʿilis*, for a discussion of al-Muʿizz's relationship with al-Sijistani.)
51. *Majalis*, pp. 467–477.
52. See, for example, *Majalis*, pp. 98, 106, 108, 119, 141, 203, 219, 220, 222, 245, 248, 255, 321–323, 561–562.
53. *Ibid.*, pp. 138–139. And yet, in another account, when a delegation of *daʿis* from various regions encourage al-Muʿizz to begin the conquest of the east, he remarks that the time has to be right, and recalls that al-Mahdi did not expect al-Qa'im to conquer Egypt when he sent him on expeditions (pp. 475–477).

54. Cf. pp. 82, 135, 155–156, 272–273, 291–293, 297, 307–308, 348–351, 357–359, 397, 428, 434, 525, 543–544, 546, 547. These accounts feature al-Nu'man in consultation with the imams on a variety of issues. In some he learns of, or remarks on, the wisdom of the imams, in others he is charged with administrative and judicial responsibilities, and of course in many he discusses the works that the imams commissioned from him. In some accounts, al-Nu'man and al-Mu'izz discuss such personal matters as marriage prospects for his sons (as mentioned above), as well as the houses al-Nu'man wants to build for his children. In addition, the imams often praise al-Nu'man's services to them, and defend him when he is criticized by others. In one account al-Mu'izz reminds al-Nu'man of once when he was slandered in the imam's presence, and adds that he could not doubt al-Nu'man's loyalty and love for the imams or treat the slanderer's insult with seriousness. Al-Nu'man rejoices at this vote of confidence from the imam (pp. 358–359).
55. A history of the Fatimid state (most probably the *Iftitah*), *Majalis*, p. 118; the *Manaqib wa-mathalib*, p. 118; a refutation of the *tafsir* of the *ahl al-Sunna*, p. 135; a record of the wisdom of Imam al-Mu'izz, p. 297; the *Majalis* itself, pp. 301–302; the *Da'a'im*, p. 305; the *Kitab al-dinar* (a short work of instruction that would only cost a dinar), p. 360; another book about the wisdom of al-Mu'izz, p. 401; an *urjuza* which is a biography of Mu'izz (the *Dhat al-minan*?), p. 462; another Book of Wisdom, p. 545.
56. *Majalis*, pp. 351–353. Al-Nu'man's worries had most probably to do more with a lack of reappointment under al-Mu'izz (he reached the post of *qadi* of Ifriqiya in the time of al-Mansur). Although he did not regain such official rank under al-Mu'izz, he nevertheless attained a greater proximity to the imam, as has already been noted.
57. *Ibid.*, pp. 232–234. See also pp. 137–138, pp. 440–441. There are times when al-Mu'izz is also driven to anger or complaint against the common people. On one occasion, he complains about their ingratitude (p. 120), and on another occasion he curses them for their wickedness (p. 290).
58. *Ibid.*, pp. 249–250. See also pp. 251 and 307–309, in which al-Nu'man endures the criticism of fellow judges indicating rifts in the judicial apparatus. Again on pp. 334–335, governors (or tax collectors) appointed by al-Mu'izz to collect the *khums* begin to bicker among themselves. On pp. 337–338, al-Nu'man convinces the inhabitants of Mahdiyya of the necessity of collecting the *khums*.

59. *Ibid.*, pp. 361–362.
60. *Ibid.*, pp. 121, 457.
61. *Ibid.*, pp. 211–212.
62. *Ibid.*, p. 259.
63. See, for example, pp. 153–156 and 304–306, in which al-Muʿizz complains that the people and government officials do not seek the knowledge of the imams as much as they should.
64. Al-Qadi al-Nuʿman's instruction of novices in the *daʿwa* here indicates his status as the imam's spokesperson on matters of doctrine.
65. *Majalis*, pp. 388–390. This account is evidence of the *majalis* sessions that the Fatimids themselves conducted in North Africa, although they were clearly not as organized as later in Egypt.
66. This appears to be the only date explicitly mentioned in the work; hence Stern's dating.
67. *Majalis*, pp. 556–560. See also al-Maqrizi, *Ittiʿaz*, vol. 1, p. 136, for another report based on this account of the event. He states that in Ifriqiya altogether 12,000 were circumcised, and in Sicily as many as 25,000.
68. P. Sanders, *Ritual, Politics and the City in Fatimid Cairo* (Albany, NY, 1994), especially pp. 75–82, 135–137.
69. F. Dachraoui, 'Muʿizz li-Din Allah', *EI2*. Dachraoui also notes the importance of this work for understanding Fatimid doctrines of this time.
70. *Majalis*, pp. 164–196. The account contains a long critique of a work on the *fada'il* of the Umayyads that their ambassador presents to al-Muʿizz. Different accounts of the same events are included, for example, in Ibn al-Athir's *al-Kamil*, vol. 6, pp. 185 ff. After the defeat of the Umayyads by the Abbasids in the 2nd/8th century, members of the Umayyad dynasty escaped to Spain, where they established an independent state in 138/756. Following the establishment of the Fatimid caliphate in North Africa, the Umayyads under ʿAbd al-Rahman III (d. 350/961) declared themselves caliphs as well, in an attempt to shore up their legitimacy and claim to the Iberian peninsula and the western Mediterranean. See W.M. Watt and P. Cachia, *A History of Islamic Spain* (Edinburgh, 1965) for a survey of this period in Spanish history.
71. These events also took place in 345/955–956. The Byzantines eventually surrendered Calabria and decided to pay a tribute to the Fatimids. In one account members of a Sicilian embassy complain to al-Muʿizz over his preferential treatment of the Kutama despite their assistance in situations such as the above. Al-Muʿizz replies

that their services were made under the compulsion of slavery, whereas the Kutama served the imams voluntarily (*Majalis*, pp. 246–247).

72. Subsequently another Fatimid offensive against the Byzantines in 359/960 resulted in the surrender of the port of Taormina across the straits from Sicily in southern Italy.
73. On genealogy see, for example, pp. 116 and 234–235 in the *Majalis*, where the Umayyads are compared to the Qur'anic 'cursed tree'.
74. *Ibid*., pp. 192–193.
75. *Ibid*., pp. 114–115, in which al-Muʿizz explains how it was that the Abbasids came to claim possession of ʿAli's sword Dhu'l-fiqar, and pp. 330–331, in which al-Muʿizz expresses contempt for a book on the *fada'il* of the Abbasids. The Abbasids also come under criticism for their immorality, as on p. 347. See also pp. 402–405 for an account of the Abbasid caliph Maʿmun's recognition of the Twelver imam ʿAli al-Rida.
76. Jawhar's appointment as general over the Kutama apparently generated some opposition because he was a former slave. In a lengthy session on al-Muʿizz's praise of the Kutama, he also justifies having put Jawhar in command over them (pp. 256–257). See also Chapter 5, note 45 below.
77. *Ibid*., p. 434.
78. Also on Ibn Wasul, see pp. 217, 388–391, 412, 417 and 458–459. Al-Muʿizz obtained the surrender or allegiance of smaller states beyond the region. One account describes the visit of a delegation on behalf of a Hasanid pretender in Yemen, whom al-Muʿizz won over to his cause (pp. 413–414).
79. Dachraoui, 'al-Muʿizz', *EI2*. Dachraoui argues further that the move to Egypt was only a response to Qarmati attacks on the Syrian provinces of Egypt, which al-Muʿizz otherwise viewed as merely an eastern appendage to his empire. This is unlikely to be the only reason given the long-standing Fatimid interest in Egypt, the evidence of their *daʿwa* there and, most importantly, al-Muʿizz's investment in the control and administration of Egypt under Jawhar.
80. *Majalis*, pp. 366–370.
81. See Dachraoui, 'al-Muʿizz', for Hamdanid–Byzantine relations. Briefly, the jihad of the Hamdanid state against the southern flank of the Byzantine empire had provoked a Byzantine counter-attack on the coast of Syria.
82. *Majalis*, pp. 442–446.

Chapter 5: The *Zahiri* Order

1. On this see P. Vatikiotis's rather dated, *The Fatimid Theory of State* (Lahore, 1957).
2. See Sanders, *Ritual, Politics, and the City in Fatimid Cairo*, and M. Canard, 'Le cérémonial Fatimite et le cérémonial Byzantin: Essai de comparison', *Byzantion*, 21 (1951), pp. 355–420. Both have used the *Kitab al-himma* for information on Fatimid ceremonial.
3. See Daftary, *The Isma*ʿ*ilis*, pp. 643–644 for a review of the scholarship on administrative aspects of Fatimid rule, and the importance of medieval sources such as al-Qalqashandi's *Subh al-*ʿ*asha*, Ibn al-Sayrafi's *al-Ishara ila man nala al-wizara* and Ibn Mammati's *Kitab qawanin al-dawawin*.
4. Al-Nuʿman, *Kitab al-himma fi adab atba*ʿ *al-a'imma*, ed. M. Kamil Husayn (Cairo, 1948), pp. 33–34.
5. This is followed by a long digression on the choice of title for the book, and an apology for its brevity and the inadequacy of the knowledge of its author (*Ibid*., pp. 34–36).
6. *Ibid*., p. 36.
7. *Ibid*., pp. 36–37.
8. *Ibid*., pp. 38–39.
9. *Ibid*., pp. 40–41.
10. *Ibid*., pp. 45–46.
11. This term is later used interchangeably with *khums* and *zakat*. Thus *amanat* refers to both *khums*, or dues given to the family of the Prophet, and *zakat* or the alms tax collected by the state on behalf of all Muslims. After the transfer of the Fatimid state to Egypt, a voluntary contribution (*najwa*) was also submitted by Ismailis attending the *majalis al-hikma* held weekly in the palace. See al-Maqrizi, *al-Khitat*, vol. 1, pp. 390–391, and vol. 2, pp. 341–342; Husayn, *Fi adab Misr al-Fatimiyya*, pp. 33–41; and Stern, 'Cairo as the Centre of the Fatimid Movement', on the institution and curriculum of, and fees collected in, the *majalis* of Fatimid Egypt.
12. *Kitab al-himma*, pp. 41–44.
13. This verse is an allusion to the pledge of a group of Muslims to the Prophet at Hudaybiyya.
14. *Kitab al-himma*, p. 48.
15. *Ibid*., pp. 50–54.
16. *Ibid*., pp. 54–56.
17. *Ibid*., pp. 56–59.

18. *Ibid.*, pp. 59–66.
19. *Ibid.*, p. 73.
20. *Ibid.*, pp. 74–78.
21. *Ibid.*, pp. 78– 81.
22. *Ibid.*, pp. 81–84.
23. *Ibid.*, pp. 85–90.
24. *Ibid.*, pp. 90–93.
25. *Ibid.*, pp. 93–96.
26. *Ibid.*, pp. 97–99.
27. *Ibid.*, pp. 99–100.
28. *Ibid.*, pp. 127–131.
29. *Ibid.*, pp. 122–125.
30. *Ibid.*, pp. 131–136.
31. *Ibid.*, pp. 136–140.
32. *Ibid.*, pp. 103–104.
33. *Ibid.*, pp. 104–109.
34. *Ibid.*, pp. 109–110.
35. *Ibid.*, pp. 110–111.
36. *Ibid.*, pp. 111–112.
37. *Ibid.*, p. 110.
38. *Ibid.*, pp. 112–113.
39. *Ibid.*, pp. 116–119.
40. See Canard, 'Le cérémonial Fatimite et le cérémonial Byzantin'.
41. Al-Nu'man, *Da'a'im*, vol. 1, pp. 350–368.
42. Wadad al-Qadi, 'An Early Fatimid Political Document', *SI*, 48 (1978), pp. 71–108. In her study of the text of the *'ahd*, al-Qadi discusses authorship and dating, and based on her findings, speculates that the *'ahd* was written in the time of al-Mahdi, in an effort both to justify the execution of Abu 'Abd Allah al-Shi'i and to appeal for support from the people against the *khassa* or notables. Although ultimately conjectural, al-Qadi presents a strong argument against the claim that 'Ali b. Abi Talib was the author, based on its representation of the conditions and political realities of a later period. See also Gerald Salinger's translation of the *'ahd* in his 'A Muslim Mirror for Princes', *Muslim World*, 46 (1956), pp. 24–39, as well as in his *The Kitab al-jihad* (Ph.D. thesis, Columbia University, 1953). Lev, in *State and Society in Fatimid Egypt*, also discusses al-Qadi's analysis of the *'ahd*. For an alternative view asserting 'Ali's authorship, see Reza Shah-Kazemi, *Justice and Remembrance: Introducing the Spirituality of Iman 'Ali* (London, 2006), especially Chapter 2 and Appendix II.

43. Al-Qadi further observes: 'In a way, then, the *'ahd* represents the first political *constitution* of the Fatimid State after its final establishment as a *Dawla*. It is for this very reason that al-Qadi al-Nu'man had to record it, perhaps under the influence of al-Mu'izz li-Din Allah, in his *Da'a'im al-Islam*. ... With the *'ahd*'s incorporation in the *Da'a'im*, the *Da'a'im* came to represent not only the paramount *divine constitution* of the Fatimid State but also the *civil constitution* of the state' (*Ibid*., p. 104).
44. *Ibid*., p. 100.
45. Al-Qa'id Jawhar b. 'Abd Allah al-Siqilli, also known as al-Katib, was a freed man of the Fatimids, possibly of Sicilian origin. He was appointed secretary under al-Mansur (hence al-Katib), and under al-Mu'izz was selected to undertake a campaign to pacify the far Maghrib. See A.I. Hasan, *Ta'rikh Jawhar al-Siqilli* (Cairo, 1963); Idris 'Imad al-Din, *'Uyun*, vol. 6, pp. 135–202; al-Maqrizi, *al-Khitat*, vol. 1, pp. 377–379; his *Itti'az*, vol. 1, pp. 105–120; Ibn Khallikan, *Wafayat*, vol. 1, pp. 34–347; al-Jawdhari, *Sirat al-Ustadh Jawdhar*; al-Nu'man, *Majalis*, pp. 217, 256, 546; and Halm, *The Empire of the Mahdi*, pp. 396–401. Jawhar is credited with having consolidated Fatimid power in Egypt both internally and externally during his rule. In terms of internal consolidation, he initiated economic and political reforms (which consisted of setting up a shadow administration composed of North Africans that acted in conjunction with the former Ikhshidid administration), held *diwans* and presided over court sessions, and was daily consulted by the vizier Abu Fadl. He also occupied himself with the expansion of the Egyptian empire abroad, namely in Syria and the Hijaz. The Qaramita attacks on Egypt had been repulsed and periodic attacks in the regions of Syria were dealt with. See also an account of this period in al-Maqrizi's *Itti'az*, vol. 1, pp. 102–150.
46. Ibn Khallikan, *Wafayat*, vol. 8, p. 341.
47. Ya'qub Ibn Killis came originally from Baghdad, and entered the service of the Ikhshidids under Kafur. Towards the end of Kafur's reign, he fell out of favour, defected to al-Mu'izz's court, and after converting, returned with him to Egypt. He was put in charge of finances and eventually appointed vizier in the time of al-Aziz. See J.W. Fischel, *Jews in the Economic and Political Life of Mediaeval Islam* (London, 1937), and Husayn, *Fi adab Misr al-Fatimiyya*, on his religious writings after converting. As for 'Usluj b. Hasan, not much is known about him; he is mentioned in connection with Ibn Killis in the sources, and with regard to his role in the financial

reforms and the administration of Egypt under al-Muʿizz. His importance is underscored by the fact that he and al-Qadi al-Nuʿman were the only two members of al-Muʿizz's train in his entry to Cairo not required to dismount. See Idris ʿImad al-Din, *ʿUyun*, vol. 6, p. 192, and al-Maqrizi, *Ittiʿaz*, vol. 1, pp. 144–145, on al-Muʿizz's decree of 363/976–977, which placed Ibn Killis and ʿUsluj b. Hasan in charge of the *kharaj* (land tax), *hisba* (market supervision), *sawahil* and *qawali* (coastal/shipping and grazing dues), *ahbas* and *mawarith* (mortmain and inheritance), and any other financial matter that might be related to revenues.

48. Jawhar's governorship of Egypt perhaps is reflected not only in the admonitions of the *ʿahd* to the governor to remember his humble beginnings, his criticism of previous rulers, his potential for arrogance and pride, but also in the need to undertake good works and pay heed to his reputation among the common people, the need to avoid oppressing the people by giving a free rein to his retainers and family, the tendency to rely too much on one's retinue and confidants and viziers of previous regimes and rulers, neglecting knowledgeable and pious people in the realm, and the need to remain faithful to the tradition (*Daʿaʾim*, vol. 1, pp. 350–357).
49. *Ibid*., pp. 367–368.
50. *Ibid*., p. 362. In the text: '*fa in shakaw ilayka thiqala kharajihim aw ʿillatan dakhalat ʿalayhim min inqitaʿi shurbin aw fasadi ardin ghalaba ʿalayha gharaqun aw ʿatashun aw afatun mujhifatun, khaffafta ʿanhum.*' The key terms here are *inqitaʿ shurbin* referring to irrigation, *ghalab gharaqin* referring to inundation, and *ʿatash* or drought.
51. Ibn Khallikan, *Wafayat*, tr. De Slane, vol. 1, p. 341.
52. Al-Maqrizi, *Ittiʿaz*, vol. 1, pp. 103–106.
53. Al-Nuwayri, *Nihayat al-arab*, vol. 28, pp. 59–62.
54. M. Shaban, *Islamic History*, vol. 2, pp. 200–201.

Conclusion: Between *Zahir* and *Batin*

1. See the discussion of *daʿwa* activity in Daftary's *The Ismaʿilis*, pp. 224–232.
2. On al-Kirmani's role, see Paul E. Walker, *Hamid al-Din al-Kirmani: Ismaili Thought in the Age of al-Hakim* (London, 1999).
3. Samuel M. Stern, 'The Succession to the Fatimid Imam al-Amir, the Claims of the Later Fatimids to the Imamate, and the Rise of Tayyibi Ismailism', *Oriens*, 4 (1951), pp. 193–255; repr. in S.M.

Stern, *History and Culture in the Medieval Muslim World* (London, 1984), article XL.

4. See the discussion of al-Nuʿman's family in Husayn, *Fi adab Misr al-Fatimiyya*, pp. 42–54, and his introduction to the *Kitab al-himma*.

Bibliography

Primary sources

Abu'l-'Arab, Muhammad b. Ahmad b. Tamim al-Tamimi. *Kitab al-mihan*, ed. Yahya Wahib al-Juburi. 2nd ed., Beirut, 1988.

Akhbar al-Qaramita, ed. Suhayl Zakkar. 2nd ed., Damascus, 1982.

al-Baghdadi, Abu Mansur 'Abd al-Qahir. *al-Farq bayn al-firaq*, ed. M. Badr. Cairo, 1328/1910.

al-Hamadhani, 'Abd al-Jabbar b. Ahmad. *Tathbit dala'il al-nubuwwa*, ed. 'A. 'Uthman. Beirut, 1966.

Ibn al-Athir, 'Izz al-Din. *al-Kamil fi'l-ta'rikh*, ed. C.J. Tornberg. Leiden, 1851–1876; repr. Beirut, 1965–1966.

Ibn Babawayh, Abu Ja'far Muhammad. *Risalat al-i'tiqadat*. ed. 1918; tr. A.A.A. Fyzee as *A Shi'ite Creed*. Bombay, 1942.

Ibn Hammad, Muhammad b. 'Ali. *Akhbar muluk bani 'Ubayd wa-sirati-him*, ed. J. al-Badawi. Algiers, 1977; ed. and tr. M. Vonerheyden as *Histoire des rois 'Obaidides*. Algiers and Paris, 1927.

Ibn Hanbal, Ahmad b. Muhammad, *Fada'il al-sahaba*, ed. W.M. 'Abbas, Beirut, 1983.

Ibn al-Haytham, Abu 'Abd Allah Ja'far. *Kitab al-munazarat*, ed. and tr. W. Madelung and Paul E. Walker as *The Advent of the Fatimids: A Contemporary Shi'i Witness*. London, 2000.

Ibn Hawqal, Abu'l-Qasim Muhammad. *Kitab surat al-ard*, ed. J.H. Kramers. Leiden, 1938; tr. J.H. Kramers and G. Wiet as *Configuration de la terre*. Paris and Beirut, 1964.

Ibn 'Idhari, Ahmad b. Muhammad. *Bayan al-mughrib fi akhbar al-Andalus wa'l-Maghrib*, vol. 1, ed. G.S. Colin and É. Lévi-Provençal. Leiden, 1948.

Ibn Khaldun, 'Abd al-Rahman. *Kitab al-'ibar wa-diwan al-mubtada' wa'l-khabar fi ayyam al-'Arab wa'l-'Ajam wa'l-Barbar*. Beirut,

1956–1961; tr. W. MacGuckin de Slane as *L'Histoire des Berbères et des dynasties musulmanes de l'Afrique septentrionale.* 1847–1851; new ed. by P. Casanova. Paris, 1969.

Ibn Khallikan, Ahmad b. Muhammad. *Wafayat al-aʿyan*, ed. I. Abbas. Beirut, 1968–1972; tr. W. MacGuckin de Slane as *Biographical Dictionary.* Paris, 1842–1871.

Ibn Qutayba, ʿAbd Allah ibn Muslim. *al-Imama wa'l-siyasa*, ed. K. Mansour. Beirut, 1997.

Idris ʿImad al-Din, *ʿUyun al-akhbar*, vol. 5 and part of vol. 6, ed. M. Yaʿlawi as *Ta'rikh al-khulafa' al-Fatimiyyin bi'l-Maghrib: al-qism al-khass min Kitab ʿUyun al-akhbar.* Beirut, 1985; vols. 4–6, ed. M. Ghalib. Beirut, 1973–1978; vol. 7, ed. and summary in English, Ayman Fu'ad Sayyid in collaboration with Paul E. Walker and Maurice A. Pomerantz, as *The Fatimids and their Successors in Yaman: The History of an Islamic Community.* London, 2002.

Jaʿfar b. Mansur al-Yaman. *Kitab al-ʿalim wa'l-ghulam*, ed. and tr. J.W. Morris as *The Master and the Disciple: An Early Islamic Spiritual Dialogue*. London, 2001.

al-Jawdhari, Abu ʿAli al-Mansur al-ʿAzizi. *Sirat al-Ustadh Jawdhar*, ed. M.K. Husayn and M. ʿAbd al-Hadi al-Shaʿira. Cairo, 1954; French tr. M. Canard as *Vie de l'ustadh Jaudhar (Contenant sermons, lettres et rescrits des premiers califes Fatimides).* Algiers, 1958.

Khams rasa'il Ismaʿiliyya, ed. ʿA. Tamir. Beirut, 1956.

al-Khushani, Muhammad b. al-Harith b. Asad and Abu'l-ʿArab Muhammad b. Ahmad al-Tamimi. *Kitab Tabaqat ʿulama' Ifriqiya* in *Classes des savants de l'Ifriqiya*, ed. Mohammed Ben Cheneb. Paris, 1915; French tr. Ben Cheneb, Algiers, 1920.

al-Kulayni, Abu Jaʿfar Muhammad b. Yaʿqub. *al-Usul min al-kafi*, ed. ʿAli Akhbar al-Ghaffari. 3rd ed., Tehran, 1388/1968.

al-Majduʿ, Ismaʿil b. ʿAbd al-Rasul. *Fihrist al-kutub wa'l-rasa'il*, ed. A.N. Munzavi. Tehran, 1966.

al-Maliki, Abu Bakr. *Kitab Riyad al-nufus fi tabaqat ʿulama' al-Qayrawan wa Ifriqiya*, ed. Bashir al-Bakkush. Beirut, 1981–1983.

al-Maqrizi, Taj al-Din Ahmad b. ʿAli. *Ittiʿaz al-hunafa' bi akhbar al-a'imma al-Fatimiyyin al-khulafa'*, ed. Jamal al-Din al-Shayyal and M. Hilmi M. Ahmad. Cairo, 1967–1973.

—— *Kitab al-mawaʿiz wa'l-iʿtibar bi-dhikr al-khitat wa'l-athar.* Bulaq, 1270/1853–1854 (known as *al-Khitat*).

al-Masʿudi, Abu'l-Hasan ʿAli b. al-Husayn b. ʿAli. *Muruj al-dhahab wa-maʿadin al-jawhar*, ed. Y.A. Daghir. Beirut, 1965.

al-Musabbihi, al-Mukhtar ʿIzz al-Mulk Muhammad. *al-Juz' al-arbaʿun min akhbar Misr*. Part 1 (historical section), ed. Ayman Fu'ad Sayyid and Th. Banquis. Cairo, 1978; Part 2 (literary section), ed. Husayn Nassar. Cairo, 1984.

Muslim b. al-Hajjaj al-Qushayri. *Sahih*. n.p., 1375/1955.

al-Nawbakhti, al-Hasan b. Musa. *Kitab firaq al-Shi'a*, ed. H. Ritter. Istanbul, 1931.

al-Nu'man b. Muhammad, al-Qadi Abu Hanifa. *Da'a'im al-Islam*, ed. A.A.A. Fyzee. Cairo, 1951–1961; English tr. A.A.A. Fyzee, completely revised by I.K. Poonawala as *The Pillars of Islam: Volume I, Acts of Devotion and Religious Observances*. New Delhi, 2002; partial trans. A.A.A. Fyzee as *The Book of Faith*. Bombay, 1974.

—— *Ikhtilaf usul al-madhahib*, ed. S.T. Lokhandwala. Simla, 1972.

—— *Kitab al-himma fi adab atba' al-a'imma*, ed. M. Kamil Husayn. Cairo, 1948; partial trans. Jawad Muscati and A.M. Moulvi as *Selections from Qazi Noaman's Code of Conduct for the Followers of Imam*. Karachi, 1950.

—— *Kitab al-iqtisar*, ed. M.W. Mirza. Damascus, 1957.

—— *Kitab al-majalis wa'l-musayarat*, ed. H. Faqi, I. Shabbuh and M. Ya'lawi. Tunis, 1978; 2nd ed., Beirut, 1997.

—— *Kitab al-manaqib wa'l-mathalib*, ed. Majid b. Ahmad al-'Atiyya. Beirut 1423/2002.

—— *Kitab asas al-ta'wil*, ed. 'A. Tamir. Beirut, 1960.

—— *Kitab iftitah al-da'wa wa ibtida' al-dawla*, ed. Wadad al-Qadi. Beirut, 1970; ed. F. Dachraoui, Tunis, 1975; tr. Hamid Haji, *Founding the Fatimid State: The Rise of an Early Islamic Empire*. London, 2006.

—— *al-Risala al-mudhhiba*, ed. 'A. Tamir in his *Khams rasa'il Isma'iliyya*. Beirut, 1956, pp. 27–87.

—— *Sharh al-akhbar fi fada'il al-a'imma al-athar*, ed. S.M. Husayni al-Jalali. Qumm, 1409–1412/1988–1992.

—— *Ta'wil al-da'a'im*, ed. M.H. al-A'zami. Cairo, 1967–1972.

—— *Urjuza al-mukhtara*, ed. I.K. Poonawala. Montreal, 1970.

al-Nuwayri, Shihab al-Din Ahmad. *Nihayat al-arab fi funun al-adab*, vol. 28, ed. M. Amin and M. Hilmi M. Ahmad. Cairo, 1992.

al-Qayrawani, Abu Muhammad b. Abi Zayd. *Kitab al-jami'*, ed. A.M. Turki. Beirut, 1990.

al-Qummi, Sa'd b. 'Abd Allah. *Kitab al-maqalat wa'l-firaq*, ed. M.J. Mashkur. Tehran, 1963.

al-Sijistani, Abu Ya'qub Ishaq b. Ahmad. *Ithbat al-nub'at*, ed. 'A. Tamir. Beirut, 1966.

al-Tabari, Muhammad b. Jarir. *Jamiʿ al-bayan ʿan taʾwil al-Qurʾan*. Cairo, 1950.
—— *Taʾrikh al-Tabari*, ed. M. Abuʾl-Fadl Ibrahim. Cairo, n.d.
al-Yamani, Muhammad. *Sirat al-hajib Jaʿfar*, ed. W. Ivanow, in *Bulletin of the Faculty of Arts, University of Egypt*, 4, Part 2 (1936), pp. 107–133; English tr. W. Ivanow in his *Ismaili Tradition Concerning the Rise of the Fatimids*, pp. 184–223.

Secondary sources

Abun-Nasr, J. *A History of the Maghrib*. London, 1971.
Afsaruddin, Asma. *Excellence and Precedence: Medieval Islamic Discourse on Legitimate Leadership*. Leiden, 2002.
Al-Azmeh, Aziz. *Muslim Kingship: Power and the Sacred in Muslim, Christian, and Pagan Polities*. London, 1997.
ʿAli, Zahid. *Hamare Ismaʿili madhhab ki haqiqat*. Hyderabad, 1954.
Barrucand, Marianne, ed. *L'Égypte Fatimide: son art et son histoire*. Paris, 1999.
Berkey, J. *The Formation of Islam*. Cambridge, 2003.
Bierman, Irene A. *Writing Signs: The Fatimid Public Text*. Berkeley, CA, 1998.
Bloom, Jonathan M. 'The Origins of Fatimid Art', *Muqarnas*, 3 (1985), pp. 20–38.
Brett, Michael. *The Rise of the Fatimids: The World of the Mediterranean and the Middle East in the Fourth Century Hijra/Tenth Century CE*. Leiden, 2001.
Brunschvig, Robert. 'Fiqh Fatimide et histoire de l'Ifriqiya', in R. Brunschvig, *Études Islamologiques*. Paris, 1976, vol. 1, pp. 63–70.
Bulliet, Richard W. *Conversion to Islam in the Medieval Period*. Cambridge, MA, 1979.
Cahen, Claude. 'Quelques chroniques anciennes relatives aux derniers Fatimides', *BIFAO*, 37 (1937–1938), pp. 1–27.
Calder, Norman. *Studies in Early Muslim Jurisprudence*. Oxford, 1993.
Canard, Marius. 'Le cérémonial Fatimite et le cérémonial Byzantin: Essai de comparison', *Byzantion*, 21 (1951), pp. 355–420; repr. in M. Canard, *Byzance et les Musulmans du Proche Orient*. London, 1973, article XIV.
—— *Miscellanea Orientalia*. London, 1973.
Cohen, Mark. *Jewish Self-Government in Egypt*. Princeton, NJ, 1980.
Cooperson, M. *Classical Arabic Biography: The Heirs of the Prophet in the Age of al-Maʾmun*. Cambridge, 2000.

Corbin, Henry. *Temps cyclique et gnose Ismaélienne*. Paris, 1982; tr. R. Manheim and J. Morris as *Cyclical Time and Ismaili Gnosis*. London, 1983.

Dachraoui, Farhat. *Le Califat Fatimide au Maghreb, 296–365 H./909–975 Jc: histoire politique et institutions*. Tunis, 1981; Arabic tr. by H. al-Sahili as *al-Khilafa al-Fatimiyya bi'l-Maghrib*. Beirut, 1994.

— 'al-Mu'izz li-Din Allah', *EI2*, vol. 7, pp. 485–489.

Daftary, Farhad. 'The Bibliography of the Publications of the Late W. Ivanow', *Islamic Culture*, 45 (1971), pp. 55–67, and 56 (1982), pp. 239–240.

—— *The Isma'ilis: Their History and Doctrines*. Cambridge, 1990.

—— 'A Major Schism in the Early Isma'ili Movement', *SI*, 77 (1993), pp. 123–139.

—— *The Assassin Legends: Myths of the Isma'ilis*. London, 1994.

—— ed. *Mediaeval Isma'ili History and Thought*. Cambridge, 1996.

—— *A Short History of the Ismailis: Traditions of a Muslim Community*. Edinburgh, 1998.

—— *Ismaili Literature: A Bibliography of Sources and Studies*. London, 2004.

Defrémery, Charles F. 'Nouvelles recherches sur les Ismaeliéns ou Bathiniens de Syrie', *JA*, 5 série, 3 (1854), pp. 373–421, and 5 (1855), pp. 5–76.

Fahd, T. 'The Dream in Medieval Islamic Society', in G. von Grunebaum and R. Caillois, *The Dream and Human Societies*. Berkeley, CA, 1966, pp. 351–363.

Fischel, Walter J. *Jews in the Economic and Political Life of Mediaeval Islam*. London, 1937.

Fowden, Garth. *Empire to Commonwealth: Consequences of Monotheism in Late Antiquity*. Princeton, NJ, 1993.

Fyzee, Asaf A.A. *The Ismaili Law of Wills*. London, 1933.

—— 'Qadi an-Nu'man, the Fatimid Jurist and Author', *JRAS* (1934), pp. 1–32.

—— 'Ibn Babawayh', *EI2*, vol. 3, pp. 726–727.

Ghalib, Mustafa. *Tar'ikh al-da'wa al-Isma'iliyya*. Beirut, 1965.

Goeje, Michael J. de. *Mémoire sur les Carmathes du Bahraïn et les Fatimides*. 2nd ed., Leiden, 1886.

Goitein, Solomon D. 'From the Mediterranean to India', *Speculum*, 29 (1954), pp. 181–197.

—— *A Mediterranean Society*. Berkeley, CA, 1967–1993.

Goldziher, Ignaz. *Introduction to Islamic Theology and Law*, tr. A. and R. Hamori. Princeton, NJ, 1981.

Gottheil, Richard J.H. 'A Distinguished Family of Fatimide Cadis (al-Nu'man) in the Tenth Century', *JAOS*, 27 (1906), pp. 217–296.
Hallaq, Wael B. 'Was al-Shafi'i the Master Architect of Islamic Jurisprudence?', *IJMES*, 25 (1993), pp. 587–605.
—— *Islamic Legal Theories: An Introduction to Sunni usul al-fiqh*. Cambridge, 1997.
Halm, Heinz. *Shiism*, tr. J. Watson. Edinburgh, 1991.
—— *Das Reich des Mahdi. Der Aufsteig der Fatimiden (875–973)*. Munich, 1991; tr. M. Bonner as *The Empire of the Mahdi: The Rise of the Fatimids*. Leiden, 1996.
—— *The Fatimids and their Traditions of Learning*. London, 1997.
—— *Die Kalifen von Kairo: Die Fatimiden in Ägypten 973–1074*. Munich, 2003.
Hamdani, Abbas. *The Beginnings of the Isma'ili Da'wa in Northern India*. Cairo, 1956.
—— *The Fatimids*. Karachi, 1962.
—— 'Evolution of the Organisational Structure of the Fatimi Da'wah: The Yemeni and Persian Contribution', *Arabian Studies*, 3 (1976), pp. 85–114.
—— 'A Critique of Paul Casanova's dating of the *Rasa'il Ikhwan al-Safa*'', in F. Daftary, ed., *Mediaeval Isma'ili History and Thought*. Cambridge, 1996, pp. 145–152,
—— 'Did the Turkicization of Asia Minor Lead to the Arabization of North Africa?', *The Maghreb Review*, 24 (1999), pp. 34–41.
—— 'Brethren of Purity, a Secret Society for the Establishment of the Fatimid Caliphate', in M. Barrucand, ed., *L'Égypte Fatimide: son art et son histoire*. Paris, 1999, pp. 73–82.
—— and de Blois, François. 'A Re-Examination of al-Mahdi's Letter to the Yemenites on the Genealogy of the Fatimid Caliphs', *JRAS* (1983), pp. 173–207.
al-Hamdani, Husayn F. *al-Sulayhiyyun wa'l-haraka al-Fatimiyya fi'l-Yaman*. Cairo, 1955.
—— *On the Genealogy of Fatimid Caliphs*. Cairo, 1958.
Hamdani, Sumaiya. 'Dialectic of Power: Sunni-Shi'i Debates in Tenth-century North Africa', *SI*, 90 (2000), pp. 5–21.
Hasan, 'Ali Ibrahim. *Tar'ikh Jawhar al-Siqilli*. 2nd ed., Cairo, 1963.
Hasan, Hasan I. *Tar'ikh al-dawla al-Fatimiyya*. 3rd ed., Cairo, 1964.
al-Hibri, T. *Reinterpreting Islamic Historiography*. Cambridge, 1999.
Hinds, Martin. 'Mihna', *EI2*, vol. 7, pp. 2–6.
Hodgson, Marshall G.S. *The Order of Assassins: The Struggle of the Early Nizari Isma'ilis against the Islamic World*. The Hague, 1955.

Humphreys, R. Stephen. 'Modern Historians and the Abbasid Revolution', in his *Islamic History: A Framework for Inquiry*. Princeton, NJ, 1991.

Hunsberger, Alice C. *Nasir Khusraw, The Ruby of Badakhshan: A Portrait of the Persian Poet, Traveller and Philosopher*. London, 2000.

Husayn, Muhammad K. *Fi adab Misr al-Fatimiyya*. Cairo, 1950.

Idris, Hady R. *La Berbérie orientale sous les Zirides, Xe-XIIe siècles*. Paris, 1962.

Ivanow, Wladimir. *A Creed of the Fatimids*. Bombay, 1936.

—— 'The Organization of the Fatimid Propaganda', *Journal of the Bombay Branch of the Royal Asiatic Society*, New Series, 15 (1939), pp. 1–35; repr. in Bryan S. Turner, ed., *Orientalism: Early Sources*, vol. I, *Readings in Orientalism*. London, 2000, pp. 531–571.

—— 'Ismailis and Qarmatians', *Journal of the Bombay Branch of the Royal Asiatic Society*, New Series, 16 (1940), pp. 43–85.

—— *Ismaili Tradition Concerning the Rise of the Fatimids*. London, 1942.

—— *Ismaili Literature: A Bibliographical Survey*. Tehran, 1963.

Jiwa, Shainool. 'The Initial Destination of the Fatimid Caliphate: The Yemen or the Maghrib?', *British Society for Middle Eastern Studies Bulletin*, 13 (1986), pp. 15–26.

Kennedy, Hugh. *The Prophet and the Age of the Caliphates: The Islamic Near East from the Sixth to the Eleventh Century*. London, 1986.

Khalidi, Tarif. *Arabic Historical Thought in the Classical Period*. Cambridge, 1994.

Kohlberg, Etam. 'Some Shiʿi Views of the Anti-Diluvian World', *SI*, 52 (1980), pp. 41–66; repr. in E. Kohlberg, *Belief and Law in Imami Shiʿism*. Aldershot, 1991, article XVI.

—— 'Imam and Community in the Pre-Ghayba Period', in S. Arjomand, ed., *Authority and Political Culture in Shiʿism*. New York, 1998, pp. 25–53.

Lambton, Ann K.S. *State and Government in Medieval Islam: An Introduction to the Study of Islamic Political Theory: the Jurists*. Oxford, 1981.

Laroui, A. *L'Histoire du Magreb*. Paris, 1970; tr. R. Manheim as *The History of the Maghrib: An Interpretive Essay*. Princeton, NJ, 1977.

Leisten, Thomas. 'Dynastic Tombs or Private Mausolea: Observations on the Concept of Funerary Structures of the Fatimid and 'Abbasid Caliphs', in M. Barrucand, ed., *L'Égypte Fatimide: son art et son histoire*. Paris, 1999, pp. 465–479.

Lev, Yaacov. *State and Society in Fatimid Egypt*. Leiden, 1991.

Levi Della Vida, Giorgio. 'Kharidjites', *EI2*, vol. 4, pp. 1074–1077.

Lewis, Bernard. *The Origins of Isma'ilism: A Study of the Historical Background of the Fatimid Caliphate*. Cambridge, 1940.

—— *The Assassins: A Radical Sect in Islam*. London, 1967.

—— 'Abbasids', *EI2*, vol. 1, pp. 15–23.

Lézine, Alexandre. *Mahdiya: Recherches d'archéologie Islamique*. Paris, 1965.

Lindsay, James E. 'Prophetic Parallels in Abu 'Abd Allah al-Shi'i's Mission among the Kutama Berbers, 893–910', *IJMES*, 24 (1992), pp. 39–56.

Madelung, Wilferd. 'Fatimiden und Bahrainqarmaten', *Der Islam*, 34 (1959), pp. 34–88; English tr. as 'The Fatimids and Qarmatis of Bahrayn', in F. Daftary, ed., *Mediaeval Isma'ili History and Thought*. Cambridge, 1996, pp. 21–73.

—— 'Das Imamat in der frühen ismailitischen Lehre', *Der Islam*, 37 (1961), pp. 43–135.

—— 'The Sources of Isma'ili Law', *JNES*, 35 (1976), pp. 29–40; repr. in W. Madelung, *Religious Schools and Sects in Medieval Islam*. London 1985, article XVIII.

—— 'Some Notes on Non-Isma'ili Shiism in the Maghrib', *SI*, 44 (1977), pp. 87–97; repr. in W. Madelung, *Religious Schools and Sects in Medieval Islam*. London 1985, article XIV.

—— *The Succession to Muhammad: A Study of the Early Caliphate*. Cambridge, 1997.

—— 'The Religious Policy of the Fatimids toward Their Sunni Subjects in the Maghrib', in M. Barrucand, ed., *L'Égypte Fatimide: son art et son histoire*. Paris, 1999, pp. 97–104.

—— 'al-Kulayni', *EI2*, vol. 5, pp. 362–363.

—— 'al-Mahdi', *EI2*, vol. 5, pp. 1230–1238.

Majid, 'Abd al-Mun'im. *Zuhur khilafat al-Fatimiyyin wa-suqutuha fi Misr*. Cairo, 1968.

Mann, Jacob. *The Jews in Egypt and Palestine under the Fatimid Caliphs: A Contribution to Their Political and Communal History Based Chiefly on Genizah Material Hitherto Unpublished*. London, 1920–1922.

Massignon, Louis. 'Esquisse d'une bibliographie Qarmate', in T.W. Arnold and R.A. Nicholson, ed., *A Volume of Oriental Studies Presented to Edward G. Browne*. Cambridge, 1922, pp. 329–338.

—— 'Mutanabbi, devant le siècle Ismaélien de l'Islam', in *Al Mutanabbi: Recueil publié à l'occasion de son millénaire*. Beirut, 1936, pp. 1–17.

Mez, A. *The Renaissance of Islam*, tr. S. Khuda Bukhsh and D.S. Margoliouth, London, 1937.

Modarressi Tabataba'i, Hossein. *An Introduction to Shi'i Law: A Bibliographical Study*. London, 1984.

—— *Crisis and Consolidation in the Formative Period of Shi'ite Islam: Abu Ja'far ibn Qiba al-Razi and His Contribution to Imamite Shi'ite Thought*. Princeton, NJ, 1993.

—— 'Early Debates on the Integrity of the Qur'an', *SI*, 77 (1993), pp. 5–39.

Momen, Moojan. *An Introduction to Shi'i Islam: The History and Doctrines of Twelver Shi'ism*. New Haven, CT, 1985.

Monès, H. 'Le Malékisme et l'échec des Fatimides en Ifriqiya', in *Études d'orientalisme dediées à la mémoire de Lévi-Provençal*. Paris, 1962, vol. 1, pp. 197–220.

Mottahedeh, Roy. *Loyalty and Leadership in an Early Islamic Society*. Princeton, NJ, 1980.

Nagel, Tilman. *Frühe Ismailiya und Fatimiden im Lichte der Risalat Iftitah ad-Da'wa*. Bonn, 1972.

Nanji, Azim. 'An Isma'ili Theory of *Walayah* in the *Da'a'im al-Islam* of Qadi al-Nu'man', in Donald Little, ed., *Essays on Islamic Civilization Presented to Niyazi Berkes*. Leiden, 1976, pp. 260–273.

—— *The Nizari Isma'ili Tradition in the Indo-Pakistan Subcontinent*. Delmar, NY, 1978.

Nasr, S. Hossein, ed. *Isma'ili Contributions to Islamic Culture*. Tehran, 1977.

—— 'Ithna 'ashariyya', *EI2*, vol. 4, pp. 277–279.

Poonawala, Ismail K. 'Al-Qadi al-Nu'man's Works and the Sources', *BSOAS*, 36 (1973), pp. 109–115.

—— 'A Reconsideration of al-Qadi al-Nu'man's *Madhhab*', *BSOAS*, 37 (1974), pp. 572–579.

—— *Biobibliography of Isma'ili Literature*. Malibu, CA, 1977.

—— 'Isma'ili *ta'wil* of the Qur'an', in A. Rippin, ed., *Approaches to the History of the Interpretation of the Qur'an*. Oxford, 1988, pp. 199–222.

—— 'Al-Qadi al-Nu'man and Isma'ili Jurisprudence', in F. Daftary, ed., *Mediaeval Isma'ili History and Thought*. Cambridge, 1996, pp. 117–143.

al-Qadi, Wadad. 'An Early Fatimid Political Document', *SI*, 48 (1978), pp. 71–108.

Quatremère, Étienne M. 'Notice historique sur les Ismaëliens', *Fundgruben des Orients*, 4 (1814), pp. 339–376.

Roy, B. and Poinssot, P. *Inscriptions Arabes de Kairouan*. Paris, 1950–1958.

Salinger, Gerald. 'A Muslim Mirror for Princes', *Muslim World*, 46 (1956), pp. 24–39.

Sanders, Paula. *Ritual, Politics and the City in Fatimid Cairo*. Albany, NY, 1994.

Sayyid, Ayman Fu'ad. *al-Dawla al-Fatimiyya fi Misr*. Cairo, 1992.

Schacht, Joseph. *The Origins of Muhammadan Jurisprudence*. Oxford, 1950.

Shaban, M. *The Abbasid Revolution*. Cambridge, 1970.

—— *Islamic History AD 600–750 (AH 132): A New Interpretation*. Cambridge, 1971–1976.

Shah-Kazemi, R. *Justice and Remembrance: Introducing the Spirituality of Imam 'Ali*. London, 2006.

Sharon, Moshe. *Black Banners from the East: The Establishment of the 'Abbasid State*. Jerusalem and Leiden, 1983.

Silvestre de Sacy, Antoine I. *Exposé de la religion des Druzes*. Paris, 1838.

Stern, Samuel M. 'Isma'ili Propaganda and Fatimid Rule in Sind', *Islamic Culture*, 23 (1949), pp. 298–307, repr. in his *Studies in Early Isma'ilism*, pp. 177–188.

——'The Epistle of the Fatimid Caliph al-Amir (al-Hidaya al-Amiriyya) – its Date and its Purpose', *JRAS* (1950), pp. 20–31, repr. in S.M. Stern, *History and Culture in the Medieval Muslim World*. London, 1984, article X.

—— 'The Succession to the Fatimid Imam al-Amir, the Claims of the later Fatimids to the Imamate, and the Rise of Tayyibi Ismailism', *Oriens*, 4 (1951), pp. 193–255; repr. in S.M. Stern, *History and Culture in the Medieval Muslim World*. London, 1984, article I.

——'Heterodox Isma'ilism at the Time of al-Mu'izz', *BSOAS*, 17 (1955), pp. 10–33, repr. in his *Studies in Early Isma'ilism*, pp. 257–288.

—— 'The Early Isma'ili Missionaries in North-West Persia and in Khurasan and Transoxania', *BSOAS*, 23 (1960), pp. 56–90; repr. in his *Studies in Early Isma'ilism*, pp. 189–233.

——'Isma'ilis and Qarmatians', in *L'Élaboration de l'Islam*. Paris, 1961, pp. 99–108, repr. in his *Studies in Early Isma'ilism*, pp. 289–298; repr. in E. Kohlberg, ed., *Shi'ism*. Aldershot, 2003, pp. 267–276.

——'Cairo as the Centre of the Isma'ili Movement', in *Colloque international sur l'histoire du Caire*. Cairo, 1972, pp. 437–450, repr. in his *Studies in Early Isma'ilism*, pp. 234–256.

——*Studies in Early Isma'ilism*. Jerusalem and Leiden, 1983.

Surur, Muhammad J. *Misr fi 'asr al-dawla al-Fatimiyya*. Cairo, 1960.
—— *al-Nufudh al-Fatimi fi bilad al-Sham wa'l-Iraq*. Cairo, 1964.
Talbi, Mohamed. *L'Émirat Aghlabide, 184–296/800–901: histoire politique*. Paris, 1966.
— 'al-Mahdiyya', *EI2*, vol. 5, pp. 1246–1247.
Vatikiotis, Panayiotis J. *The Fatimid Theory of State*. Lahore, 1957.
Wali, Taha. *al-Qaramita*. Beirut, 1981.
Walker, Paul E. 'The Isma'ili Da'wa in the Reign of the Fatimid Caliph al-Hakim', *Journal of the American Research Center in Egypt*, 30 (1993), pp. 161–182.
—— *Early Philosophical Shiism: The Ismaili Neoplatonism of Abu Ya'qub al-Sijistani*. Cambridge, 1993.
—— *Hamid al-Din al-Kirmani: Ismaili Thought in the Age of al-Hakim*. London, 1999.
—— *Exploring an Islamic Empire: Fatimid History and its Sources*. London, 2002.
Watt, W. Montgomery and Cachia, P. *A History of Islamic Spain*. Edinburgh, 1965.
al-Ya'lawi, Muhammad. *al-Adab bi Ifriqiya fi'l-'ahd al-Fatimi, 296–365 H*. Beirut, 1986.
Zaman, M. Qasim. *Religion and Politics under the Early 'Abbasids: The Emergence of the Proto-Sunni Elite*. Leiden, 1997.

Index

www.ingramcontent.com/pod-product-compliance
Lightning Source LLC
Chambersburg PA
CBHW070615310726
48982CB00001B/87

* 9 7 8 1 8 5 0 4 3 8 8 2 3 *